The Complete Book of Airships — Dirigibles, Blimps & Hot Air Balloons

The Complete Book of Airships — Dirigibles, Blimps & Hot Air Balloons

BY DON DWIGGINS

TAB BOOKS Inc.
BLUE RIDGE SUMMIT, PA. 17214

FIRST EDITION

FIRST PRINTING—AUGUST 1980

Library of Congress Cataloging in Publication Data

Dwiggins, Don.
   The complete book of airships.

   Includes index.
   1. Airships. 2. Hot air balloons. I. Title.
TL605.D84   629.133'2'09   80-20021
ISBN 0-8306-9696-2
ISBN 0-8306-9692-X (pbk.)

Preface

The history of dirigibles has been told before, but with this book you will discover many thrilling episodes of forgotten history appearing in print for the first time. The successes and failures that marked the appearance of earlier lighter-than-air dirigible craft are traced and explanations are given for why they suddenly went out of style.

Now that modern materials and construction techniques are available, we can expect to see rapid progress toward bringing back the sky giants with new peacetime and military missions to perform. Already millions of dollars in government funds have been earmarked for research and development and construction of hybrid helium dirigibles mated to helicopter propulsion systems. Yet, even these novel concepts had their origins in designs that appeared decades ago. I hope the reader will find the story of the return of the sky giants both informative and exciting.

Don Dwiggins

Acknowledgements

I wish to express my gratitude to all those who have helped assemble the material for this history of dirigibles since the project began as a hobby 45 years ago. Many airmen, inventors and dreamers have passed from this temporary world on to a future that knows no limits of happiness and creativity.

Others still aboard spaceship Earth will, I hope, share with me the fun and excitement of envisioning new ways to travel on journeys both real and of the imagination. After all, man first had to dream of flying before he could give life and spirit to his desires to share the sky with the birds.

Among those who assisted, I should like to thank the Smithsonian Institution, NASA, FAA, U.S. Navy, American Philosophical Society Library, American Historical Association, Franklin Institute, Crerar Library in Chicago, Henry E. Huntington Library in Pasadena, National Archives, California State Library, and many others who gave of their help.

The following periodicals and special publications receive my thanks: *American Journal of Science and Arts, American Engineer and Railroad Journal, American Aeronaut, American Inventor, American Historical Review, American Journal of Science, Aerial Age, Aeronautics, Aeronautical World, Aero Club of America Bulletins, Aeronautical Annual, Century Magazine, Fly, Franklin Journal and Mechanics Magazine, Harper's New Monthly Magazine, Journals of Congress, Magazine of History, Popular Science Monthly, Popular Flying, Pennsylvania Magazine of History and Biography, Smithsonian Miscellaneous Collections, Scientific American, Senate Documents (U.S.), Scientific Mechanic, Transportation, Yankee Pilot, National Aeronautic Association Review.*

Special volumes consulted include: Andrews, Solomon, *The Aereon*, Washington, 1864; Chanute, Octave, *Progress in Flying Machines*, N.Y.,

1894; Dolfuss & Fouche, *Histoire de l'Aeronautique*, Paris, 1932; Hodgson, J.E., *The History of Aeronautics in Great Britain*, London, 1924; Miller, Francis T., *World In The Air*, N.Y. 1930; Wise, John, *Through The Air*, Philadelphia, 1873; Myers, Carlotta, *Aerial Adventures of Carlotta, or Skylarking in Cloudland*, 1883; Zahm, *Aerial Navigation*, 1911; Turnor, Hatton, *Astra Castra*, London, 1865.

Other works include: Robinson, Douglas, *The Zeppelin In Combat*, Oxfordshire, England, 1962; Robinson, Douglas, *Giants In The Sky*, Seattle, 1973; Collier, Basil, *The Airship*, N.Y. 1974; Nobile, Umberto, *My Polar Flights*, N.Y. 1961; Wellman, Walter, *The Aerial Age*, N.Y. 1911; Holland, Robert S., *Historic Airships*, Philadelphia, 1928; Shute, Nevil, *Slide Rule*, N.Y., 1954; Santos-Dumont, Alberto, *My Air-Ships*, N.Y. 1904; Mooney, Michael M., *The Hindenburg*, N.Y. 1972; Toland, John, *Ships in the Sky*, N.Y. 1957; and Vaeth, J. Gordon, *Graf Zeppelin*, N.Y. 1958.

Among corporate friends who have helped, I would like to mention the Goodyear Aerospace Corp., Piasecki Aircraft Corp., Aeron Corp., Boeing Vertol Corp., and Raven Industries Inc.

There are others, many others, who shared their time and thoughts with me to help get this all together in what, I hope, will entertain and inform you with a new look at the ageless dream of flying on silent air currents and listening to the silence of space in a way that recaptures an almost forgotten mode of travel and sport—by the lighter-than-air route.

Thanks also to the Lighter Than Air Society of Akron, Ohio, and attorney Dudley Nichols for helping me with the story of an aeronaut I knew well and whose tales I found fascinating—the late Roy Knabenshue.

Contents

Chapter 1

Cloud Country

Man, unlike other living creatures of this curious world on which we live, is endowed with both imagination and inventiveness. Man is fortunate in not just adapting to his environment, but in constantly seeking to change it, to overcome its limitations, to go beyond horizons—across the seas, underneath them and above them.

The human brain possesses a miraculous power unique to our species. Properly utilized, it can give mankind something new and beneficial—something of real value. But how many of us use it? True genius—the ability to spread wings of imagination and soar sublimely—is unfortunately rare.

In 1932, Thomas Alva Edison told an inquiring reporter: "Genius is 1 percent inspiration and 99 percent perspiration." Yet even among the world's greatest geniuses such as da Vinci, Edison, and Franklin, their work has been, essentially, not original but imitative. Man observes, and copies, until, with his intellect, zeal, and work, some new and different concept is shaped that was not there before (Figs. 1-1, 1-2, 1-3 and 1-4).

Man's long struggle to master the sky began imitatively. Today's crowded skies filled with heavier-than-air machines resulted because a few men of genius accepted the challenge as an intellectual problem and turned to man-made laboratories to grasp simple aerodynamic laws that had no visible counterpart in nature.

Strangely enough, with all his bent of imitativeness, man has yet to imitate true bird flight successfully with a mechanical ornithopter, or wing-flapper. The mechanics of such devices were known to da Vinci and others, yet the physical problems of duplicating bird flight have been beyond man's intellectual grasp. Until this century, heavier-than-air flight

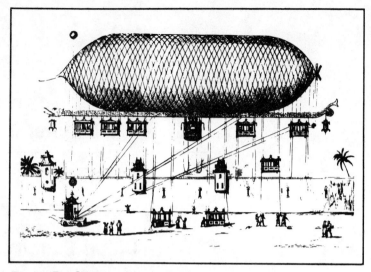

Fig. 1-1. The Chinese say this aerostat flew in 1306.

was ranked with perpetual motion, squaring the circle or designing an indefinite arch—all unattainable daydreams.

Mankind does from time to time produce a genius who changes the course of history with a brand new idea—like the unrecorded inventor of the wheel. In all nature, the wheel has no direct counterpart unless you want to consider the microscopic rotifer. The rotifer is a multi-celled, aquatic invertebrate animal whose anterior has been modified into a retractile disc bearing circles of strong cilia that give the appearance of rapidly revolving wheels as they set up vortex patterns to draw food to them or move about. Perhaps not until some Mesopotamian of the fourth millenium B. C. accidentally overtuned a potter's wheel did the true wheel come into use for travel. History hasn't been the same since.

And what of the sky?

What besides birds can navigate the air, men asked when they failed to duplicate their feathered friends. There were fluffy, white thistledowns that drifted like tiny parachutes for miles on zephyrs and insects that hovered—their wing membranes beating invisibly 300 times a minute.

And clouds—white, creamy, cumulus formations that floated effortlessly against previously azure summer skies. What kept them up? The answer seemed absurdly simple. They were lighter than air and floated upon it as a cork floats on a millpond. Yet men of science did not understand why clouds were lighter than air or even if they were. The mechanics of meterology were not fully understood and it escaped attention that cumulus formations marked the tops of rising bubbles of sun-warmed air. Rather, it was supposed that such clouds contained a mysterious vapor—referred to as ether.

THE MONTGOLFIER BROTHERS

Similar "vapors" also made smoke rise, decided two inventive French brothers, Etienne and Joseph Montgolfier. They liked to spend summer afternoons burning leaves and watching them drift upward with the curling smoke. Intellectually curious, they wondered if they could capture those mysterious vapors inside a paper bag? Would the bag rise too, like the leaves?

The Montgolfier brothers thought of paper because their ancestors had returned to France from the Sixth Crusade to Damascus in the 14th

Fig. 1-2. Francisco Lana's "Flying Vacuum" of 1670. It didn't work.

Fig. 1-3. The Sacrum Miverva was a fanciful concept of balloonist Eugene Robertson. It never flew.

century with secret knowledge of paper making. Their father, Pierre Montgolfier, had been made a Squire by Louis XVI for inventing a special paper, called Vellum, which he manufactured inside the base of a windmill in the village of Annonay.

The Montgolfier brothers begain reading all they could find on the subject of vapors. One volume, *On Different Kinds of Air*, had been written by Joseph Priestly, an English chemist, who also served as pastor at Mill Hill near Leeds where he resided next door to a brewery.

Pastor Priestly became so fascinated with "fixed air" (carbon dioxide) that hung suspended over the brewery's fermentation vats that he devoted a lifetime to the study of gases. Considered something of a radical, he showed that water is composed of two combined gases—oxygen and hydrogen. But he did agree with other scientists that things burned because of something else in their makeup—called *phlogiston*.

This idea excited the Montgolfiers. Perhaps phlogiston was the secret ingredient that made smoke rise! They quickly set about making a paper balloon. On June 5, 1783, they filled it with stinking smoke from burning wet straw and sheep's wool. The balloon swelled and tugged at the mooring rope. When let go, it rose majestically to an altitude estimated at 6000 feet. Man had discovered a way to reach the high sky!

Concerned, however, that toxic vapors filled the higher reaches of the atmosphere, the brothers debated whether it was safe to ascend themselves in a basket suspended beneath a phlogiston filled balloon. It seemed a better idea to use "barnyard aeronauts" first, to see if they would return to earth alive. They collected a sheep, a rooster and a duck and piled them into a wicker basket. Although they appeared to become a bit airsick (was it due to phlogiston?), all returned alive. There was only one mishap. The sheep angrily kicked the rooster on takeoff.

LIGHTER-THAN-AIR TRAVEL BEGINS

However, it was neither Etienne nor Joseph Montgolfier who first dared to make a human ascension, but a French scientist named Pilatre de Rozier. On October 17, 1783, having made out his will and said goodby to friends and relatives, de Rozier climbed into the basket of a Montgolfier-type balloon tied to a rope and rose skyward. He did not die. Lighter-than-air human travel, had in a sense, begun.

Although it would be some time before the means to make a lighter-than-air (LTA) craft travel from one point to another at the will of the operator, exploration of the sky moved ahead rapidly.

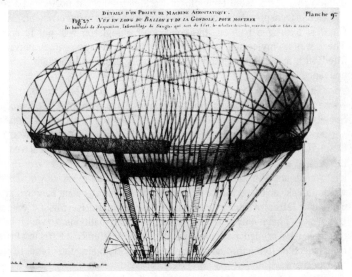

Fig. 1-4. The first dirigible proposal of Captain J. B. M. Meusiner. Jules Verne found the papers in the Academy of Science archives in Paris, France.

World attention to ballooning was focussed on Paris on August 27, 1783, two months prior to de Rozier's captive ascent, when a hydrogen-filled balloon ascended from the Champ de Mars. The aerostat was built by a French physicist named Jacques Alexander Cesar Charles and four days were required to fill the highly inflammable gas. An excited witness to the affair was the United States Minister Plenipotentiary to France, Benjamin Franklin.

After the show, the crowd that had assembled to watch got to arguing over bubbles of wine in nearby bistros. "What good can a balloon be?" someone demanded of Franklin.

Franklin shrugged and smiled. His retort was the bon mot of the day: *"Eh, a quoi ben l'enfant qui vient de naitre?"* ("What good is a newborn babe?").

Later, Franklin would write to Sir Joseph Banks of the Royal Society of London: "This experiment . . . may be attended with important consequences that no one can foresee . . . It may be sufficient for certain purposes, such as elevating an engineer to take a view of the enemy's army, works, etc., conveying intelligence into or out of a besieged town, giving signals to distant places, or the like."

Franklin's grasp of the balloon's potential (Fig. 1-5) as a practical device was typical of America's vigorous youth, of her desire to find her place in the family of nations. Even then, at the beginnings of American history, conquest of the sky was a subject in the thoughts of the nation's leaders.

The best minds, both political and scientific, came to regard the balloon as a remarkable technological achievement that portended a revolution in transportation equally as important as that in government. With Charles' hydrogen balloon, the concept of phlogiston was put to rest. There was no mysterious substance involved in creating lift. An aircraft filled with a gas lighter than air was simply sustained through natural bouyancy.

Thomas Jefferson, America's top tinkerer, on February 18, 1784, wrote to a friend, Francis Hopkinson, of Philadelphia's Philosophical Society: "What think you of these balloons? They really begin to assume a serious face . . . this discovery seems to threaten the prostration of fortified works unless they can be closed from above, the destruction of fleets, and what not."

At Mount Vernon, General George Washington sat down at his writing desk, adjusted the false teeth made for him by Paul Revere, and penned a letter of inquiry to a friend living in Paris, Major-General Duportail: "I have only newspaper accounts of air-balloons, to which I do not know what credence to give. I suspect that our friends at Paris in a little time will come flying through the air, instead of ploughing the ocean, to get to America . . . "

Washington's thoughts about a trans-Atlantic airline would be more than a century in coming to reality, yet he had touched on the very point that concerned everyone involved in ballooning. How could balloons be made self-propelled and steerable so that they would not simply rise and float at the mercy of the winds.

Seeking to describe such an aircraft, a new phrase came into use—*balloon dirigere* Latin words meaning "to direct" or steer. The phrase would subsequently be changed to *dirigible balloon*, or simply *dirigible*.

Franklin continued to concentrate on the problem of dirigibility of balloons after witnessing the first hydrogen balloon ascension from Paris. On November 21. 1783, he witnessed the first free balloon ascent from La

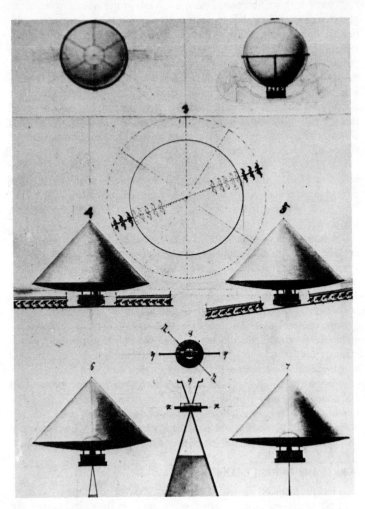

Fig. 1-5. A sketch for an eagle-powered conical baloon was found among Benjamin Franklin's papers in the American Philosophical Society library.

Muette, the royal chateau in Passy, by Pilatre de Rozier and the Marquis d'Arlandes. They managed to get their huge "montgolfier" up some 300 feet, only to drift across the Seine River.

That some day, Franklin wrote to Sir Joseph Banks in England: "These machines must always be subject to be driven by the winds. Perhaps mechanic art may find easy means to give them progressive motion, in a calm, and to slant them a little in the wind. This experiment is by no means a trifling one. It may be attended with important consequences that no one can foresee . . ."

Something of a libertine, Franklin was known in Paris as a romanticist as well as a scientist and diplomat. Apparently, Franklin had an eye for the beautiful wife of Jean Baptiste Le Roy—the scientist in charge of the king's laboratory at Chateau de la Muette in Passy with whom he enjoyed puttering and discussing ballooning. Madame Le Roy he called affectionately "Ia Femme de Pouche" (the pocket-wife) because of her diminutive size. After his return to the United States, he received a letter from her announcing that she had separated from her husband. She also revealed that she had made a balloon ascension. Madame Le Roy wrote that she had wished the balloon might have carried her to Franklin in America, for whom she held the "greatest love and admiration."

If Madame Le Roy never made the trans-Atlantic balloon flight to her love, Franklin's son, William Franklin, did manage to send the world's first airmail letter to the American statesman's grandson, William T. Franklin. The letter was carried aboard the first aerostat to cross the English Channel.

John Jeffries was the first American to make a balloon ascension. He crossed the English Channel as a passenger in a balloon piloted by the French aeronaut Jean-Pierre Blanchard. Jeffries, a Boston medical student had gone abroad in 1768 to study and he received his medical degree at Aberdeen the following year.

Returning to America during the period of political unrest, Jeffries became one of Samuel Adams' Sons of Liberty. Later he switched sides and in 1776 joined British General Howe's troops as a surgeon on their campaign to Nova Scotia. In 1779, Dr. Jeffries returned to England and won considerable attention both as a physician and a meteorologist.

When Blanchard appeared in London with his balloon, Jeffries paid 100 pounds for a seat to become the first American citizen to go aloft. The trip lasted two hours and the ascent from London on November 30, 1784 was witnessed by such notables as the Prince of Wales. The Duchess of Devonshire personally held one of the restraining ropes.

ACROSS THE ENGLISH CHANNEL

Jeffries financed Blanchard on January 7, 1785, when the latter made the first successful Channel-crossing attempt from Dover to France—but there was a hitch. Despite Jeffries' backing, Blanchard decided at the last minute to fly alone in order to keep for himself the honor of making the world's first international flight. With typical Yankee directness, Jeffries quitely gathered together a small mob of sailors and presented himself at Dover Castle. Blanchard discreetly took him along.

The crossing was a thrilling one. Blanchard took a along a pair of silken oars to row against any adverse wind. Half way across, when a downward rush of the balloon threatened to plunge them into the icy Channel waters, all ballast had to be jettisoned—including the silken oars. The aerostat rose and continued to drift. Nearing the French coast it again began to settle, as Blanchard noted the barometric pressure falling.

Ripping off their heavy clothing and tossing it overboard, the balloonists checked the descent log enough for them to reach land. But once more disaster threatened as they sank toward the treetops of the forest of Guines. Jeffries wrote later that they were saved by one last and "curious" expedient to lighten the balloon. The American passenger reached out then and grabbed a treetop, ending the historic voyage. He personally delivered the letter to William T. Franklin in Passy.

Blanchard's carreer was a turbulent one. On a visit to Austria, he was arrested on a charge of spreading anti monarchist propaganda during the French Revolution. He escaped to the United States, where he made numerous balloon ascensions, before returning to France.

BALLONETS

Fresh attempts were being made to convert spherical balloons into dirigibles with no success. In England, Charles Green introduced coal gas as a cheaper substitute for hydrogen and in 1784 a young officer in the French Army's engineer corps came up with a concept for a dirigible balloon remarkably like today's airship designs. The officer, Jean-Baptiste Meusnier, had, in 1793, submitted to the French Academie des Sciencesa paper on aerostatics in which he proposed the first concept for ballonets. These were air-filled reservoirs inside an outer ellipsoidal envelope, which, when inflated with pumps, would keep the pressure inside the envelope constant and thus hold its shape. The method also would dispense largely with the need for valving off gas or dropping ballast to regulate the dirigible's bouyancy in relation to the air that it displaced.

Meusnier's "Ellipsoidal Airship" design was 260 feet in length and included such advanced ideas as a rudder, elevator, and three huge airscrews of the Archimedean type, to be powered by a crew of forty men turning a crank linked to the propeller shafts by ropes. It never got off the ground or off the drawing board. Original water color drawings of the Meusnier dirigible are preserved in the Musee de l'Air at Chalais-Meudon.

More than half a century passed before a successful dirigible flight was achieved. But in the meantime, inventors were having a field day trying. In 1784, a member of the French Academy, the geometrician Monge, proposed linking 25 spherical balloons together like beads on a necklace, supposedly, they would undulate through the sky powered with silken oars in the manner of a water snake.

In the following year, M. Vallet, director of a chemical factory at Javel, made a number of ascents in a spherical balloon outfitted with a pair of wheels, or four-bladed propellers, which he had previously tested to propel a boat along the Seine. It has been suggested that Meusnier got his idea for his dirigible propulsion system from Vallet.

Meusnier's airship employed a triangular suspension system which hung the passenger car from suspension cords attached to girths around the balloon itself. He further proposed that a portable tent could be used to hangar the dirigible during military field operations, as well as a permanent shed. His idea of employing an ellipsoidal balloon, according to M. J. B. Davy of the British Science Museum, "unquestionably marks the inception of the airship, and his plan for propulsion was far ahead of any hitherto proposed."

General Meusnier never lived to see his dirigible actually built. In the year 1793, at the age of 39, he died in battle before Mayence. It is recorded that the King of Prussia ordered a cease-fire for his army until Meusneir was buried, as a tribute to his genius.

Two Parisians, the brothers Anne-Jean and M. N. Robert, were the first actually to employ Meusnier's ballonet idea in an actual aircraft. It was an ellipsoidal balloon financed by Louis Phillipe Duc de Chatres which measured 52 feet in length. It was filled with 28,274 cubic feet of hydrogen gas and included a ballonet of 3571 cubic feet displacement.

THE FIRST DIRIGIBLE ASCENT

There was a great sendoff on the morning of July 15, 1784. Hundreds of watchers gathered at the Parc de St. Cloud to watch the world's first dirigible rise. The dirigible carried three passengers—the Roberts brothers and the Duc de Chatres. Silken oars had been provided to row the craft over the Parisian housetops. But as it turned out, there was no opportunity to try them. As the dirigible rose, the hydrogen gas expanded. But no safety valve had been installed, and in alarm, the trio watched the silken gas bag swell almost to the point of bursting. Duc de Chatres saved the day, however, by grabbing a flagstaff with a pointed spearhead and jabbing the envelope, permitting gas to escape. A second trial flight was made from the Tuileries on September 19 that year. The craft was carried by air currents as far as Beauvry, near Bethune, but no credit can be given to the oars for directing its flight path or increasing its speed.

The public was becoming exasperated with such foolishness and was prepared to heap ridicule on other daring aeronauts of the period who attempted to make their lighter-than-air machines sail against the winds. On July 11, 1784, a crowd gathered at the Luxembourg to watch two experimenters named Miolan and Janinet attempt controlled flight in a dirigible "Montgolfiere." They planned to propel the craft by means of jets of hot air escaping from ports along the meridian of the hot-air bag. It also had a large, fan-shaped rudder. They never got off the ground, due to high winds, and in an ensuing riot the machine was burned by the mob.

The problem of aerial navigation by a dirigible balloon in fact seemed so difficult to achieve that the Academy of Lyons in France at this time offered a prize for a worthy essay on *"la maniere la moins dispendieuse et la plus efficace de diriger a volante les machines aerostatiques."* A total of 101 entries were made. However, the prize was not attained, although one entry did come close. Distinguished physicist and chemist L. B. Guyton de Morveau (1737-1816) began experimenting in December 1783, at the instance of the Academy of Dijon, with ways to steer a balloon through the sky. Guyton de Morveau was no idle dreamer. He had proposed using balloons to lift water from flooded mines and suggested making the gas bag of metal—an idea that would be the forerunner of metalclads of the 20th century.

The Dijon balloon carried a pair of oblong winglike surfaces attached to the gas bag. One served as a prow and the other as a rudder. A pair of smaller wings on either side served as oars, with another pair worked from the car. A number of flights was carried out in the summer of 1784 without success. While silken oars never would prove useful in future attempts, the ellipsoidal shape and use of ballonets would prove practical in modern dirigibles.

One such craft was a fish-shaped balloon proposed in 1789 by the French Baron Scott, an officer of the Dragoons, in a work entitled *Aerostat Dirigeable a Volante*. Scott envisioned using a pair of air pockets outside the gas bag fore and aft. By drawing them inside the gas bag, one at a time, the lift at that end would be decreased, causing the dirigible to tilt. The principle of air pockets did prove successful more than a century later when adapted to the German Parseval non-rigid airships of 1908. Scott's design inspired S. J. Pauly, a Genevan gunsmith, to construct a fish-formed balloon in 1804 that was to be propelled by silken oars.

In 1815, Pauly visited London and together with Durs Egg built a second similar craft called the Dolphin Balloon. He proposed using movable ballast (weight shift) to tilt the nose of the craft up or down. The project was abandoned before completion.

On July 9, 1825, the famous French aeronaut, Eugene Robertson, made the first manned balloon ascent from New York City—in return for a $1200 subscription from Castle Garden. A special tent was provided for the visiting Marquis de Lafayette and the affair was spectacular to say the least.

Promptly at 7 o'clock, Robertson took his place in the balloon basket. "Remaining in the same attitude," the *New York Post* reported, "holding in one hand the flag of the United States and in the other the French flag," Robertson was towed once around the amphitheater. Then Lafayette severed the last ribbon, sending the aeronaut aloft to glory. Shortly afterward another balloon, smaller and without a passenger, was sent up. This balloon was intended to represent the great racehorse Eclipse. Surmounting it was the gallant figure of a knight in armor.

GENET'S FOLLY

About this time, an ex patriate Frenchman living upriver from New York City precipitated a sensational battle of opinion between the leading American scientists of the day with the publication of a work entitled: *"On the Upward Forces of Fluids and Their Applicability to Several Arts, Sciences, and Public Improvements: For Which a Patent Has Been Granted by the Government of the United States to the Author, Edmond Charles Genet."* The storm centered around a proposal in Genet's book for a gigantic dirigible airship to be driven by a fan arrangement powered with two furiously running horses galloping on a circular treadmill (Fig. 1-6).

Dr. Thomas P. Jones, editor of the *Franklin Journal and Mechanics Magazine*, reprinted in July 1826 a scathing article which had appeared in the *Boston Journal of Philosophy and the Arts*. The article ridiculed Genet for daring to suggest such an absurdity. Jones described Genet's airship as "a monstrous balloon, which is to be loaded with windmill and two horses, three men, their attendants, a chemical apparatus, an anchor, fodder and provender, water, provisions for three men, and errors and omissions to the amount of 13,400 pounds."

Genet leaped to his own defense with an article which Benjamin Silliman condescended to run in his *American Journal of Science and Arts* early the following year. However, Genet seems to have succeeded only in getting into deeper and deeper water. After lamenting that the editors of the *Boston Journal of Philosoply and the Arts* had "endeavored to recreate their readers at my cost", Genet went on to explain that "there are two different kinds of upward forces in fluids, the one due to the principle of gravity, and the other to what I call the principle of levity."

Genet himself was not altogether sure just what the "principle of levity" was, but he took a stab at explaining it. He claimed that it was "due to the action of another fluid, which draws upward toward the ethereal regions certain particles of matter and aerial fluids, in proportion to their degree of affinity with the unknown cause of that ascensive and centrifugal force."

Silliman was a bit gentler with Genet, stating that "there is a wide difference between attempting that which is absurd, and that which is only very difficult. Perpetual motion is an absurdity, but it involves no absurdity to attempt to rise into the atmosphere, or to attempt to steer our way when we have arrived there . . . that it is physically possible to raise horses, and even relays of horses, into the atmosphere, with sufficient provender for a few days, is certain."

Edmond Charles Genet might have been a dreamer, but he did have a considerable reputation as a statesman. In 1874, France noted with alarm England's rapid industrial rise and sent Genet to that country as a special envoy to study means of improving France's manufacturing facilities. In Birmingham, Genet met Watt and Boulton, the noted pioneers of steam engine construction, who willingly gave him valuable information on the subject.

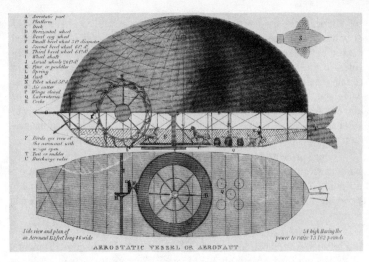

Fig. 1-6. Edmond Charles Genet's 2-horsepower dirigible.

Genet was appointed French Minister to the United States in 1793 and immediately began organizing military expeditions against Florida and Louisiana. Then he commissioned a number of privateers to prey on British shipping. These actions were not in accordance with President George Washington's ideas of American neutrality and the French minister was hastily recalled.

Finding America to his liking, Genet settled down and became a citizen of the United States. In 1814, he married Miss Martha Brandon Osgood, daughter of Samuel Osgood, the first United States Postmaster General. Thereafter, he spent much of his time in scientific research and publishing a number of papers on various scientific matters.

A champion of Genet's horse powered balloon was Dr. Felix Pascalis, President of the American branch of the Linnean Society of Paris, who favorably reviewed Genet's book in *The American Journal of Science and Arts* at about the same time Boston was condemning it. Dr. Pascalis pointed out that Genet had been a contemporary of Montgolfier, "was present at the first balloon ascension which he performed before the King of France, and soon after, in 1783, he read a memoir to the Royal Academy, of which he was a member, on the means of applying steam power for the propulsion of balloons, and he obtained the applause of that learned society."

Genet's "Aerostatic Vessel," for which he obtained the second United States aeronautic patent ever granted (on October 31, 1825) consisted of an "elliptic hemisphere." It was designed to resemble a fish, 152 feet long, 46 feet wide, and 54 feet high and it contained an astonishing 1,023,000 cubic feet of hydrogen—similar to that of 20th century Zeppelin rigids. He computed its lifting power at nearly 37 tons.

Beneath the gas bag was suspended a platform, or deck, in the center of which was placed a horizontal wheel. The wheel was journaled and geared to two large paddlewheels, each 20 feet in diameter. On opposite sides of the huge drive wheel, two horses were harnessed so that in running their hooves would cause the treadmill to turn and drive the paddle wheels at a speed of 21 rpm. In front, Genet provided an "air cutter" or elevator for pitch control, and at the stern was fitted a rudder, "not only to steer the machine, but also to supply it with an additional force of propulsion by means of an oscillatory motion, like that of sculling a boat."

Wings projected from either side and were so rigid that they could be withdrawn in flight or extended to produce a parachute effect while descending to land. Equipment was to be carried at each end of the deck to generate gas and the space between was left clear for passengers and freight.

Genet interested Robertson in his proposal and received an encouraging letter from the balloonist urging him not to let the plan lie dormant.

"Having read attentively the Memorial," wrote Robertson, "I do not see why the scheme should not work . . . The Americans have applied steam power, combined with mechanics, to the regular navigation of water; let them now apply the aerostatic power to the navigation of the air, a double conquest, which will spread an immortal fame over their national character."

The French aeronaut regretted that "indispensible engagements have obliged me to visit New Orleans for an ascent," but he told Genet he hoped to return shortly and assist him with construction and operation of a full-scale horse powered balloon.

Genet meanwhile conceived a plan to employ his horse powered balloon in search of a Northwest Passage. The Northwest passage was a topic foremost in the public mind since Sir John Franklin's expedition of 1821-22. Franklin had traveled 5500 miles and followed the Coppermine River to its mouth. On January 16, 1826, Genet wrote from Albany to a friend in Washington City, urging him to present copies of his paper to political leaders—one to President John Quincy Adams; one to "Mr. Henry Clay, who has so conspicuously signalized himself by his zeal for the promotion of the useful arts; and, if a committee has been appointed on that very interesting part of the President's Message, relative to astronomy, to voyages of discovery and to a geographical survey of the Northwest coast of this Continent, with another copy."

Genet wished to impress Washington with the "incontestible principles upon which rest the hope of succeeding in the construction of an aerial vessel or aeronaut, by the means of which our fellow citizens could in a very short time, and very conveniently, explore all the Polar Circle, while the British and the Russians are enduring all sorts of difficulties and disappointment in the vain attempt of finding a passage to those unknown regions."

"If in reality there is a Polar sea free from ice," Genet added, "the only practical method of penetrating there is by Aeronautic means, which would afford the facility either of hovering above all the extent of that great unknown, or of transporting to its shores, either from the Behring or Melville Straits, the materials necessary to construct better vessels than the crazy canoes used by Captain Franklin in his first expedition from the Coppermine River . . . "

Washington D.C. apparently did not share Genet's enthusiasm for his horse powered balloon as a means for polar exploration. His scheme was never officially acted upon. However, his proposal was perhaps the first to suggest dirigibles might be used to explore the frozen Arctic regions. This was a prophetic concept that would come true a century later.

Chapter 2

The Search for an Engine

Of all the problems relating to development of a successful dirigible, unquestionably the most important was the lack of an adequate means of propulsion. An engine that was both lightweight and sufficiently powerful was needed to overcome the high skin drag of a giant, elongated gas bag and to provide sufficient thrust to give it a practical headway.

THE FIRST PRACTICAL APPROACH

Everything imaginable had been tried soon after the Montgolfiers first ascended in their hot air balloons—silken oars, man-powered Archimedean screws, horses and even harnessed birds. Without a doubt, the first practical approach to the problem was made by Sir George Cayley of England. He is widely recognized as the "father of aeronautics" in Great Britain for his work on mechanical flight, but also widely overlooked for his contributions to the problems of navigable balloons.

Cayley was born at his ancestral home at Brampton in Yorkshire on December 27, 1773, and was admittedly inspired by the Montgolfiers to study aeronautics. In the years 1816 - 17 Cayley first published his ideas on navigable balloons in the pages of Tilloch's *Philosophical Magazine*, where he suggested the formation of a 'Society for Promoting Aerial Navigation', and in the *Mechanics' Magazine* in 1837. In 1809, he expressed his faith in the future of "Aerial Navigation" writing that "an uninterrupted navigable ocean, that comes to the threshold of every man's door, ought not to be neglected as a source of human gratification and advantage."

While his earliest experiments in aeronautics concerned mechanical flight, his ultimate faith in navigating the sky lay in the potential of the navigable balloon. Shortly before his death in 1857, Sir George wrote that

"On a great scale, balloon floatage offers the most ready, efficient, and safe means of aerial navigation. Elongated balloons of large dimensions, thus offer greater facilities for transporting men and goods through the air, then mechanical means alone . . . and when the invention is realized, it will abundantly supply the increasing locomotive wants of mankind."

Pointing out that the surface of a balloon increases as the square of its diameter, and hence its resistance to forward motion due to increased skin drag (not then defined), he also reminded that the volume of bouyant gas increased as the cube of the diameter.

It was thus obvious to Cayley that giant navigable balloons would require "acres, not yards of cloth" to construct. He also was sanguine about the need for changing the balloon's form from spherical to cylindrical and suggested the need for dividing the gas into several compartments "like the stomach of a leech."

He foresaw the coming of a rigid dirigible shape as a requirement to protect its shape against air resistance—a matter then not fully understood. A steam engine, about the only type of engine that appeared practical at that time should, he felt, be suspended in a car well below the balloon itself to keep the fire well away from the inflammable hydrogen gas.

In 1816, Cayley's first design (Fig. 2-1) employed a hot-air "Montgolfier" type gas bag 300 feet long and 45 feet in diameter by 90 feet wide. It consisted of two elongated balloons linked side-by-side. This design reappeared in mid-century in the *Aereon* of Dr. Solomon Andrews of Perth Amboy, New Jersey. A crew of seven would man the craft and it was expected to travel at 15 miles per hour with steam propulsion. Actually an

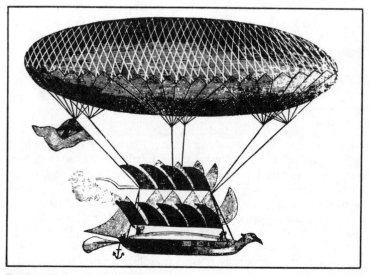

Fig. 2-1. Cayley's navigable balloon.

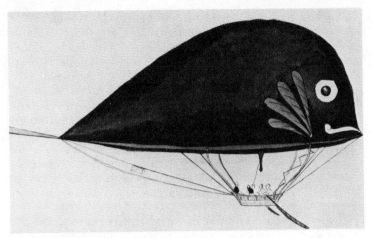

Fig. 2-2. Pauley and Egg's "Dolphin."

elongated spheroid with conical head and a tapered stern, it followed the advice of seamen that a ship, to sail well, should have a "cod's head and a mackerel's tail."

Subsequently, Cayley expanded his design into a craft 432 feet long requiring 11,880 square yards of cloth weighing one-half pound per square foot and with a lifting power of 163,000 pounds. Deducting 1700 pounds for the weight of the craft and another 15,210 pounds for engine, boiler, etc., he arrived at a payload of 34 tons. That would have been equivalent to carrying 500 men for one hour or 50 men for a full 48 hours. Range was given as 960 miles in calm air. The steam powerplant was to drive twin pusher propellers, or as an alternative, a set of wings to flap in the manner of a bird, or ornithopter. His published data on engine power, speed, pressures, and fabric were well advanced for his day. No record exists that Cayley built such a navigable balloon as he proposed, yet he is known to have conducted many preliminary experiments to prove his ideas.

OTHER SCHEMES

By contrast to Cayley's scientific approach to dirigibles, a few nuttier schemes should be mentioned in passing. Among them is the Dolphin fish-shaped balloon mentioned in Chapter 1. In 1816, Pauly and Egg, both Swiss nationals, built a huge wooden hangar 100 feet long at Knightsbridge in London in which to fabricate their dirigible, 85 feet long, 32 feet high, and sporting a rudder of whalebone and silk, 15 feet in length (Fig. 2-2).

The main balloon casing was made from goldbeater's skin, the product of seventy thousand oxen, in sevenfold layers built up over a framework of wooden ribbing. A ballonet 21 feet in diameter also was built to "regulate the dilation and condensation" of hydrogen and so preserve its fish shape. Pauly hung a gondola beneath the balloon with a netting of white tape and employed a shifting ballast of a box of sand to be moved forward and backward to shift the center of gravity and tilt the head up or down. An "atmospheric" steam engine was suggested but not installed.

Egg's Folly, as the craft became known, was finally abandoned when Pauly died. This left Durs Egg to support the entire cost of the project— L10,000. Though it never flew, use of the ballonet was made to raise the famed dwarf, Tom Thumb, in a small car from the Surrey Zoological Gardens during an exhibition by the American showman P.T. Barnum.

In 1834, a French infantry colonel, Comte de Lennox, promoted a scheme to establish a dirigible airline between Paris and London. A stock company called the European Aeronautical Society was formed and a rowing balloon called the *Eagle* was built. The *Eagle* was actually built in Paris and an overseas office was set up in Golden Square, Soho, to sell stock in the venture.

In August of 1834, a crowd gathered to witness an ascent from the Champ de Mars in Paris. But before Lennox could climb aboard, the netting gave way and the balloon lurched skyward until it burst in midair. As was to be expected, a mob moved in and completed the destruction.

Thomas Monck Mason, was an operatic manager who at one time leased His Majesty's Theater, and who had been invited in 1836 by Charles Green to become one of eight passengers to make a historic balloon voyage from Vauxhall Gardens in London to Weilburg, Germany. The trip covered 480 miles in 18 hours.

Mason became so enthused with ballooning that he published a volume entitled *Aeronautica, or Sketches Illustrative of the Theory and Practice*

Fig. 2-3. Thomas Monck-Mason's ellipsoidal dirigible (1843).

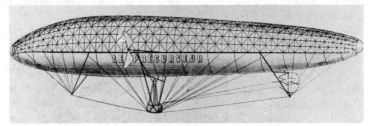

Fig. 2-4. Pierre Jullien's Le Precurseur flew as a model (1852).

of Aerostation in which he proposed means of making a free balloon dirigible. Mason actually did build a working model of an ellipsoidal balloon 44 feet long with a displacement of 320 cubic feet, weighing 20 pounds and inflated with hydrogen. In 1843, it was exhibited at the Royal Adelaide Gallery in the London Strand and cheered by viewers as it circumnavigated the gallery at a speed of 6 miles an hour, propelled by clockwork (Fig. 2-3).

The success of this model dirigible inspired a French clockmaker, Pierre Jullien of Villejuif, to build a model dirigible in 1852. He optimistically called it *Le Precurseur* (Fig. 2-4). Of clean, streamlined form tapering to the stern, it was driven by clockwork geared to a pair of propellers mounted on either side of the craft. *Le Precurseur* was fitted with both vertical and horizontal control surfaces, but lack of funds prevented Jullien from building a full scale model. One Parisian who viewed the model *Le Precurseur* making its way around the Hippodrome gallery would go away with his head full of ideas. Henri Giffard built the world's first successful airship two years later as the result of this inspiration (Fig. 2-5).

In 1850, another experimenter in England, Dr. Hugh Bell, (a physician by profession) constructed a 50-foot dirigible (Fig. 2-6) he called the *Locomotive Balloon*. It was based on a British patent (No. 12,337) granted in 1848. The silken gas bag held 15,000 cubic feet of coal gas and reportedly could lift approximately 500 pounds of payload.

Bell's inventiveness let him design the craft's passenger car in the form of a canoe in the event it came down over the sea. At the stern, he installed a screw propeller to be turned manually. Curiously, this employment of a screw propeller drew a protest from J. J. O. Taylor. In 1802, Taylor had invented a screw propeller for marine navigation and he claimed to have been the first to think of it for use in aircraft.

Nevertheless, a trial flight was made in May, 1850, from the Phoenix Gas Works at Kennington Oval. Bell was alone in the canoe-car. Cranking furiously to turn the 6-foot propeller, Bell also had to manage the gas valve and steer the craft. After drifting nearly 30 miles in 1½ hours, he came down near High Laver, Essex, where a tragedy occurred. Bell lowered his grapnel to stop the craft's progress and it struck a lad in the head as he ran up to assist in the landing. The boy was killed.

Fig. 2-5. Frenchman Henri Giffard experimented with this dirigible. It was powered by a steam engine (1855).

Lest we forget the dreamers at this stage of dirigible development, consider the excitement caused by a gentleman named James Nye. In 1852, he published a pamphlet entitled *Thoughts on Aerial Travelling and on the Best Means of Propelling Balloons*. He proposed to propel his 337-foot long dirigible through the air by means of successive firing of

Fig. 2-6. Dr. Hugh Bell's 50-foot dirigible flew in 1850.

3-pounder rockets, one every seven seconds, with the goal of covering 200 miles in seven hours. Fortunately, the craft was never built.

John Luntley was another imaginative Britisher. In 1851, he published a pamphlet entitled *Air Navigation* describing a dirigible 120 feet long built in a corkscrew shape. The idea was for the whole balloon to rotate and screw its way across the heavens. It was supposed to burn hydrogen gas as fuel and travel 700 miles at 30 mph with a cargo of 23 tons.

Do you think he was crazy? Then how about Richard Boyman? In 1866, he proposed a steel balloon of cylindrical shape with conical ends and using jet propulsion for motive power? Consider Philip Brannon's *Arcustat* of 1871. It was designed with three sections—the upper one containing hydrogen gas for lift, the middle one fitted with a heating apparatus to produce rarefied air, and the daring aeronauts risking their lives below!

THE FIRST PRACTICAL DIRIGIBLE

Henri Giffard, constructor of the first truly navigable balloon was best known for his invention of the steam injector. The stream in sector produced sufficient royalties to allow him to experiment at leisure with matters aeronautical. Giffard, who had worked with Le Berrier (Lennox's colleague in the *Eagle* project of 1834), made his first ascent as a free balloonist in 1851 with the prominent aeronaut Eugene Godard.

In the same year, Giffard built a small, lightweight steam engine of three horsepower. Subsequently, in a patent application for a means of "application de la vapeur a la navigation aerienne," he described in detail a model oblong aerostat with a steam-driven screw propeller. In 1852, Giffard designed and built a full-scale dirigible roughly 144 feet long and 40 feet in diameter, with a displacement of 88,000 cubic feet.

Slung 20 feet beneath the envelope was a small single-cylinder steam engine of three horsepower, with a vertical boiler and enclosed firebox, that drove a three-bladed propeller at 110 rpm and produced a speed of 6 mph. On September 24, 1852, Giffard ascended from the Hippodrome in Paris to make history with the world's first successful dirigible flight. He demonstrated its control in a light breeze and landed safely near Trappes.

Giffard was well aware of the hazard of setting the dirigible's hydrogen gas afire with his steam engine. He took the special precaution of screening the stokehole with wire gauze. This was an application of the precaution taken by Sir Humphrey Davey who was the inventor of the miner's lamp that bears his name. The initial flight covered a distance of some 17 miles at an airspeed estimated at 5.5 mph.

During this flight, Giffard made some experiments with a triangular sail that served as a rudder and which enabled him to deviate his course from the direction the wind was blowing him. However, he was not able to complete a circle or return to his starting point—no doubt because of the underpowered engine.

Giffard's dirigible has been described as notable not only as the first moderately successful navigable airship, but also as a prototype of the future semi-rigid type. His achievement was more remarkable due to the fact it contained no ballonet to maintain its streamlined shape under influence of pressure of the relative wind. However, he did not attempt to rise to any great altitude so there was no great need for a ballonet to compensate for pressure changes due to altitude.

Giffard built a second airship in 1855, slightly larger than the first, and had a still bigger one on the drawing board. But for all his pioneering work and brilliant achievement as an inventor of the first practical dirigible, his life ended tragically when he became blind and died prematurely in 1882.

It is interesting to speculate what might have transpired had Giffard lived to build the third dirigible he planned—one of truly gigantic proportions even by today's standards. It was to be 1970 feet long, 98 feet in diameter at midsection and have a displacement of 7,800,000 cubic feet. To power this giant, he designed a steam engine weighing 30 tons which he believed would provide a cruising speed of 45 miles an hour.

Realizing that he was limited by the engine's high power-to-weight ratio, Giffard felt that the only answer was to construct a gigantic envelope able to support the heavy powerplant. The high cost of such a project rendered it impractical and in later years Giffard confined his aeronautical work to the building of large captive balloons.

AMBITIOUS PLANS

Free balloons were widely employed as a means of escape during the siege of Paris imposed by the Prussian army during the Franco-German War. Leon Gambett, France's Premier, escaped in a remarkable flight from Montmartre on October 6, 1870, to establish a new government seat

Fig. 2-7. Eight "galley slaves" powered Dupuy de Lome's 1872 airship.

Fig. 2-8. Dupuy de Lome's man-powered dirigible flew in 1872.

at Tours. There he soon formed a dozen army corps representing 36 divisions.

A still more ambitious craft (Figs. 2-7 and 2-8) was planned by Stanislas-Charles Henri-Laurent Dupuy De Lome (1816-1885). He was a noted French naval architect who was a member of the government's Committee of Defense that took over the reins of government when Napoleon III fell in September 1870. He was given a credit of 40,000 francs to build a giant steerable dirigible. Capitulation ended the project before the craft was completed, but two years later he felt ready to try again. This time he built a small dirigible, similar to Giffard's, measuring 108 feet in length and 47 feet in diameter.

With no lightweight engine available, he was forced to depend on manpower. In a large wicker car slung by a network of triangular ropes, he provided room for eight "galley slaves" to turn a long crankshaft linked to a 4-bladed propeller at the bow.

The Dupey de Lome dirigible made only one flight, from the fortress at Vincennes, on February 2, 1872, and proved to be somewhat successful by veering 12 degrees off course under power—defying a light wind. A safe landing was made at Mondecourt after achieveing an airspeed estimated at 5 miles an hour. The aircraft had all the features of a modern non-rigid airship with control and stability, suspension system, ballonet and blower and an envelope of double-ply rubberized and doped fabric. Only an adequate powerplant was missing. Later in that decade two other balloonists, Albert and Gaston Tissandier (who had also built war balloons during the Siege of Paris), fitted an electric motor to a dirigible.

In the meantime, a daring project was initiated by the German engineer Paul Haenlein (1835-1905). He wanted to power a dirigible with an

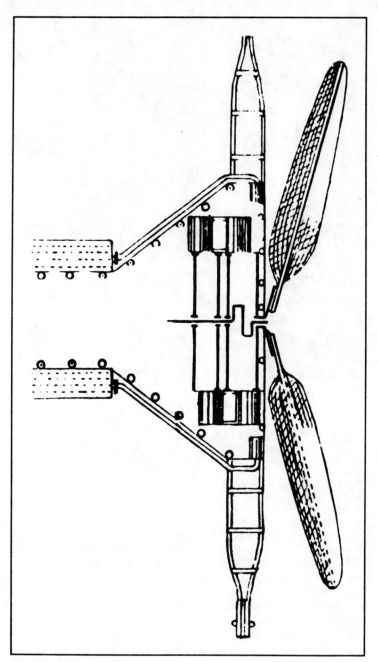

Fig. 2-9. Paul Haenlein's 164-foot dirigible flew in 1872. It used a Lenoir gas engine.

Fig. 2-10. The Tissandier brothers experimented with a dirigible powered with an electric motor. (1833).

internal combustion engine designed to operate on gas drawn from the balloon itself. In 1865, Haenlein patented a design for an elongated dirigible fitted with a horizontal framework underneath to serve as a rigid keel (Fig. 2-9). He proposed to use a primitive gas engine of the Lenoir type, burning coal gas, and meant to keep the dirigible rotund by using a ballonet and blower.

Haenlein completed his dirigible at Brunn, Bavaria, in 1872. The 4-cylinder Lenoir engine swung a 4-bladed propeller at 40 rpm and delivered an estimated 5-brake horsepower. The engine, which has been patented in 1860 by Etienne Lenoir, did not operate on the 4-stroke cycle. Instead, like most of the existing steam engines, it was double-acting. A mixture of coal gas and air was drawn into each end of the cylinder alternatively by means of an eccentric driven sleeve valve. The charge was fired by an electric spark, but the operation was inefficient since the fuel-air mixture was not compressed inside the cylinder. In fact, it developed less power than a steam engine of equivalent size and weight. However, it did dispense with the need for carrying a heavy boiler.

. Haenlein's dirigible was 164 feet long and 30 feet in diameter with a displacement of 85,000 cubic feet. It has been described as resembling a pair of ship hulls fitted together. A ballonet was employed and the car was slung close to the belly of the gas bag for rigidity. The engine was designed to draw 250 cubic feet of gas per hour from the balloon and the loss was to be compensated for by further inflating the ballonet and by discharging ballast.

The weight of Haenlein's engine and the use of coal gas rather than hydrogen severely limited its lifting power and the craft was never flown freely. However, it was flown at tether on December 13, 1872, at Brunn. Soldiers held the restraining ropes and its speed was estimated at 10 mph.

REACHING THE SUBSTRATOSPHERE

Two other French aeronauts figure prominently in the history of the development of the dirigible. Gaston and Albert Tissandier made many scientific ascensions to the substratosphere. On one such flight, Gaston Tissandier reached a height of 27,950 feet with no supplemental oxygen and was rendered unconscious. Two companion scientists, H.T. Sivel and J.E. Croce-Spinelli, lost their lives through asphyxiation. The Tissandier brothers served in the French aeronautic corps during the Franco-German

Fig. 2-11. Albert and Gaston Tissandier flew a 92-foot dirigible powered by an electric motor.

Fig. 2-12. Renard and Kreb's Dirigible La France flew in 1884 on electric power.

War. With this practical and scientific background, they felt ready in the early 1880s to attempt construction of a dirigible to be powered with an electric motor.

The Tissandier dirigible was similar in form and size to that of Dupuy de Lome. They fitted a Siemens electric motor of 1.5 horsepower in the car. The current came from a series of 24 bichromate of potash batteries hooked up in series (Fig. 2-10). The batteries alone weighed a hearty quarter ton. Their first trial flight was made on October 8, 1883 (Fig. 2-11), from the infield of the Autiel racetrack near Paris. Despite a light zephyr, some control was achieved using a sail-like rudder at the stern. On September 26, a second test flight was made with more positive results. However, when the craft encountered a slight wind its low-powered motor was not up to combatting it and the experiments were abandoned.

It should be noted that Gason Tissandier's son, Paul, would become one of France's first pilots of heavier-than-air crafts. Paul Tissandier was checked out in the Wright Flyer by none other than Wilbur Wright. In addition, Paul Tissandier was a competition pilot during the world's first airplane races at Rheims in 1909.

THE LA FRANCE

More successful than the Tissandier dirigible was one constructed the following year by Charles Renard and Captain A.C. Krebs. It was a torpedo-shaped affair 165 feet in length and 27 feet in diameter at the widest section. They gave it the name *La France* (Figs. 2-12 and 2-13). Both officers of the French Corps of Engineers, these men had been planning their navigable balloon since 1878 and they had hoped to persuade the Minister of War, (through their commander, Colonel Laussedat) to finance the project. The government, however, had decided against spending more francs on dirigibles after the Dupuy de Lome effort. Fortunately, they found a champion in Premier Leon Gambetta who had not forgotten that he owed his escape from Paris during the Siege to a balloon. Gambetta personally invested sufficient funds to carry out the project.

With a displacement of 66,000 cubic feet, *La France* was gracefully streamlined with the widest part forward. Beneath the gas bag it carried a long and slender car 108 feet long consisting of a canvas-covered bamboo framework 6 feet high. At the prow was fitted a 23-foot, 4-bladed wooden propeller which was driven by a multi-polar electric motor (Fig. 2-14) developed by Krebs. The motor delivered 7.5 brake horsepower and was operated on current produced by a series of light chromium chloride batteries designed and built by Renard. The motor subsequently was

Fig. 2-13. Krebs and Renard's dirigible balloon (1884).

replaced with one of Theophile Gramme's series-wound motors that developed an extra horsepower. The batteries and motor weighed 210 pounds with an awkward 85 lb/hp power-to-weight ratio.

A curious feature of the big propeller was its ability to be gimballed upward on landing to prevent the blades from striking the ground. A rectangular rudder and elevator control plane were fitted at the rear of the car and a sliding weight was provided to shift the center of gravity. A heavy guide-rope of the type invented by balloonist Charles Green was installed both to control height and to facilitate landings.

La France was built at the military balloon establishment at Chalais-Meudon near Paris. Krebs was a former director. Once completed, their dirigible was ground-bound for two months while its builders awaited calm weather for the initial trial. Finally, on August 9, 1884, at 4 p.m., the meterological conditions were favorable for the historic trial.

The aeronauts climbed aboard their car and started the motor. With the guide rope released, they rose slowly above treetop level. With the propeller turning slowly, the craft moved forward and they could feel the coolness of relative wind blowing on their faces. They dried out the rudder and it worked. Turning from south to west and encountering a north wind, they decided to complete the turn and head back to Chalais.

Delighted, they returned to their starting point and crossed Chalais at a height of 1000 feet. This was the first dirigible in history to accomplish a round trip voyage. The trip took 23 minutes and covered some five miles. Another seven flights were made during the next two years. Two flights were over the city of Paris, and on five flights *La France* returned to the starting point. The speed was 14.5 mph over the ground.

Even though Renard and Krebs had proven them fully controllable in a light wind, it was evident that a new source of power had to be found before dirigibles could become practical. Steam, electricity, compressed air, all had been tried and found insufficient to overcome the huge drag of skin friction—even flying at low Reynolds Numbers.

IMPORTANT BREAKTHROUGHS

Then in the 1880s, two important breakthroughs were achieved that would significantly improve the performance of dirigibles in the areas of power and weight. In 1885, the German engineer Gottlieb Daimler patented his historic benzine motor. This motor was an internal-combustion petrol engine developed from Nikolas Otto's improved 4-stroke gas engine. The following year, the electrolytic process for producing aluminum on a commercial scale was invented independently by P.L.T. Heroult in France and C.M. Hall in America.

The internal combustion engine not only made practicable dirigible aircraft, but revolutionized society by bringing the age of the automobile. As early as 1677, the Abbe Jean de Hautefeuille attempted to pump water to a higher level by combustion of gunpowder brought into contact with

Fig. 2-14. An electric multi-polar engine used on the La France (1884).

water. The vacuum formed by cooling the hot products of combustion was used to lift the water.

In 1824, the most thorough study of thermodynamic aspects of internal combustion engines was published in a pamphlet by Sadi Carnot in France. It also included the theory of diesel engine operation.

In 1838, William Barnett was granted a patent on a different idea—the first engine in which a charge was compressed before burning. Barnett also designed a 2-stroke engine with an external charging pump. The 2-stroke cycle is completed in a single up-and-down stroke of the piston, unlike the 4-stroke cycle which requires two up-and-down strokes (or two turns of the crankshaft). Barnett further devised an ingenious igniting cock that provided a pilot flame for igniting the charge and a relighter to rekindle the pilot light after it was extinguished when the oxygen inside the cylinder was consumed in the burning charge. This system was used in many engines prior to the development of electrical ignition. Another method of ignition, the hot plug, was introduced by Alfred Drake in 1843.

J.J.E. Lenoir's engine, used by Paul Haenlein in 1872, operated on illuminating gas but actually was not a new concept. In essence it was a converted double-acting steam engine with slide valves to admit gas and air and to discharge exhaust products. Although it developed little power and utilized only about 4 percent of the energy in gas, hundreds were sold.

In 1861, G. Schmidt proposed an engine in which the charge would be supercharged to three times atmospheric pressure before entering the cylinder. This would attain a greater transformation of heat energy.

In the following year the operating cycle of the modern automotive engine was proposed by Alphonse Beau de Rochas in Paris. He stated the four conditions required for maximum economy as:

—Maximum cylinder volume with a minimum cooling surface.
—Maximum rapidity of expansion.
—Maximum ratio of expansion.
—Maximum pressure of the ignited charge.

He next described the sequence of operation for attaining this maximum economy as:

—Suction during an entire outstroke of the piston.
—Compression during the following instroke.
—Ignition of the charge at dead center and expansion during the next outstroke (the power stroke).
—Forcing out the burned gases during the next instroke.

Today we describe the 4-cycle function simply as intake, compression, fire, and exhaust.

Because Beau de Rochas' work was entirely theoretical, his name is largely overlooked as the originator of the 4-stroke cycle. Instead, the credit is commonly given to Nikolas Otto. In 1867, the firm of Otto and Langen began producing a 3-piston engine in Deutz, Germany. Engines of this type had already been build by Barsanti and Matteucci.

THE OTTO SILENT ENGINE

In 1876, Otto applied the Beau de Rochas principle in a new engine that became known as the Otto silent engine. This was the first 4-stroke engine employing compression and operating on the basic principle of today's automobile engines. Although quite heavy and having poor efficiency, some 50,000 engines were sold in 17 years. Its success led to development of a wide variety of competitive engines under different brand names.

First to employ the new internal combustion engine in the air was Doctor Karl Woelfert of Germany. Woelfert had become a professional aeronaut making public ascensions at county fairs in an elongated balloon known as *The Cucumber.*

THE DAIMLER ENGINE

In October 1887, a publisher account of Woelfert's early dirigible experiments was read by the German engine builder Gottlieb Daimler. He had developed a vertical single-cylinder engine that ran on petrol. It had been used successfully in a boat and in road and rail cars and Daimler wondered whether his engine could be used in the sky as well. He invited

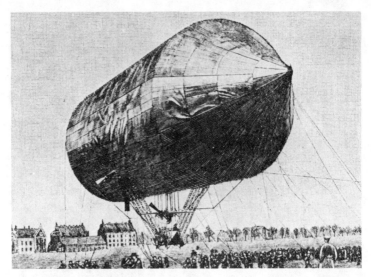
Fig. 2-15. David Schwartz' aluminum airship.

Woelfert to visit his plant at Cannstadt and Woelfert accepted. Daimler installed a 2-horsepower, single-cylinder engine into Woelfert's small dirigible that formerly had been manually-powered.

Initial trials were made at the Daimler plant site on August 12, 1888, but as Woelfert was too heavy to be carried aloft along with the engine, a slender young Daimler mechanic took the dirigible up. The ignition system of the Daimler engine used a platinum tube heated to a high temperature by the flame of a petrol burner. This was a considerable fire hazard. The young mechanic, named Michael, carried a lighted candle screened from the wind to relight the ignition burner when the propeller blast blew it out. He survived.

An improved dirigible 100 feet long and carrying a Daimler engine that swung a 7-foot aluminum propeller was tried out on June 12, 1897, at Templehof Field, Berlin. Woelfert planned to fly cross-country to Findorf and return. He was accomplished by his mechanic, Robert Knabe. At 3000 feet, the fuel tank exploded, apparently ignited by the burner, and the whole airship was engulfed in flames. Both men died in the fiery crash.

Another Daimler internal combustion engine of 12 horsepower was used to power the world's first aluminum hulled rigid airship. The airship was designed by the Austrian inventor David Schwartz and built in Berlin in 1895-97. Schwartz died before the craft was completed, but his widow was determined to carry on the project. The craft had a somewhat cylinderical appearance, but it actually was elliptical in cross-section and was 46 feet deep and 39 feet wide. The nose was conical and the stern slightly concave. Its length was 156 feet. Displacement was 130,000 cubic feet. The shell consisted of a tubular aluminum framework covered with

Fig. 2-16. David Schwartz' "Tin Can" airship crashed in 1897.

aluminum sheets .008 of an inch in thickness. The Daimler engine, placed in the car attached to the metal shell by aluminum struts, drove two tractor and one pusher propeller s linked by belts at 480 rpm.

Inflated at Temeplehoffer Field on November 12, 1897 (Fig. 2-15), the Schwartz metalclad dirigible was piloted by an inexperienced aeronaut unfamiliar with the craft. In the teeth of a 15-knot wind, the dirigible rose rapidly to a height of 82 feet. It was then blown off the field toward a group of buildings. The aeronaut apparently panicked and opened the relief valve. This caused the craft to plunge to earth. The aeronaut leaped to safety at the last moment, but the ship lay in twisted ruins and resembled a collapsed beer can (Fig. 2-16).

The obvious success of the Daimler engines for aeronautical use finally caught the attention of two men who would become prominent dirigible designers—Count Ferdinand Von Zeppelin, and Alberto Santos-Dumont.

Chapter 3

Go West By Airship

Ever since the first Montgolfier hot-air balloon probed the sky in 1783, the urge to make LTA vehicles go places at the will of the pilot rather than simply drift with the winds had been largely "goal-oriented." There was the desire to end England's insularity by linking her far-flung empire by air, the lure of the frozen north and the expectation of discovering the North Pole from the sky, and the excitement of searching for a Northwest Passage to the riches of China and the spices of India by a direct airline route, rather than rounding the "Horn" by clipper ship.

In the mid-19th century, the discovery of gold in California was the catalyst that would launch a number of schemes to carry prospectors directly from the Eastern Seaboard states to the Western gold fields by air, rather than crossing the wide prairies and mountains by wagon train or spending weeks and months following the sea route around South America.

PORTER'S PROPOSAL

A leading proponent of this concept was a Yankee jack-of-all-trades named Rufus (Fig. 3-1). His ideas were amazingly prophetic in regard to design and operation of passenger dirigibles. Porter built and successfully flew a scale model of his giant aircraft, and but for an unfortunate accident might have had America's first multiplace dirigible flying.

The war with Mexico was in full stride in 1847 when Rufus Porter began thrilling New York crowds with amazing demonstrations of his model of the world's first rigid dirigible. A full-size version of 160 feet in length actually was built later on. The ideas was, of course, not new. In 1784, Francis Hopkinson, a signer of the Declaration of Independence, had

Fig. 3-1. Rufus Porter formed the Aerial Navigation Company in 1852 to fly passengers to the gold rush country in a 160-foot dirigible. The dirigible was wrecked in a storm (courtesy of F. Rufus Porter).

thought of giving a balloon the shape of "a fish, or a bird, or a wherry," and other Americans like John Pennington and Citizen Genet had worried over the same problem with little practical success. Rufus Porter had the right answer.

Porter was a member of that odd fraternity of American inventors who, without benefit of special training or special laboratory facilities, stumbled blindly ahead, carving and whittling into reality golden ideas that flashed before them in crystal-clear visions. By only the narrowest margin, these men escape the lunatic fringe of individuality, but their freedom of spirit made them pioneers of science.

THE AEROPORT

Porter first turned his attention to aeronautics as early as 1820. In that year he applied for a United States Patent on an aerial ship he named for himself—the *Aeroport*. Far in advance of its day, the *Aeroport* consisted of a long, finely tapered gas bag from which was suspended a similarly shaped passenger car. Midway between the hull and car was mounted a large screw propeller that was geared to a steam engine placed within the car. Lack of finances prevented Porter from immediately developing the idea to a practical point. He turned for a time to developing other inventions to support a large and growing family.

Among his many accomplishments, Porter published in a trade paper called *Scientific Mechanic* (Fig. 3-2). He also found time to renew his work on the dirigible *Aeroport*. In the Christmas, 1847 issue of his inventor's newspaper, Porter featured on the front page a remarkable engraving of his airship under the caption: THE TRAVELLING BALLOON. The illustration showed clearly the manner in which Porter provided a rigid framework to hold the gas bag in a streamlined shape. This was an innovation that was to prove prophetic.

THE AERIAL STEAMER MODEL

Porter then constructed a spring-operated working model of the *Aeroport* that was some 6 feet in length and he gave a number of demonstration flights in the Merchant's Exchange Building to raise funds for the construction of a larger passenger carrying airship. The model was a huge success and crowds daily gathered to see the wonderful vessel churn its way in a circular path around the inside of the hall.

The New York press was loud in its acclaim of the *Aeroport*. The *New York Sun* reported: "The Aerial Steamer Model was again tried at the Merchant's Exchange yesterday afternoon and with brilliant success. It described the circle of the rotunda eleven times in succession, following its rudder like a thing instinct with life. With its description of each circle, burst after burst of applause arose from the excited throng, and followed it throughout its journey. At the close of the performance, three loud cheers were given for the steamer, and the auditors quitted the rotunda with every manifestation of pleasure and delight."

According to the *New York Sun*: "The Model Aerial Steamer was exhibited again in the Merchant's Exchange, and satisfied some of its greatest opponents that it could navigate the air."

With New York City practically at his feet, Porter prepared to exhibit a still larger model at Boston and another in Washington. The Massachussets capital shared New York's enthusiasm over the Aeroport and the *Boston Bee* reported favorably a demonstration given in Temple Hall.

Fig. 3-2. Rufus Porter's publication, the Scientific Mechanic, featured a story on his plans for a transcontinental dirigible.

"Mr. Porter's flying machine," reported the *Bee*, "did all that it promised on Wednesday evening. It rose above the audience, and went around the hall, exactly as he said it would, and the spectators gave three cheers for the successful experiment."

The *Boston Mail* was equally impressed, but reversed a small doubt about its future: "The flying machine did fly last evening, though rather slow. At the second and third attempts, the apparatus went round the hall, just over the heads of the auditory, very satisfactorily, and elicited three hearty cheers from the spectators. Mr. Porter may be considered as having fairly demonstrated the theory of aerial navigation; but it is only in the open air that the practicability of the theory can be demonstrated."

In Washington, Porter built a giant model, 22 feet long and 4 feet in diameter that was powered with a real steam engine. Two fan-bladed propellers drive it and a double tail comprised of horizontal and vertical surfaces provided directional and pitch control. Three feet below the bag was suspended a car 7 feet in length, 10 inches wide and tapered in outline to a double point. A row of tiny windows on each side of the car showed "the representation of many happy looking passengers looking out."

The *Scientific American* remarked that "when adjusted above the stage of Carusi's large hall—furnished with flags and gaily painted—and standing still without contact with anything, there was considerable sensation, and many rose to their feet; but in a moment the steam valve was opened and the miniature *Aeroport* started forward, and with rapid speed sailed round the circumference of the hall and returned promptly to the position whence it started."

Schools were let out in Washington to allow the children to "witness the phenomenon of a steam vessel sailing through the air," and Porter was discussed by the elite of Washington's society. The *Washington Evening Star* nicely summed up the day's opinion: "A mode of traveling rapid and safely through the air, in any required direction, has been desired by man in all ages of the world. But never prior to the introduction of Mr. Porter's model *Aeroport*, has anything appeared upon which creeping humanity could base a rational anticipation of the long-desired art; and even with the reality of a bona fide aerial steamer, men are inclined to imagine that what they see is but an optical illusion, or some peculiar affection of the imagination. But there is the tangible fact before them—a real, mechanically-constructed steam ship, with its wheels, engine, and cargo, floating in air, and occasionally shooting forward in directions or circles, according to the dictates of its engine and helm."

THE AERIAL NAVIGATION COMPANY

Despite this warm reception, Porter was unable to raise sufficient capital to construct a full-sized passenger carrying *Aeroport*. Finally, in the spring of 1852, he formed the Aerial Navigation Company. It was America's first company organized for the commercial exploitation of an aircraft. The company issued stock certificates at a par value of $5 each (Figs. 3-3 and 3-4). On March 19, 1852, Porter announced in the columns of the *National Intelligencer* his intention to establish an airline from Washington to California, and an airline to Europe. Operating on a two-day schedule each way, he hoped to derive profits amounting to $60,000 a week.

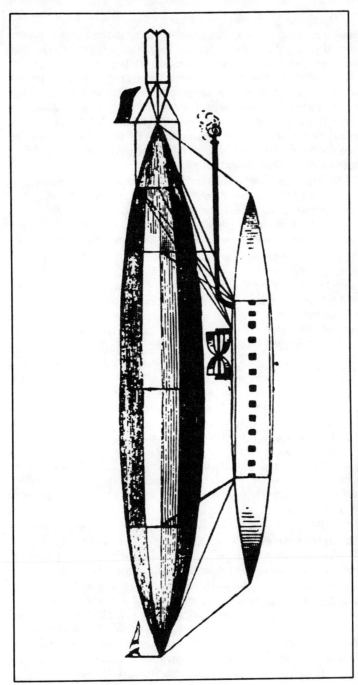

Fig. 3-3. The gold rush transcontinental dirigible of 1852.

America's first airline proposal met with favorable reception. Within three months after the announcement appeared in the *National Intelligencer*, Porter had disposed of no less than 779 shares of stock—bringing in the sum of $3895. Porter's goal was to raise $1500 for the construction of a 5-passenger *Aeroport* (150 feet long). From its operating profits, he wanted to construct a monster dirigible 700 feet in length and capable of "carrying one hundred fifty persons safely at the rate of ninety miles per hour." The largest *Aeroport*, he estimated would cost $15,000 and require only six weeks to complete. Apparently he did not cease selling stock immediately upon reaching his goal of 300 shares. He found the public's response better than anticipated.

Porter immediately launched into construction of 5-passenger *Aeroport* and except for an unlucky combination of circumstances, might have brought to America the honor of producing the world's first successful passenger-carrying rigid airship. An interesting account of what happened appeared in the *Scientific American* a few years afterward:

"After having tested the main principles of his invention on a small scale, Mr. Porter made arrangements, procured materials, and commenced the construction of an *Aeroport* at Washington, on a scale large enough to good service, provided it had been carried through to completion, and had performed according to anticipation. He constructed an aerial float 160 feet long, by 16 feet in diameter, made of varnished linen cloth, supported internally by twelve rods extended the entire length.

"Suspended about sixteen feet below was a saloon sixty feet long and eight feet in diameter, tapering on a curve each way from the center, and furnished with seats for passengers, and glass windows in the sides. In the center was an engine room, six by five feet, in which were a four-horsepower boiler, and two-cylinder engines. The float was furnished with a rudder with four leaves, two vertical and two horizontal, with four steering lines descending to the saloon cabin. Between the float and the saloon were mounted a pair of 6-fan propelling wheels 10 feet in diameter, connected to the engines by endless-chain belts. The bouyant power of the *Aeroport* over all the weight of float, saloon, engine, etc,, would have been 700 pounds.

"All parts of the apparatus were finished, ready for operation, and the inflating boxes arranged, with a full supply of acid and zinc for inflation, when it was discovered that the varnish, which had been used for preparing the float, had so weakened the linen that it would support but little more than its own weight; and while the workmen were engaged in repairing and strengthening it—the float having been partly inflated for that purpose—a sudden and severe storm, with a violent gale, rent the float so extensively that, winter coming on at the same time, the work had to be abandoned. Mr. Porter has since discovered a varnish that will not injure the fiber of linen, and intends to construct an *Aeroport* to carry sixty passengers as soon as he can command the requisite funds for that purpose."

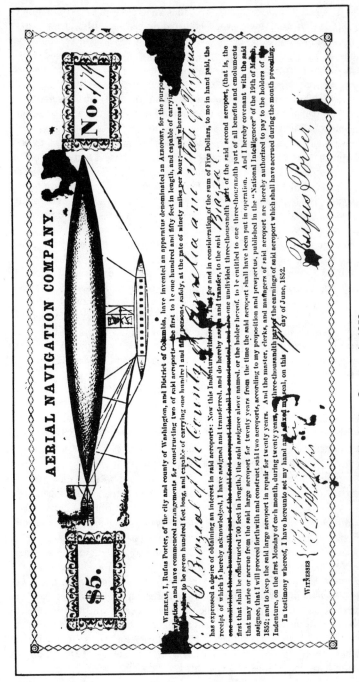

Fig. 3-4. Rufus Porter sold stock in his Aerial Navigation Company in 1852.

The noted balloonist John Wise took an interest in Porter's scheme. In 1850, he wrote: "It was proposed to build a balloon with which to carry passengers to the gold regions of California at the rate of two hundred miles an hour . . . the exhibition of this model created a considerable sensation in the minds of the credulous, and it was asserted at the time that many persons engage passage in the contemplated 'Aerial Steamer' . . . It was also stated in a respectable journal of New York City, in the year 1849, that the machine was actually in course of construction, and the steam engine was finished."

Evidence that Porter's scheme was seriously considered as a means of transportation to the California Gold fields, is the fact that it was given several pages in a contemporary publication entitled: *The Pocket Guide to California; A Sea and Land Route Book, Containing a Description of the El Dorado, Its Geographical Location, etc.*. Beneath an alluring engraving purporting to show the *Aeroport* crossing the Rockies, the editor, J.E. Sherwood of New York City, wrote:

"Aerial Route to California. — The practicability of travelling rapidly and safely through the air, has been established as far as theory can establish a point without actual experment; and all the essential principles on which success mainly depends, have been thus established . . . Should such an apparatus be constructed, and succeed according to the anticipations of the inventor, the voyage from this city to California may be made in some four or five days. The inventor, Mr. Rufus Porter of this city, proposes to carry passengers to California for $100, including board and a passenger-ticket to return. We advise our readers to look out for the fast line."

The Yankee inventor seems to have been doomed to failure as an airship builder, for there remains no record that the project was ever renewed. Stockholders of the *Aerial Navigation Company* held numerous meetings to decide on a future course, but finally forgot about flying when the nation's capital was confronted with a graver problem—the Civil War.

A FORERUNNER OF AERONAUTICAL ACHIEVEMENT

Nevertheless, Rufus Porter's *Aeroport* was an important milestone of aeronautical achievement both in America and abroad. Porter had also envisioned a number of airship construction and operation details that later would come into general usage. He foresaw the necessity of mooring airships to tall masts and proposed to lift the passengers to the cabin by means of a basket-like elevator. He planned to provide each passenger with an "improved parachute." To regulate the bouyancy of the gas bag, he included an ingenious arrangement whereby the framework could be "contracted" from within the cabin—compressing the gas to decrease its lifting power on the principle of the ballonet. A generating plant was added to replenish the bag with any gas that might escape. He further provided the float with several compartments, so that "if a rent should occur in either one, the descent of the *Aeroport* would be so moderate that the pilot would have ample time to select his ground to land upon."

In later years, others would recall Porter's *Aeroport* not as an idle inventor's dream, but a forerunner of the successful rigid dirigibles that roamed the skies in the next century. H. V. Wiley, commander of the United States Navy dirigible *Macon* in 1935, wrote that he was "surprised to find how many of the things incorporated in a modern airship had been forecast by Mr. Porter."

If Porter had been overly enthusiastic in predicting dirigible airspeeds in excess of one hundred miles an hour, he was on solid ground in designing the *Aeroport* with rudder and elevator surfaces for dynamic control in flight and in believing that airships would be safe from lightning strikes in the sky, since they would assume the same polarity as the clouds in penetrating thunderheads.

He firmly believed in the safety of airships for commercial travel, as exemplified in the early operations of the German Zeppelins in transatlantic and intercontinental service prior to the *Hindenburg* disaster. Failing to obtain an appropriation from the United States Congress to develop his ideas, he struggled alone, as an independent inventor, carrying dreams that one day would become realitites.

Chapter 4

The Antigravity Machine

Washington D.C.'s lack of interest in the Genet horse powered balloon did not deter the boom of lighter-than-air activity in the United States by American aeronauts bent on launching an Air Age in the New World. On September 10, 1830, New Yorkers would read in the papers:

"Balloon Ascension.—A person, named Durant, ascended yesterday in a balloon from Castle Garden. The spectacle drew many persons to the Battery, which was literally covered with an immense multitude of every age, sex, condition, and color, whose faces, as they were all turned upwards gaping at the show, and twisted by various contortions and grimaces from the effects of the dazzling sunshine, presented a ludicrous appearance. It is estimated that upwards of twenty thousand persons were collected to see a man risk his neck for their amusement and their money.

"We understand that the aeronaut came safely to land on the farm of Mr. Johnson, near South Amboy."

Thus did the *New York Post* lightly report a great milestone in America's quest to conquer the sky. The "person named Durant"—a New Yorker, Charles Ferson Durant—had in fact become the first American-born airman to explore the airways.

On the following evening, the *Post*, atoned somewhat for its disregard of hard news coverage by belatedly printing a fuller account of the historic ascension—filed by a New Jersey correspondent:

"PERTH AMBOY, Friday Morning, Sept. 10—Gentlemen—Mr. Durant, the Aeronaut, who ascended from Castle Garden yesterday at half past 4 o'clock, p.m., arrived safe in this place last evening. At about 6 o'clock the balloon was discovered gliding gently but rapidly over our city, in a southwesterly direction, at an elevation as judged when first seen, of a mile and half; at this height, by the aid of a spy glass, the aerial voyager was distinctly seen by a number of persons waving his flag. After crossing the Raritan, he descended on terra firma, a little more than a mile south of the ferry at the mouth of the river. Early this morning the car, flag, etc., were conveyed on a carriage through the principal streets accompanied with music, and at half past seven, Mr. Durant embarked on board the steam boat Thistle, Capt. Diehl, for your city, accompanied with the felicitations of the inhabitants of Amboy at the successful result of his journey. We are informed that Mr. Durant is the first American that has ever ascended alone in a balloon."

Among the persons who had assembled at the Battery to witness Durant's ascent was forty-five-year-old Samuel Woodworth, poet-author of a favorite tavern song, *The Old Oaken Bucket*, who prophetically saw in the event a harbimger of future dirigible travel to the far corners of the world. In honor of the occasion, Woodworth penned a poem, printed copies of which Durant scattered from his balloon immediately after rising from Castle Garden:

Good bye to you people of earth,
  I am soaring to regions above you;
But much that I know of your worth,
  Will ever induce me to love you.
Perhaps I may touch at the moon,
  To give your respects as I pass, sirs,
To learn if the spheres are in tune,
  Or if they are lighted with gas, sirs.

I then shall descend to the earth,
  And visit the chief of the Tartars,
Ascertain what his turban is worth,
  And the cost of his favorite garters.
At China I think I'll take tea,
  At India, some fruit I'll regale on,
And then over mountain and sea,
  To Africa fearlessly sail on.

With William the Fourth I will waste
  No language of sycophant flattery.
But cross the Atlantic in haste,
  And safely return to the Battery.
Then Huzza! for the land of the West,
  The country of freedom and honor,
A home for the brave and opprest,
  May blessings be lavished upon her."

THE KEY TO FLIGHT

Durant's admirers in Perth Amboy included a young man who for years had carried in his heart a burning desire to fly. Solomon Andrews

(Fig. 4-1) first felt the urge one warm Sunday afternoon five years before Durant's historic ascension while sitting in his father's church listening to the elder Andrews deliver a lengthy sermon to a dozing congregation.

"Looking out of a window at the soaring of an eagle in his winding way through the air," Andrews later wrote, "I caught as with an electric shock the key to the whole system of aerial flight. From that moment my aim in life was fixed. The study of medicine, and of science generally, were influenced by one idea . . . The acquirement of various trades, and skill in workmanship, was determined by the resolution to construct a flying machine."

Young Andrews set about building small models of his aerial navigator to test "the principle and mechanical application for locomotion." He constructed a paper kite which, he reported, "was made to go three hundred feet in the open air against a pretty strong wind. This was done in the presence of two witnesses."

When Charles Durant dropped from the sky virtually in his back yard, Andrews lost no time in meeting the aeronaut. Andrews suggested politely that Durant might try out his secret principle during his next ascent "by an attachment to his balloon in a simple and economic way." Durant refused.

Undismayed, Andrews suggested his plan in a letter to another balloonist, Richard Clayton, who lived in Cincinnati and who had attained considerable notoriety by once ascending without a car. Though Andrews offered to pay for the cost of installing his device on Clayton's balloon, his letter was ignored. Shrugging, Andrews resolved to work out his plan alone. He did not divulge its nature to anyone else—even when in London he had a chance conversation with the veteran British aeronaut Charles Green on the possibilities of navigating the air. "Green believed it would be done," Andrews wrote later, "but did not pretend to know how. I did not divulge my plan to him."

Not until 1849, when he was 43, did Solomon Andrews finally begin construction of the strange craft that had been inspired by a look through a church window years earlier. For months, curious citizens of Perth Amboy puzzled over what was going on inside the huge shed Andrews had erected in a vacant lot. On July 4th of that year, they would find out.

Get-rich-quick America literally fell into the Mexican War and came up with a gold nugget. By the Guadalupe-Hildago Treaty, it got California just as gold was found at Sutter's Mill. Soldiers fresh from the war deserted and were among the mad rush of 49 ers to the far-flung diggings. But in Perth Amboy, New Jersey, Solomon Andrews had other things on his mind. Quietly, he got out his hammer and saw and went to work building America's first airship hangar.

Andrews had not been idle since that day in 1830 when Charles Durant's balloon dropped in from New York City at the end of the first all-American balloon flight. He had spent long, hard years as inventor and public servant with one goal in mind—to fly.

Fig. 4-1. Dr. Solomon Andrews.

Rising from a Justice of the Peace to a three-term mayor of Perth Amboy, Andrews had still found time to serve as alderman, councilman, president of the Board Of Health, and Collector of the Port of Perth Amboy. He invented and patented more than a score of gadgets. The most outstanding invention was a profitable combination lock. This led to a contract with the Post Office Department for a foolproof padlock for mail sacks, that he manufactured for thirty years.

SECRET IDEAS

In 1849, Andrews at last found time and the finances to put into concrete from his "secret" ideas for a navigable airship. He had intended to complete the craft in his Perth Amboy hangar without letting anyone see it "until it made its first trip through the air to New York," but the appearance of Rufus Porter and his highly-touted *Aeroport* made Andrews change his mind. "The recent notices of Messrs. Porter and Robjohn of a model, without a large machine to match, so totally different in every respect," he said, "make this public exhibition necessary . . . In case of success its inventor may forestall any doubtful claim which otherwise might occur, as in the case of Fulton and Fitch in steam navigation . . ."

Accordingly, Andrews filed a caveat with the Patent Office and, on June 21, inserted an advertisement in the *New York Sun*:

"AIR SHIP. —The public is informed that the Inventor's Institute at Perth Amboy, N.J., will exhibit on the Fourth of July next, and during that day only, the Aerial Ship which they are now building, and which they hope to complete during the present summer.

"It is now in a state so forward as to show the full size, form, and internal structure; the framework being complete, and the envelope of silk (already procured) only to be put on, to be ready for the first trial."

Andrews could not resist adding a touch of mystery: "Whoever, after having witnessed this structure, shall discover and make known to the undersigned, the motive power, and its mode of action, shall be entitled to a share of stock in the invention . . ."

The crowd that assembled in Andrews' hangar on the Fourth of July saw a large framework, 80 feet long, 20 feet wide, and ten feet deep, suspended from the roof. Speculation ran high as to what was supposed to make the thing go and if it would go. Andrews was careful not to let his secret out at the time. He wanted first to prove that it was workable.

The general air of mystery which surrounded Andrews' airship was reflected in the following notice in the *Knickerbocker Magazine* in New York: "We believe it to be a fact, that a gentleman of Perth Amboy, New Jersey, has actually built a flying machine with which he expects to cross the Atlantic, carrying many passengers. Thousands of dollars in stock have already been subscrived and expended in this project, and the proprietor has written and obtained permission to descend through the roof of the great glass palace in Hyde Park, London, on his arrival there in his balloon."

Whether or not Andrews was influenced by Porter's *Aeroport* in constructing his airship with a rigid framework is uncertain. However, he ultimately abandoned this mode of construction.

Andrews completed his "secret" airship and inflated it during the summer months. Yet for some unknown reason, he never took it outside the hangar doors. For several weeks he experimented with it inside the building. Finally, he deflated the bag, slipped one of his padlocks on the door and turned to other matters. Fourteen years would pass before Andrews would again turn to work on his airship. With the nation in the Civil War, he felt compelled to offer its services to President Abraham Lincoln as an aid to steaming the rebellion. His amazing success in this venture was to cause such astonishment in New York City that for some time the Civil War was nearly forgotten.

At the outbreak of the Civil War, Dr. Solomon Andrews, the genius of Perth Amboy, forsook his various duties as physician, politician, inventor, and padlock-manufacturer to join the Union Army. He served with the Sanitary Commission caring for wounded soldiers on transport vessels. In the Spring of 1862, Dr. Andrews was with the Army of the Potomac at Harrison's Landing following the bloody Seven Days Retreat of McClellan's forces from the Chickahominy.

RENEWED EXPERIMENTS

The frequency captive balloon ascensions made by Professor Thaddeus S. C. Lowe, chief of Lincoln's Balloon Corps, attracted the doctor's interest so much that he resigned his commission as Assistant Surgeon to return home and renew his experiments with his mysterious dirigible.

On August 9, 1862, Dr. Andrews wrote a letter to President Lincoln seeking to secure government funds to construct his airship as a military aircraft. He went so far as to offer as collateral all his personal real estate holdings which he valued at $50,000.

Further to convince the President that he was sincere, he added: "I will sail the airship, when constructed, five to ten miles into Secessia and back again, or no pay."

It was Andrews' scheme to construct a dirigible airship that could travel over rebel lines, pause while the pilot made observations of enemy positions, draw maps and then return to base behind Union lines—independent of the wind direction. The plan sounded feasible, yet Lincoln did not answer his letter.

Dr. Andrews next wrote to the Secretary of War on August 18, 1862 and obtained an invitation from Assistant Secretary of War P.H. Watson to submit drawings and a description of his airship. Andrews complied on September 1, 1862 and his papers were referred to the Bureau of Topographical Engineers. When no response was forthcoming, Andrews decided to forge ahead on his own and prove his airship by an actual flight test.

He purchased 1300 yards of muslin and employed the noted American balloonist John Wise, who earlier had failed in an attempt to form a Balloon Corps, to varnish the cloth. Andrews ordered that the material be made up into 21 small ballonets, each from 7 feet to 12 feet in diameter. But balloonist Wise erred and made them pear-shaped instead of round.

Speculation ran high in Perth Amboy as to how Dr. Andrews proposed to propel his dirigible. There was no evidence of a motor of any kind. Was it some kind of anti gravity scheme? A perpetual motion device? Even John Wise was tight-lipped and only smiled knowingly when the townspeople questioned him about the good doctor's invention.

Dr. Andrews next purchased 1200 yards of Irish linen, and instructed Wise to make it up in the form of three cylindrical bags, each 80 feet long and 13 feet in diameter. Wise shook his head; he didn't want to be the laughing stock of the country in a time of war. So, Dr. Andrews pushed all other matters aside and did the job himself.

When completed, the larger containers (reinforced with wooden battens) were stuffed with the smaller ballonets filled with hydrogen gas. Dr. Andrews reasoned that if the gas were fed directly into the long envelopes it would rush to one end whenever the airship was tilted on the pitch axis, unless they were tightly inflated, and thus in danger of exploding in climbing to higher altitudes.

Beneath the three long cylinders, which were laced together like cigars in a box, Dr. Andrews slung a catwalk 12 feet long and 15 inches wide so suspended that its weight would be evenly distributed over the whole lifting bag area regardless of the craft's pitch inclination. A sliding box, containing the ballast, could be slid along the catwalk to displace the center of gravity fore or aft, to alter the pitch attitude.

THE AEREON

One day in June, 1863, Dr. Andrews (then 57 years of age) had his strange craft gently hauled out of its wooden hangar for its maiden voyage. When the gathered crowd asked him what it was to be called, he replied: "It is my *Aereon* (Fig. 4-2). A name I have coined from *Aero* and *Eon*, to represent the *Air Age*." Although the craft was moderately successful that calm morning, all of the ballonets that Wise had made up collapsed from leakage. The outer cylinders, which Dr. Andrews had sewn up with care, held, and *Aeron* returned to earth safely after the trial flight.

Now Dr. Andrews set about remodeling his airship, removing the collapsed ballonets and substituting in their place cloth partitions to keep the gas evenly distributed inside individual compartments just as Rufus Porter had proposed to do in his giant *Aeroport*. In applying this feature, Dr. Andrews actually anticipated by many years the similar design practice used by Count Ferdinand von Zeppelin in his giant dirigibles.

In July and August two more flights were made to test modifications. Dr. Andrews' *Aereon* made a final flight on September 4, 1863 both President Lincoln and his Secretary of War were invited to witness the demonstration. They did not attend.

These remarkable flights—America's first successful man-carrying dirigible voyages—attracted such interest in New York City that they were the subject of gossip in all quarters. The press followed Dr. Andrews' flight with enthusiasm and reported eye-witness accounts for the Aeron's performance. On September 4, *Aereon's* flight drew this comment from the *New York Herald*:

Fig. 4-2. Dr. Solomon Andrews' Aeroeon.

"We have this week the pleasure to record the success of the most extraordinary invention of the age if not the most so of any the world ever saw—at least the greatest stride in invention ever made by a sigle individual. On Friday, the 4th . . . (Dr. Andrews) made his last experiment, and demonstrated to an admiring crowd the possibility of going against the wind, and of guiding her in any and every direction.

"After a few short flights, to satisfy himself and a few friends that all was right, he set her off in a spiral course upwards, she going at a rate of not less than 120 miles per hour, and describing circles in the air of more than one and one half miles in circumference. She made twenty revolutions before she entered the first strata of clouds and was lost to view. She passed through the first strata of dense white clouds, about two miles high, scattering them, as she entered, in all directions.

"In her upward flight could be distinctly seen her rapid movement in a contrary direction to the moving clouds, and as she came before the wind passing them by with great celerity. As she was distinctly seen thus to move both below and above the clouds on the clear blue sky at five o'clock P.M., with the sun shining clear upon her, there could be no mistake or optical delusion to the beholder.

"As to her propelling power and motive apparatus, it behooves us not now to speak. It might be considered contraband of war, or affording aid and comfort to the enemy, for with such a machine in the hands of Jeff Davis, the armies around Washington would become powerless to preserve the Capital."

This voyage apparently was made without the inventor on board according to Dr. Andrews' own word. In a subsequent application for a patent covering the airship's design, he described an accompanying illustration of *Aereon* on her September 4, 1863 flight in which the airship "described a spiral circle upward of not less than one and one half miles in circumference. She made twenty revolutions in fourteen and a half minutes, when she was lost to view in the upper strata of clouds. The first eleven revolutions were made in seven minutes, the last three revolutions in three and one half minutes. The weight in the car was about one hundred thirty pounds . . . I found but one occasion to move the dinner car with the ballast from its central position, and that was when she made her spiral flight, when I was not in the car."

Following this flight, Dr. Andrews tore *Aereon* to pieces to prevent discovery of its modus operandi. He felt that he had at last found the secret of aerial navigation. He then submitted a number of testimonial letters to President Lincoln, at Lincoln's request, and further offered the services of *Aereon* to a number of European governments. Queen Victoria and Louis Napoleon politely acknowledged his letters, but Washington D.C. remained silent. The War Department had pigeonholed all his correspondence.

Not one to give up easily, when Congress convened in December, 1863, Dr. Andrews laid a petition before each member of the House and the Senate and finally gained official interest. The House Military Affairs Committee requested the Secretary of War to appoint a commission to report on *Aereon* and Dr. Andrews gave a demonstration flight with a number of small models in the basement of the Capitol building.

Witnesses to this demonstration were top figures in government and the academic world. Included were Professor Joseph Henry, first secretary of the Smithsonian Institution and founder of the United States Weather Service; Professor Alexander D. Bache of the Coast Survey; and Cpatain Israel C. Woodruff of the Bureau of Topographical Engineers. All were impressed favorably, but government red tape quickly snarled the project and the Commission's recommendation was not laid before the House Committee until February, 1865. By then the Civil War was virtually over and no further official action was taken on the *Aereon* project.

Dr. Andrews did not remain idle during these trying times, and on July 5, 1864, he finally won his patent for an "Improvement in Aerostats." The same year he published a pamphlet that at last partially lifted the veil of secrecy that had surrounded *Aereon*'s dirigibility from the start. The pamphlet was entitled:

The Aereon . . . A Protest, Addressed to the Senate and House of Representatives by the Inventor of a War Aerostat, Complaining of the Conduct of the War Department in Regard to the Matter. Then he disclosed the manner in which *Aereon* could navigate against the winds by using his "mysterious principle:"

"To navigate the air with this vessel," he wrote, "it is only necessary to step to the rear of the car, thus elevating the bow five to ten degrees, and by throwing out a little ballast she will go ahead on the ascending plane. When she has ascended as high as the aeronaut wishes to go, he opens one of the valves and discharges some gas, at the same time stepping toward the forward end of the car, which will depress the bow, elevate the stern, and so change the angle of inclination, when she will go ahead on the descending plane.

"On a near approach to the earth he has only to step to the middle or rear end of the car, and thus elevate the bow. To stop her momentum at any rate of velocity, sail horizontally for a short distance, or throw out more ballast and go ahead again on the ascending plane. Having forward motion, she is turned by the rudder just like a boat on the water. Stern way may also be had if desired. Before the ballast is exhausted, come down to a depot, replenish the wasted gas, and go on again.

"One pound of ascending or descending power will give to this vessel a forward movement of one mile per hour, and each additional pound will increase her speed in about the same ratio, so that by ascending or descending with a power of two hundred pounds a speed of two hundred miles per hour may be attained . . ."

In hindsight, it appears quite obvious that Dr. Andrews and the New York newspaper accounts of *Aereon*'s speed were overly optimistic. Yet the idea did work, and his patent covered the potential use of his principle of flight with an ordinary balloon attached to a flat surface to achieve the same resultant force as with his elongated triple-bag aerostat.

It is worth nothing that a similar patent—one of the first aeronautical patents ever granted in America—was issued to Italian inventor Muzio Muzzi on October 16, 1844. Muzzi's balloon was of lenticular shape and was fitted with two wing-like projections and a rudder.

Muzzi explained: "By the resistance of the atmosphere against these planes, either in the ascending, or the descending of the balloon, such ascending or descending motion may be resolved into a horizontal one." There is no record Muzzi's invention ever got beyond the planning stage.

COMMERCIALIZATION

Meanwhile, Dr. Andrews met with no encouragement from the Army and, having spent some $10,000 of his own money on the *Aereon* project, was determined to develop his airship on a commercial basis. With the weight of Professor Henry's endorsement behind him, in November, 1865, he incorporated in New York state the Aerial Navigation Company. It was America's first chartered organized for the exploitation of aircraft actually to get a passenger-carrying dirigible into operation. Rufus Porter's Aerial Navigation Company of 1852, although incorporated thirteen years earlier, never got beyond the model stage.

The new *Aereon* was shaped rather like a lemon. It was constructed from material salvaged from four war surplus military balloons used by the military aeronaut Thaddeus S. C. Lowe. It proved difficult to steer on its initial flight (May 25, 1866) from the corner of Green and Houston Streets in New York City. It carried three passengers—Dr. G. Waldo Hill, Charles M. Plumb, and George W. Trow, all officers of Dr. Andrews' Aerial Navigation Company.

Trow was a leading New York publisher in 1865 and he printed a pamphlet describing the new *Aereon* that gave its history. It was entitled: *Aerial Navigation and a Proposal to Form an Aerial Navigation Company*. This was followed the next year with a 15-page pamphlet: *The Aereon, or Flying-Ship, Invented by Solomon Andrews*.

The May 25 flight was described in glowing terms by the press. Reported the *New York World*: "The *Aereon*, passing over Fourteenth Street and Fifth Avenue, shot along at a rate that threw the astonished miles behind her. That course conclusively tested, the *Aereon* was headed due southeasterly, or directly against the wind. Changing her course, the gallant vessel, freighted with so many hopes, veered around as directed and, for full five minutes, whose luxurious duration seemed hours, she bore on her unswaying, undeviating way, with tremendous velocity, annihilating space, and spurning the wind across whose path she rode, and whose advancing hosts she met and conquered."

Reported the *New York Tribune*: "Dr. Solomon Andrews of this city essayed the performance of aerial navigation on the 25th, and met with much better success than some of the critics had expected. His flying machine went up from Houston Street and came down at Astoria, Long Island, to the consternation of the people there residing and passing, having concluded to make some alternations in his apparatus before trying further experiments."

Dr. Andrews finally invited the press to visit his hangar and ask any questions they chose about the aerial wonder. *Harper's* correspondent viewed the whole episode with some cynicism:

"The Brobdignagian lemon," he wrote, "is 'bound in boards' at the corner of Green and Houston Streets, a locality ill adapted for the success of heavenward experiments, inasmuch as the physical and moral character of that region has a decided downward tendency . . ." The writer concluded that *Aereon* had little chance of commercial success. Prophetic, perhaps, but failure would come from a different direction.

Having replaced a defective rudder to make *Aereon* more controllable, Dr. Andrews made a final flight on June 5th, with Charles Plumb on board. *Aereon* gracefully crossed and recrossed a designated landmarked time and again to prove that it was capable of navigating independent of air currents. Shortly thereafter, however, a bank failure plunged the Aerial Navigation Company heavily into debt. Dr. Andrews quitely terminated his flying career. He had realized his life long dream and proved his concept workable.

AN AERIAL BOAT

Once Dr. Andrews' secret was out, others attempted to fly on gravity power, or anti gravity power, as the case may be. Daniel L. Rhone, a judge of Luzerne County, Pennsylvania, for a number of years had closely observed birds to learn their secret of flight. He was assisted by a younger brother, Freas B. Rhone. But when he designed and patented an "Aerial Boat" it was very unbirdlike. The patent was granted June 23, 1874—some twenty years after the *Aereon* flights.

Like some other airship inventors, Judge Rhone was short of funds and resorted to publishing a pamphlet in an effort to raise capital to construct a full-sized machine. Entitled *A Novel Air Ship*, the pamphlet bore a likeness of his craft on the cover (Fig. 4-3). In outline, it rather resembled an early ferry boat and it had two large flat surfaces extending along its sides. A section of these surfaces at the rear was hinged in a manner that permitted them to be retracted or extended in order to elevate or depress the front end.

"Force always expends itself in the direction of least resistance," Judge Rhone explained. "The boat is put in shape for at least resistance in front. The wings are to create great resistance to any perpendicular ascent or descent. Suppose we have a surplus bouyancy of five hundred pounds; this will tend to lift the boat perpendicularly upward with the same force as if it were so many pounds falling, and the air will press perpendicularly downward, so that the boat will take the course of least resistance—a diagonal—the resultant of the two forces. Besides, after falling upward

Fig. 4-3. Judge Daniel L. Rhone's "Anti-Gravity" machine.

some distance, a force will be developed which, on depressing the bow of the boat, will drive it some distance downward, on further on a horizontal . . ."

Judge Rhone made numerous tests of the principle with small models. He remained firmly convinced that he had learned the secret of aerial navigation from his bird watching and from the study of falling leaves and corks bobbing in water.

"A model with gliding planes was built and operated by gas, the retort of which was in the cockpit of his 'man-bird,' as he called it," recalled his brother, Freas. "The construction of his assembled parts began in 1860; the experiments and testing of his finished model began in 1872, in his own yard of his resistance at Wilkes-Barre. His model never made an actual flight because of lack of mechanical propulsion, and at last, in 1897, he despaired of success and declared to me his belief that the world was right and he was wrong, and gave up. He died in 1901."

Chapter 5

The San Francisco Avitor

Of all the tales to come out of California's Gold Rush country in the mid-1800s, none is more enchanting than the story of Frederick Marriott's flying steam engine, the dirigible *Avitor*, and his million-dollar promotion, the Aerial Steam Navigation Company. It is a story with roots that go back to England two decades earlier, when Marriott, an energetic young British journalist turned press agent for an extraordinary scheme to conquer the sky by opening an air route to China.

Born in Somerset, England, in 1805, young Marriott (Fig. 5-1) became one of the founders of *The Illustrated London News*. He then helped form the Aerial Steam Transit Company in order to raise funds for the construction of a giant silk and bamboo monoplane to carry passengers half way around the globe.

THE AERIAL STEAM CARRIAGE

Resembling a modern airplane in its general design and appearance, the proposed *Aerial Steam Carriage* was to carry a wing area of 4500 square feet and a tail surface one third as large (Fig. 5-2). This area was calculated to lift half a pound per square foot, including machinery, fuel, and payload. A steam engine of 35 to 40 horsepower was planned to drive the cloud colossus through the air with a pair of 6-bladed propellers.

The *Aerial Steam Carriage* was the invention of William Samuel Henson of Somerset, England. He had been very successful in building and flying small, workable models of his passenger airliner. He was joined in his enterprise by John Stringfellow, a manufacturer of lace-making machinery, who developed a light steam engine to power Henson's models. Marriott, who lived nearby, spent long evenings with these two inventors discussing the potential of their flying machine.

70

Fig. 5-1. Frederick Marriott.

In 1842, Marriott arranged with a lawyer, D.E. Columbine, for the patenting of the *Aerial Steam Carriage*. With the help of J.A. Roebuck, Member of Parliament for Bath, provisional protection was secured in September of that year. On the following March 24, Roebuck introduced a bill in the House of Commons for the incorporation of the Aerial Steam Transit Company—the world's first incorporated "airline."

Marriott seized upon the moment to fire the public's enthusiasm with prospects of flying swiftly to the far corners of the earth. On March 28, complete specifications of the aircraft were filed and a patent was obtained. The press devoted considerable space to the venture and fantastic conceptions of the Steam Carriage in flight over foreign lands were drawn by George Cruikshank and other leading British artists.

"If ultimately successful," Marriott announced, "this extraordinary invention will be without parallel even in the age which produced gas and steam."

Public subscriptions were not forthcoming, however, and Henson and Stringfellow were forced to continue their experiments on their own. Marriott's enthusiasm did not wane. He wrote to his daughter: "If any success attends this Aerial Company, I shall do well, as I have a big holding in shares. I have composed a song which is being set to music, and you will be able to sing it. The first stanza follows:

> "We're afloat, we're afloat on that ambient tide
>   That long has the boldest and bravest defied;
> Up! Up! Let us mount like a falcon set free,
>   We're afloat, we're afloat on a measureless sea."

In November, Henson proposed that he and Stringfellow buy out Marriott's shares in the company. Later, discouraged and impoverished, Henson married his landlady's daughter, a Miss Jones, and moved to America to forget flying. Before leaving England, however, Henson in 1847 obtained a patent for *Improvements in the Construction of Razors for Shaving*, the forerunner of the modern safety razor. He died at Newark, New Jersey, on March 22, 1888.

Stringfellow kept up his work on flying machines, in June, 1848, he successfully flew a steam-powered model, with a 20-foot wingspread, inside his lace factory at Chard. It was the first sustained flight of a powered airplane.

Marriott, after selling his interest in the Aerial Steam Transit Company, founded a paper called *Chat*. This venture was financially unsuccessful and, having spent most of his fortune, he sailed for San Francisco after being lured by tales of gold nuggets you could pick up on the streets of that waterfront town.

While London scoffed at the Aerial Steam Transit Company, Americans, from their perspective of transatlantic distance, were inclined to consider it a bit more seriously. The Henson and Stringfellow steam engine, actually a marvel of lightness and strength, attracted a good deal of interest in the New World. In 1843, the *Journal of the Franklin Institute* observed:

"The difficulty of flying machines consist less in devising an apparatus capable of floating in, and being moved through the air in any given direction, than in freighting it with mechanical power sufficient to enable it to maintain its pace through long distances against the constantly adverse influence of gravitation, and the frequently occurring opposition of the wind and weather. The means by which Mr. Henson hoped to overcome this difficulty, that is to say, the boiler by which he proposes to generate steam enough for any given length of flight, deserve, therefore, a little more consideration than they have as yet received . . ."

Frederick Marriott could not have picked a better place to go to in the United States than San Francisco. When he left England, following the

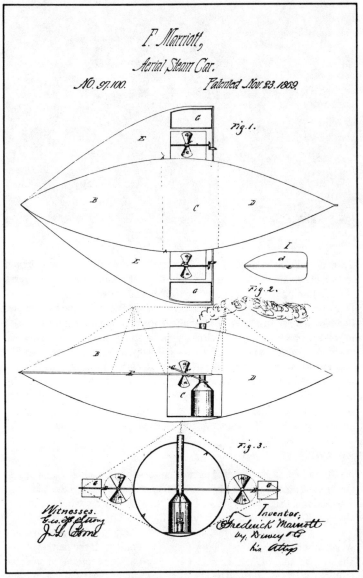

Fig. 5-2. In 1869, Marriott patented his "Aerial Steam Car."

collapse of the Aerial Steam Transit Company he had set his heart and mind working toward recouping his losses to allow him once again to tackle the problem of aerial navigation—by now an obsession with him.

The Silver Era already had brought thousands of men of all description through the Golden State into San Francisco Harbor where ships

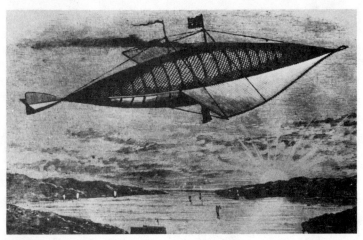

Fig. 5-3. An early woodcut of Marriott's San Francisco "Avitor" of 1869.

flying nearly every known flag rode at anchor while their crews gambled and fought along the waterfront. Gold began to pour in from the Sierra Nevada mining camps and the city thrived and grew.

Shrewdly, Marriott did not head for the gold fields to find his fortune. Instead, he opened a bank. It did not take long for him to establish himself in San Francisco as a leading citizen and eventually he was financially in a position to return to his first loves—journalism and flying machines.

He founded the *San Francisco News Letter* and once again tried promotion of an "aerial navigation company"—this time his own. He fully believed that he held a simple answer to the chief problem that blocked success of the Henson-Stringfellow machine. He would overcome the unyielding weight of a steam engine simply by adding a gas bag.

THE AVITOR

In his spare moments, Marriott reworked his plans for a navigable airship, which he named the *Avitor*, and at length evolved a plan that satisfied him (Fig. 5-3). On October 22, 1863, he wrote to his son-in-law. General W. H. Noble of the Royal Artillery in London:

"Put this picture of the *Avitor* in your scrapbook. If the machine works, there will be some money for you and others. If the laurels should alight upon some loftier head, let the Spartan's epitaph be 'upon some mother's worthier son than he.' I am content to abide by the result. If I win, all those I most value will be all right. If it is a splendid fizzle, why, then, I must calmly resign the prospect and swallow the bitter pill with loss of money, prestige, and lofty hopes . . ."

A number of years would pass before Marriott was able to complete his plans for the formation of a company to build his flying machine, but his enthusiasm never wavered. On April 18, 1866, Marriott wrote to a grand-

Fig. 5-4. In 1866, Marriott incorporated the "Aerial Steam Navigation Company."

75

daughter, Ida Kirkpatrick, the daughter of Captain T.S. Kirkpatrick, Governor of Newgate Prison in London:

"I send you a picture of *'Marriott's Aeroplane Steam Carriage'* for navigating the air . . . we shall say nothing or beat the big drum until we can fly—then we will all take a ride. She carries four passengers. Let us pray!"

Four months later, on August 31, Marriott incorporated the Aerial Steam Navigation Company—capitalized at one million dollars. Ten thousand shares at $1000 each were put up for sale (Fig. 5-4). The editor-inventor-promoter-banker aroused such interest throughout San Francisco—with lurid stories of the flying machine's possibilities appearing regularly in the columns of the *News Letter*—that within two years he had raised more than $10,000. San Francisco followed with interest the progress of Marriott's flying machine and on November 17 *The Californian* commented in verse:

> "The time is drawing near
>> When the world, amazed, shall see
> The Avitor appear
>> In her wondrous flying gear,
> To sail the upper sea,
>> With an undulating motion,
> Like a swan on Woodward's Lake,
>> Or a gull upon the ocean!"

Certain of success, Marriott eagerly made preparations for the construction of a prototype machine about 37 feet in length. Early in 1867, he wrote a relative in England:

"Your ancestors are fixed in history for navigating one element. I may probably be fixed on a more popular and universal notoriety for some historical prominence or other. I mean the name of Frobisher is unapproachable on water, but I may have a name on navigating the air as the first discover of how to do it. I think I may have made a discovery in the way of propulsion, but I am not quite sure."

On July 2, 1869, Marriott's *Avitor* finally made its maiden flight over Shell Mound park—a race track located not far from the present site of San Francisco Municipal Airport (Figs. 5-5 and Fig. 5-6). This flight was historically significant. It was the first in which an aircraft propelled itself through the air of the Western United States. Marriott's *News Letter* gave this account of the flight the following day:

"An engineer's trial trip of the model steam carriage just completed at the Avitor Works, Shell Mound Park, was made yesterday (Friday) morning, in the presence of the constructing engineers, several of the shareholders of the *Aerial Steam Navigation Company*, a number of employees of the San Jose Railroad who happened to be in the vicinity, and of residents in neighborhood. The morning was beautiful and still—scarcely a breath of air stirring. All conditions were most favorable to success.

"The gasometer was fully inflated at 15 minutes past six o'clock and the model was floated out of the building and across the race track to the

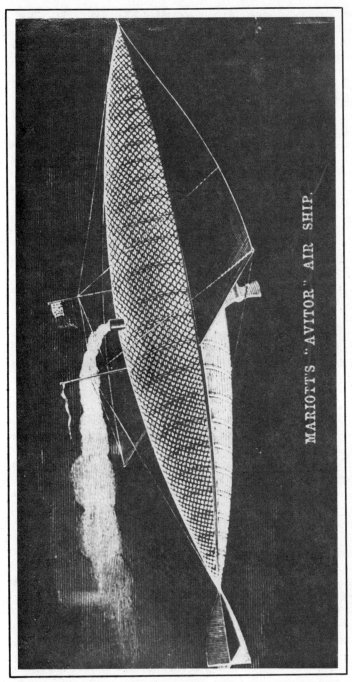

MARIOTT'S "AVITOR" AIR SHIP.

Fig. 5-5. Frederick Marriott's Aviator flew in 1869.

open space in the center. In six minutes steam was got up—the rudder set to give a light curve to the course of the vessel—and the valves opened. With the first turn of the propellers she rose slowly into the air, gradually increasing her speed until the rate of five miles an hour was attained.

"The position of the rudder caused her to describe a great circle, around which she passed twice, occupying about five minutes each time. Lines had been fastened to both prow and stern, which were held by two men who followed her track and had sufficient ado to keep up with her at a dog trot.

"As she described her second circle, a pull given to the head line unintentionally caused the rudder to shift to a fore-and-aft position, when the model pursued a straight flight up the race track about a quarter of a mile; she was then turned around, and retraced her flight to the point of departure; whence, being duly guided, she entered the building. The fires were 'drawn' and the first extensive flight of a vessel for aerial navigation was accomplished. The total distance transversed was a little over a mile.

"The appearance of the vessel in the air was really beautiful. As seen in the building, she looks cumbrous and awkward—just as a ship looks cumbrous and awkward on the docks. The change of appearance, as she is circling gracefully through the air, is equal to that of the same ship when seen in the water. The first moment of opening the steam value was one of suspense; as the vessel rose and forged slowly ahead, the suspense was scarcely dissipated; but in a very few seconds her speed increased—in obedience to the rudder she commenced to swing around the curve—the men at the guys broke into a trot, and cheer upon cheer arose from the little group. In years to come it will be something for these men to tell, that they were present at, and saw the first mile flight ever accomplished in the grand discovery of aerial navigation."

Two days later, on the Fourth of July, a public demonstration was given. But as a considerable wind had sprung up, the flight was made inside the building. The *Avitor* rose from the floor as soon as the steam was started, traveled from one end of the hall to the other, and returned to her starting point.

Marriott was awarded Letters Patent No. 97,100 for the *Avitor* on November 23 the same year. In his specifications he curiously referred to the airship as the "Aerial Steam-Carriage"—the same name by which he had publicized the Henson-Stringfellow airplane of 1842 (Fig. 5-7). The patent reveals the construction details of Marriott's craft as:

"A vessel or carriage constructed of light and strong material, made pointed at both ends, each being inflated with hydrogen gas. This structure is divided into three compartments, the engine being carried in the compartment in the middle of the vessel. Extending from the forward point of the carriage to about the middle of the vessel on each side is a vane or wing. These wings serve to carry the carriage steadily through the air.

"The carriage is caused to move through the air by screw propellers driven by a steam engine. In the rear of each of these vanes or wings, at the

Fig. 5-6. Frederick Marriott's Avitor. It flew!

sides of the vessel, is attached a plane, which turns upon an axle, by which any desired elevation can be given to the vessel. A tail or rudder is also attached to the rear pointed end, by which desired direction can be given to the vessel when it is in motion.

"The *Avitor*, when fully inflated, does not contain sufficient gas to cause it to rise, but remains in position until the propellers are started into operation, and begin to beat the atmosphere, when it rises with the greatest ease."

In this description, Marriott reveals an astuteness of the need for such a craft to fly "heavy." This design feature is to be found in such advanced technology craft as the *Heli-Strat* of the Piasecki Aircraft Corporation—a hybrid heavy-lifter combining a gas envelope with four helicopter rotor systems. Appearing before the Senate Subcommittee on Science, Technology and Space on February 27, 1979, the company's president, Frank N. Piasecki, observed that "the envelope is sizes such that when you have a machine with the engine stopped on the ground, it almost weighs nothing—that is, it's almost weightless."

As futuristic as the Avitor was, the local San Francisco press covered the maiden flight rather objectively. The *San Francisco Daily Times* commented: "At once life was imparted to the whole body, and it arose promptly and gracefully and took its flight into the air under guidance of the rudder, thus establishing the astounding fact that it had power and could fly; and giving proof that the grand problem had been solved.

"The carriage mounted nearly to the roof with a firmness and steadiness equal to the movement of an ocean steamer on smooth water. The guests cheered long and loud, and many fairly danced with delight at the success."

Exaggerated Press Reports

Elsewhere in the United States and abroad, excitement grew over exaggerated reports of the California based dirigible. The *London Dispatch* wrote: The wonderful California flying machine, we are informed, will soon wing its way across the Rocky Mountains from San Francisco to New York, to the great loss, no doubt, of the now-superfluous Pacific Railway." The *Dispatch* was referring to the Central Pacific Railroad which finally had reached Oakland in September, 1869.

In New York City the *Scientific American* reported: "Within four weeks the first aerial steam carriage, capable of conveying six persons, and propelled at a rate exceeding the minimum speed of thirty miles an hour, will wing its first flight over the Sierra Nevada, on its way to New York and remoter parts. We do not doubt that our citizens will organize to give a hospitable welcome to the celestial visitor."

The fine hand of Frederick Marriott can be seen in such far-out reports in the world press, considering his background as journalist and promoter, and he spared no words in filling the columns of his own *News Letter* with glowing tributes to the *Avitor*: "No savage in war paint shall

Fig. 5-7. Marriott promoted the "Aerial Steam Carriage" of 1842.

interrupt its passage over and across our continent," he wrote. "No malaria or hostile tribes nor desert sands shall prevent the exploration of Africa, or ice mountains the search for the Northwest Passage. No tax for crossing New Jersey; no extortions from huge corporations who monopolize the great routes of travel. Man rises superior to his accidents when for his inventive genius he ceases to crawl upon the Earth and masters the realm of the air."

Demonstration Flights

Following the early demonstration flights, Marriott moved his *Avitor* from Shell Mound Park to the Mechanics Pavilion in the heart of downtown San Francisco. Daily exhibition flights were made—twice in the morning and twice in the afternoon. Adults paid 50 cents admission and children 25 cents to witness the amazing spectacle of a steam-powered airship chugging nonchanantly around the big hall, dodging rafters and gas-light fixtures.

"Thousands visited it here," the *News Letter* affirmed, "and all expressed themselves satisfied that aerial navigation was an established fact . . . The *Avitor* fulfilled the requisitions for aerial flight, viz . . . sustaining power, propelling power, and guiding power."

A NEW PROJECT

Eventually *Avitor* fell victim to a disastrous fire that razed the Mechanics Pavillion, but Marriott already had planned a larger, man-carrying dirigible. This new *Avitor* was to be 150 feet long and capable of lifting one and one-quarter tons. It was estimated to cost only $475 to build and sale of stock in Marriott's company suddenly boomed. More than $5,000 poured into the company coffers within a few days.

The giant *Avitor* was never built, however, and Marriott turned his efforts to the design of a heavier-than-air flying machine that did not incorporate a gas bag for lift. Nevertheless, Marriott seems to have worked on his *Avitor* as late as September, 1881. On September 5, 1851 he wrote to his son-in-law, Captain Prescott William Stevens, R.N., of *H.M.S. Thetis*, then stationed at Esquimault in Vancouver:

"If you can come down here, I can put you up at my house at the corner of Jones and Lombard Street. About the aeroplane, I have already expended fifty thousand dollars on it and now the best engineers of this country say that *it is discovered*. It is too simple a method to be doubted, and a mechanical discovery which will enable people with five hundred dollars to obtain a machine and proceed in any direction they elect, and will bring about a revolution which neither steam or electricity have as yet effected. I am contemplating a mundane 'News Letter' to be delivered by the constructing engineer on the trips daily to be made, and we hope to carry mail all over America."

On October 10, 1881, Marriott submitted to the United States Patent Office drawings and specifications for his heavier-than-air craft, an odd looking design somewhat resembling a giant sailing vessel with masts replaced with upright Archimedean screws. Two similar screws were placed horizontally along the sides of the vessel for forward propulsion and, like the *Avitor*, it was fitted with flat wings.

Although it is not remarkable that Marriott's patent application was turned down, the grounds for refusal by the Patent Examiner, J.E.M. Bowen, provide a commentary on the Patent Office's attitude toward all proposals for heavier-than-air craft in the Nineteenth Century:

"It is the opinion of the Examiner," wrote Bowen, "that an apparatus for navigation the air which does not depend upon a gas field for elevating means, is an impracticable structure." As a consequence, scores of other aeronautical patents granted in future years had gas bags, even though the gas bags had nothing whatever to do with the inventions themselves.

A disappointed old man, Frederick Marriott finally gave up his lifelong dreams of founding a transcontinental dirigible airline or building a workable helicopter. He devoted the remaining three years of his life to publishing his *News Letter*. In 1884 at the age of 79, Marriott, builder of the West's first navigable flying machine, stepped on a carpet tack and died of blood-poisoning.

Chapter 6

Mistress of the Winds

Where others had failed in their attempts to achieve aerial navigation by gliding under gravity power up and down, it remained for an enterprising married couple of Frankfort, New York to conquer the sky in this manner. Carl E. Myers operated a "balloon farm," constructing spherical weather balloons and small man-carrying aerostats. Carlotta Myers served as chief test pilot (Fig. 6-1). In 1880, she began a career as a carnival performer and in 1882 published a book of her experiences: *Aerial Adventures of Carlotta, or Sky-Larking in Cloudland.*

Carlotta enjoyed studying the wind currents along the Mohawk and frequently used them to visit friends for tea in distant cities—returning on different wind currents at different elevations. She became a familiar figure up and down the Mohawk Valley and earned the sobriquet: Mistress of the Winds (Fig. 6-2).

On these excursions, Carlotta took along a mysterious bundle of rods and cloth. When curious folks asked what they were she replied: "These are my fishing poles." But rather than fish for birds in the high sky, Carlotta unfurled the package and assembled what she called her "screwsail"—a cloth tractor propeller that assumed a helical shape when she spun the crank. With this device Carlotta found she could actually navigate into the wind.

Her secret for making spot landings was equally simple and effective. She simply used her feet to tilt the half-inch plywood bottom of the balloon basket, suspended by a rope netting, and jettisoned some hydrogen from the gas bag. As the craft sank, the slanted basket bottom gave her a measure of lateral control. She simply tilted the plywood floor toward her intended landing site and down she came.

Fig. 6-1. Carlotta Myers.

Carl Myers, at this time, designed and built a lemon-shaped gas bag to support a light framework resembling a bicycle. It was fitted with pedals for propulsion that were chain-linked to a screw-sail tractor propeller of Carlotta's design. The bottom half of the gas bag was flat, forming an inclined plane, against which the propeller slipstream pushed to give it ascension power.

THE SKY CYCLE

Crude as the design was, Myers' *Sky Cycle* (Fig. 6-3), as he called it, really worked. He could navigate the sky at will at speeds up to 10 miles per hour. He frequently performed at carnivals up and down New York state. By 1895, Myers had modified the design to include a full cylindrical, spindle-shaped gas bag and a pair of bat wings to serve as lifting surfaces.

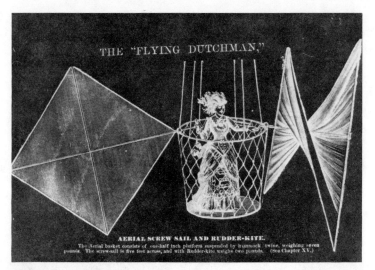

THE "FLYING DUTCHMAN."

AERIAL SCREW SAIL AND RUDDER-KITE.
The Aerial basket consists of one-half inch platform suspended by hammock twine, weighing seven pounds. The screw-sail is five feet across, and with Rudder-kite weighs two pounds. (See Chapter XV.)

Fig. 6-2. Aeronaut Carlotta Myers won fame as the "Mistress of the Winds" by navigating a free balloon over New York.

On August 3, 1895, Myers invited a reporter from the *New York World* to go for an aerial spin in his bat-wing *Sky Cycle* (Fig. 6-4). It was the first dirigible ever to fly over the rooftops of New York City. In the paper's Sunday edition, a sketch of the craft bearing the logo: THE WORLD showed it sailing high above Manhattan. The story was headlined:

THE WORLD'S AIRSHIP
Sails Over New York and Brooklyn
Both With and Against the Wind

- - - -

A Reporter its Sole Operator

- - - -

First Trial In New York of a Device
By Which Man May Really Soar.

- - - -

The Problem Seems to be Solved

The reporter was impressed and described his thrilling flight in detail. After taking off from a vacant lot near the Brooklyn Navy Yard, he made several short runs back and forth over a cheering crowd to prove that he could fly upwind as well as downwind. He then waved goodbye and pedaled across the river to New York. He swung north and flew the entire length of Manhattan Island, over the Bronx, and on to Yonkers—where he landed.

Professor Myers continued his ballooning by working with the United States Weather Bureau, building small weather balloons to carry instruments aloft, and conducting experiments with rain-making devices for the

Department of Agriculture. On his first attempt, he sent up a balloon of 10 feet diameter filled with a mixture of hydrogen and oxygen gases to a height of 1500 feet—and there detonated it. He explained:

"An insulated wire terminating in a small fulminate cartridge inserted in the neck of the balloon allowed it to rise to about 1500 feet elevation. The balloon was exploded by a hand dynamo while I lay flat upon my back to watch it through a good binocular.

"At the moment of discharge, the 10-foot sphere instantly dilated to ten times its former diameter, looking like a gorgeous yellow globe of dazzling fire, like the sun suddenly moved near at hand. This instantaneously disappeared, leaving an equal space filled with twinkling fragments of the envelope, looking like 'star dust' or snowflakes.

"The spectacle, surpassing any I have ever yet seen, was followed about a second later by the most stunning CRASH I have ever heard. Following this, in rattling and reverberating succession, came the jarring roar of thunder-like echoes, reflected again and again from earth and air, as the shock rolled along the hilltops, and through the vaults of the sky.

"Following the explosion, the roof and walls of the casino, the clubhouse, and the bowling alley, situated directly below the point of discharge, spread and then collapsed. Small fish in the brook below were found dead in large numbers. As a coincidence, the skies burst open before we could pick up and store our apparatus, and a heavy shower of nearly an hour's duration pursued us into the city from where we operated, the day having been a fine one, warm and clear, previous to the discharge."

FLIGHT TECHNIQUES

While Myers was toying with his rain-making experiments as a balloon-buster, Carlotta was continuing her experiments with ways of

Fig. 6-3. Myers' Sky-Cycle.

making spherical balloons dirigible and studying their actions in free flight under difficult circumstances. One thing interested her particularly:"If you turn about, the rim of your car rotates in the opposite direction and you still stare at the landscape before you," she wrote. "Turning quickly around seems like walking forward in a railroad train slowing down, and your very footing seems alive and conscious of you. You begin to realize that you are free in space, and the dominating influence.

"If you wave your fan your bubble responds, like the zephyr you invoke. If your fan is big enough, you begin to realize that force directed on 'empty air' is not wasted, but may be utilized. I have wafted myself across a river when the breeze died at nightfall, and would have left me on the lonesome side, while a radiant city invited me to take the airline ferry to a warm meal. I worked my passage by wafting a folded newspaper, as an air paddle."

VECTORED THRUST

In the summer of 1888, Carl Myers received an order from Peter C. Campbell of Brooklyn, New York for three small working models of a dirigible and one large enough to carry two men. Years before, Campbell had been granted a patent for his dirigible airship which, like that of another inventor named Charles Ritchel, mounted both horizontal and vertical propellers to obtain dynamic lift and forward thrust. It was the genesis of a persistent concept, later repeated by Simon Lake, and in recent years would become the "vectored-thrust" concept for future heavy-lifters.

Campbell formed a company to finance construction of a large dirigible to navigate between Brooklyn and New York. It was not as ambitious a scheme as Porter's transcontinental dirigible airline proposal, but one calculated to achieve modest financial success in the manner of today's feeder airlines.

James Allen, who had served the North as a military aeronaut during the Civil War, was summoned to Brooklyn to pilot the newly completed Campbell aircraft. But after an initial test flight that included a climb to 200 feet, Allen immediately descended and warned that the control system was inadequate. He advised Campbell to abandon the scheme, but Campbell decided to go ahead anyway.

In the following year, Campbell hired a Canadian balloonist named E. D. Hogan to continue the trial flights. On July 16, Hogan ascended from the Nassau Gas Company lot in the teeth of a stiff westerly wind that immediately swept the dirigible out over the Atlantic Ocean.

According to the report of an eyewitness to the event, Hogan had begun cranking the elevating propeller so fast that it literally spun off. It fell to the ground and left the aeronaut helpless to bring the dirigible down. Both the aircraft and its pilot vanished over the Atlantic and were never again heard from (Fig. 6-5).

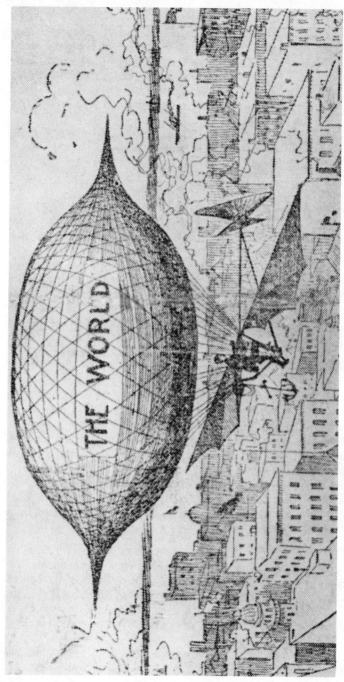

Fig. 6-4. A New York World reporter flew the bat-winged Sky-Cycle in 1895.

THE ZEPHYR

Campbell was not a man to give up easily. Two days following the loss of Hogan and the aircraft, Campbell called on Carlotta Myers, the famed lady aeronaut, to keep interest alive in the Campbell Airship Company with an ascension from the Washington Park baseball grounds. As Carlotta gracefully stepped into the car of her free balloon, The *Zephyr*, a small aerostat only 20 feet in diameter and weighing 65 pounds, Campbell cleared his throat and proclaimed:

"Now, Carlotta, if you only had my airship you could sail around Brooklyn, and then over to New York and to Jersey City, and that would really boom air navigation!"

Carlotta laughed. "Is that all you would like me to do?" she asked. "Cannot you map me a course you wish me to follow?"

Campbell responded eagerly: "Mrs. Myers, if you will fly to the Brooklyn City Hall, then down to the Battery, and turn up the river to the bridge, and sail along it to City Hall, New York, you will be seen by more people than ever together saw any human being or airship!"

Without a word, Carlotta smiled at Campbell. After all, Carl Myers had followed such a course in his *Sky Cycle*, and had permitted a newspaper reporter to duplicate the feat. Although her aircraft was a simple free balloon, she was, after all, mistress of the winds. For a long minute she gazed inquiringly at the drifting clouds overhead—studying their motion. Then she signalled her husband to shove her off.

Perfectly balanced, her tiny balloon moved away silently and gently as a thistledown. It rose smoothly until it caught an air current that carried her off toward the Brooklyn City Hall. Picking up speed, Carlotta passed over the turning point, valved a wisp of gas and settled lower to earth where she felt the rustle of a contrary wind. Now her balloon followed the river to the bridge while thousands of spectators yelled and waved their hats and river boats tooted their whistles and rang their bells. Within one hour she had completed the course which Campbell had outlined for her, and gently descended to earth.

Packing her balloon into a small bundle not two feet square, she returned to her starting point by wagon, street car, ferry, and elevated train—changing conveyances nine times—showing how much more quickly and easily air travel was.

GUIDING APPARATUS

Carlotta made the secret of her control system public on May 26, 1885, when she and her husband were granted United States Letters Patent No. 318,575 for a "Guiding Apparatus for Balloons." Her secret was simple. It lay entirely in the construction of the balloon basket's floor which was made from thin ply veneer suspended from the balloon by a flexible netting.

It was a refinement of the experimental control system she had developed for her casual excursions up and down the Mohawk Valley a few

90

Fig. 6-5. E.D. Hogan was lost at sea in Peter Campbell's airship.

years before. She explained: "The platform serves as a support for the aeronaut, and also as a rudder capable of adjustment in various planes by changes in the position or weight of the aeronaut. Upward or downward movements may be diverted toward any point of the compass and its course in calm air guided in any special direction when the platform is impelled or drawn forward by rotating a screw-sail attached for propulsion."

Carlotta's experimental rudder sail was (Figs. 6-6 and 6-7) dispensed with as unnecessary when navigating by her adjustable floor. She explained: "The platform alone is competent to modify the direction of flight when the balloon arises, and especially to influence the direction of its fall. A spherical balloon, by the aid of the platform alone, can be so influenced or diverted in calm air as to land in any desired quarter of a considerable area below."

Another innovation in the Myers' patent was a system of anchoring spikes that could be dropped through holes in the platform so that, when landing in a crosswind, they would dig into the ground as the balloon's platform slid over it. The aeronaut stood at the rear of the car much like riding an aquaplane behind a speedboat.

The Myers' Balloon Farm at Frankfort, New York became a busy place as their business boomed. In 1891, Myers set an admirable production record by completing 60 balloons in 60 days. In five successive days he turned out 10 balloons—two per day.

Myers experimented from time to time with a wide variety of propulsion and control systems. He was determined to find a suitable way to achieve dirigibility with his free balloons and his lemon-shaped *Sky Cycle*, or *Gas Kite*, as he sometimes called it. He tried out both hand- and foot-driven cranks to operate his screw sails, vibrating wings, movable planes, and a universally mounted rudder—all together or one at a time. He made as many as one hundred flights in his little sky runabout and put on demonstrations in 14 states.

On February 5, 1900, Myers concluded from his experiments with three such aircraft that "with practice acquired by the use of the *Sky Cycle*, and with some variation in structure and equipment, including a light aero-motor engine of the best type, there should be no difficulty in accomplishing an overland transcontinental journey by two or three persons, with this type of aircraft, in less time than the same trip could be made by the same party on the ground."

BEAUTIFUL SKY COUNTRY

While her husband was continuing his *Sky Cycle* experiments, Carlotta was making almost daily ascensions up and down the Mohawk Valley. Describing a typical journey from Utica to the Frankfort Balloon Farm, she revealed the pleasures of controlled ballooning this way:

"My balloon just floated from the hands that held it, and gently bore me straight away from the haven I sought . . . Higher and higher I went without a change till my little mountain barometer watch marked a mile. Then a little thrill vibrated my gas bubble with a silken rustle as the changing air current made it shiver. My wayward course checked, and then changed more and more, till nearly reversed, and I began to approach the beautiful Mohawk Valley which I knew would lead me homeward, as its normal winds wind and run with the stream lower down.

"It was a very slow ride. At times the balloon at this height hardly seemed to move . . . Higher still, nearly two miles above the Valley, I crossed eastward over Schuyler, where I wasted a wisp of gas by pulling a cord which opened one leaf of my double valves . . . As I turned again into the valley current, I felt my way downward till quite past my own home. Here I stopped my falling balloon with a handful or two of sand, and hovered, balancing, over the valley charms, meanwhile guessing how I should reach my home most directly by windage.

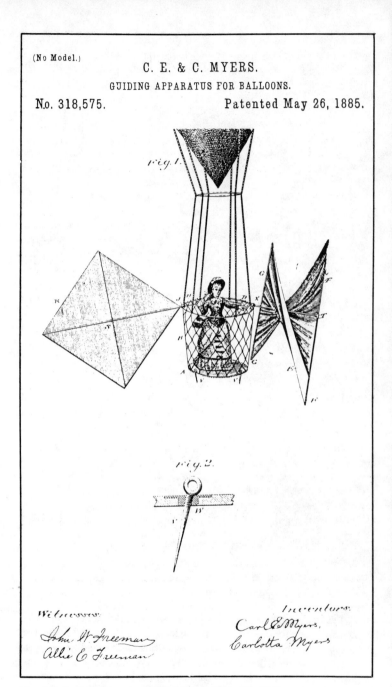

Fig. 6-6. Carlotta Myers' patented screw sail and rudder.

Fig. 6-7. The aerial "basket."

"I watched my barometer, as it marked below one mile high, and I looked anxiously for the wind I was expecting to meet me and escort me homeward . . . The looked-for wind was waiting for me, and we went on together across the valley, the river, and the canal, and in the green fields of the upland plateau I brought my car to the ground within a few rods of my house, in the western edge of Frankfort Village.

"I could have landed anywhere within a mile of my last elevation, simply by slanting the edge of my hammock-netting car . . . With a lightweight balloon, a five-pound car, and handy winds, one can wander at will in space, and feel in touch with home . . . "

Carlotta made roughly a thousand ascensions during the 1880s and 1890s to outnumber those of all other aeronauts in America during the same two decades. Never did she encounter any serious difficulty with her aerostats and it is doubtful that a more skilled aeronaut ever lived. Should you care to navigate the beautiful sky country with the memory of Carlotta, find a copy of the volume she wrote in 1883: *"Aerial Adventures of Carlotta; or, Sky-Larking in Cloudland, Being Hap-Hazard Accounts of the Perils and Pleasures of Aerial Navigation. By the Lady Aeronaut, Carlotta."*

Chapter 7

The Man Who Sailed
Down the Streets of Paris

It was the dawn of a beautiful day. The morning sun threw slanted rays down the tree-lined Champs Elysees past the Arc de Triomphe. Traffic was light. The morning promenaders were not yet out and only a horse-drawn carriage clattered over the cobblestones.

On the top floor a luxurious apartment building at the corner of Champs Elysees and the Rue Washington, a lovely young American tourist had completed her shower and was drying herself before the window while taking in the exhilerating view.

Suddenly she held her hand to her mouth to stifle a scream. A large dirigible had silently slid down the sky to poise before her. At eye level, a slender young man stood on a narrow catwalk beneath the hulk and smiled at her.

Lifting his wide-brimmed panama hat, he bowed graciously at the startled maiden, who now sought to cover her nakedness with her towel.

"Bon jour, madamoiselle! Permettez-moi de vous presenter . . ."

But before the aeronaut could present himself properly the girl had slammed the shutters.

"You . . . CAD!" she screamed.

"J'ai faim!" the aeronaut persisted. "I'm hungry! Would you be so kind as to join me for coffee and croissants?"

In a moment the shutters opened and the girl peeked out, smiling. "Merci, monsieur!" she said. "I should be delighted. But first—your name?"

Alberto Santos-Dumont frowned. Was there really someone in all Paris who did not know the famed Brazilian playboy (Fig. 7-2), the son of a millionaire coffee plantation owner who had proven that dirigibles could be made to go anywhere at the will of the operator? The sportsman who explored the streets of Paris at rooftop level from his aerial machines? The very same hero who had won the Deutsch Prize by sailing from St. Cloud around the Eiffel Tower (Fig. 7-1) and back in under half an hour?

Fig. 7-1. Alberto Santos-Dumont circles the Eiffel Tower.

Quickly Santos-Dumont recovered his aplomb. After all, the girl *was* beautiful. He had been trying for days to make her acquaintance since she moved into the apartment just across the street from his apartment at the opposite corner.

It had been an inspiration. What would society say at the next cocktail party. After he had proven he could navigate his *Number 9* dirigible down through the heart of Paris' Right Bank district to his home for a cup of morning coffee! It had been fortuitous that the American girl had appeared at the window *en dishabille*—an unexpected thrill.

THE GUIDE ROPE

The secret of his ability to fly low and slow across the Parisian rooftops lay in his employment of what he called his "guide rope." This was a variation of the drag rope invented by Charles Green, the noted British balloonist. Green had developed his drag rope, fitted with copper floats, for use in a projected crossing of the Atlantic by balloon (a project that never took place).

Both in theory and in operation, the ideas was sound. To keep an aerostat on an even keel on cross-country trips, it had been the custom to jettison gas or ballast as the occasion required. This was a practice that severely limited range. Santos-Dumont, like Green before him, learned that dragging a rope across the ground or water served as a compensating device to regulate altitude.

Santos-Dumont's guide rope weighed about 66 pounds. In free flight, it represented the bulk of the aircraft's ballast except for a few extra pounds of sand or water for emergency use. When his dirigible sank lower than the total length of the guide rope, the weight of the length trailing on the surface was subtracted automatically. This permitted the balloon to stabilize or rise as the occasion demanded.

ARCTIC EXPLORATION

Santos-Dumont has the greatest faith in his guide rope and saw a great future in it for Arctic exploration by dirigible. In his autobiography, *My Airships*, published in 1904, Santos-Dumont wrote: "Some day, explorers will guide-rope to the North Pole from their ice-locked steamship after it has reached its farthest possible point north. Guide-roping over the ice pack, they will make the very few hundreds of miles to the pole at the rate of forty to fifty miles an hour. Even at the rate of thirty miles, the trip to the pole and back to the ship could be taken between breakfast and suppertime. I do not say they will land the first time at the pole—but they will circle round about the spot, take observations, and return for supper!"

Santos-Dumont can be forgiven for overlooking the disastrous attempt to reach the pole in this manner by Sweden's Salomon August Andree. With two companions, Knut Fraenkel and Nils Strindberg, Andree sailed off from Danes Island, Spitzbergen, in their balloon *Ornen* (Eagle) on July 11, 1897—only to vanish in the whiteness (Fig. 7-3).

Fig. 7-2. Alberto Santos-Dumont.

Shortly before Santos-Dumont died in 1932, a strange sequel to the Andree mystery unfolded. For 33 years, nothing had been heard from the ill-fated balloonists, with the exception of a message brought by carrier pigeon, and a letter in a buoy found floating with a report that all was well on their first two days out.

Then on August 6, 1930, Norwegian explorers visited White Island, some 300 miles east of Andree's launch point, and stumbled onto the remains of a silent camp. There they found the frozen bodies of the three aeronauts, a diary in Andree's handwriting, and a roll of undeveloped film, wrapped in a sweater. The film was carefully developed (Fig. 7-4) and with the diary, the fate of the Andree expedition finally became known to the outside world. Three days out of Spitzbergen, ice and snow on their balloon had forced them down on the ice. They abandoned the balloon and spent a terrifying two and one-half months stumbling over the Arctic icepack to the small island where they died. One poignant photo showed Frankel and Stringberg, guns in hand, standing beside a polar bear they had shot for food.

THE RUNABOUT

Santos-Dumont was luckier and his choice of locale for aerial experimentation far more salutary than a trip to the pole. He loved Paris and delighted in sailing down the lovely streets, waving at the pretty girls and cheering men on the sidewalks below (Figs. 7-5 and 7-6). Typical was his venture down the Champs Elysees on Tuesday, June 23, 1903. Up at 2 a.m., he relates, "in my handy electric automobile I arrived at my airship station at Neuilly Saint James while it was yet dark."

Rousing his ground crew, he boarded his little *Number 9 Runabout* and slanted skyward over the wall and across the Seine River. Coming to the Bois de Boulogne, he crossed the woods following open areas to guide-rope as much as possible. Coming to the Porte Dauphine, he swung down the broad Avenue du Bois de Boulogne and headed for the Arc de Triomphe. He was tempted to sail through the arch. But instead, he recalled, "I rounded the national monument, to the right, as the law directs."

Already Santos-Dumont had built and flown several dirigibles far larger than the little *Number 9 Runabout*, which the young Brazilian had constructed purely for pleasure flying.

"*Number 9* was the smallest of possible dirigibles," he wrote, "yet it was very practical indeed. As originally constructed, its capacity was but 7770 cubic feet, permitting me to take up less than 66 pounds ballast; and thus I navigated for weeks, without inconvenience.

"Even when I enlarged it to 9218 cubic feet, the balloon of my *Number 6*, in which I won the Deutsch Prize, would have made almost three of it, while that of my still bigger *Omnibus* is fully eight times its size. Its 3-horsepower Clement motor weights but 26½ pounds, and with such a

Fig. 7-3. In 1897, Andree vanishes in the Arctic while seeking the Pole.

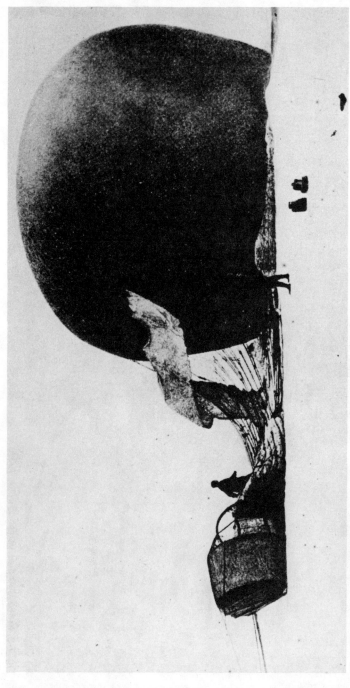

Fig. 7-4. This photo of the Eagle was developed from film lost in the Arctic for 33 years.

motor one cannot expect great speed; nevertheless this handy little runabout takes me over the Bois at between twelve and fifteen miles per hour, and this notwithstanding its egg-shaped form which could seem little calculated for cutting the air. Indeed, to make it respond promptly to the rudder, I drive it thick-end first."

Santos-Dumont found himself momentarily confused as he rounded the Place de Etoille with the Arc de Triomphe at its center. All the radiating avenues looked to be the same from the air! Finally he looked back, saw the monument with its arch facing his intended route, and set off down the Champs Elyssees—now lovely in the dawn's light.

He traveled slowly, his little Clement motor chugging merrily, as he trailed his 132-foot guide rope along the rooftops with 66 feet of it sliding over chimney pots and slate shingles with a soft rustle. Ahead, he spotted a light in a window. The American girl was up and about! He softly closed the throttle and nosed down so that he was on a level with her windowsill.

The sight that greeted him was unnerving, as she turned toward him—a sight he would long remember. Santos-Dumont had had little time for romance during his years in Paris. He was always too busy with his aeronautical projects. Yet he did find time now to follow up his unusual dawn meeting with his lovely neighbor. Following their formal meeting over the white tablecloth of a sidewalk cafe, he was startled to hear her ask to go sky-riding in his *Runabout*. Santos-Dumont Revealed:

"My heroine, a very beautiful young lady well known in New York society, confessed an extraordinary desire to navigate the airship.

Fig. 7-5. Alberto Santos-Dumont sails over the streets of Paris, France.

" 'You mean that you would have the courage to be taken up in the free balloon, with no one holding its guide-rope?' I asked. "Madamoiselle, I thank you for the confidence!"

" 'Oh, no!' she said. "I do not want to be taken up. I want to go up alone and navigate it free, as you do!"

Santos-Dumont thought hard for a moment, looked into her pleading eyes, and smiled. "If you will take a few lessons," he offered, "so that you can handle the motor and the machinery, perhaps it can be arranged!"

On the appointed day, Santos-Dumont's lady friend climbed onto the framework of *Number 9* dirigible at the Neuilly Saint James airship station, started the engine and rose into the air. Santos-Dumont reported: "The guide-rope trailing some 30 feet gave her an altitude and equilibrium that never varied. I will not say that no one ran alongside the dragging guide-rope, but certainly no one touched it until the termination of the cruise at Bagatelle, when the moment had arrived to pull down the intrepid girl-navigator."

Santos-Dumont's gallantry was equal to the occasion. Not only did he give the young lady full credit for soloing his *Runabout* dirigible, he discreetly kept her name a secret. Not that he was a rooftop peeping Tom—he simply enjoyed the spark of romance that added to his pleasures in skirting Paris' chimney pots in search of adventure. As a matter of fact, Santos-Dumont felt that aeronauts who attempted to rise to greater heights were fools. In his opinion, dirigibles were best suited to contour flying (as it is known today).

TO BE AN AERONAUT

Born in Brazil on July 20, 1873, he had early become fascinated with machinery and as a teenager was allowed to drive the plantation steam locomotive that hauled sacks of coffee to market. At a fair in San Paulo, he saw his first balloon ascension in 1888 at the age of 15 and knew then and there he would some day become an aeronaut.

In 1891, he first visited Paris with his family. From his avid reading, he knew this was the capital of balloon activity for the whole world. The Montgolfier Brothers had started it all in 1783. Then had come Charles, Henri Giffard, and others such as the Tissandier brothers, who only a few years before had attempted dirigible flight under power of an electric motor. The youth consulted the city directory in search of a professional balloonist who could take him up, but their prices were outrageous. Discouraged, he turned to the latest fad—automobiling—and spent his allowance on a 3½-horsepower Peugeot.

Santos-Dumont's natural interest in machinery was a help. Whenever the car broke down, which was often, he got out his tools and repaired it himself. On returning to Brazil with his family, the Peugeot went along. Back in Paris the following year, Santos-Dumont, the rich man's son, bought one of the fancy new tricycle autos and staged a race at the Parc des Princes Velodrome—a bicycle track.

Fig. 7-6. "No. 5" landing at Trocadero for repairs.

Back in Rio in 1897, he stumbled on a volume by M. M. Lachambre on the ill-fated Andree expedition: *Andree: Au Pole Nord en Balloon*. Lachambre was the man who had built the Andee balloon and Santos-Dumont was determined to meet him. And so, that winter he made his first ascent with Lachambre at a cost of 250 francs. He was hooked.

"Suddenly the wind ceased," he recalled later in describing the thrill of ballooning. "The air seemed motionless around us. We were off, going at the speed of the air current in which we now lived and moved. Indeed, for us there was no more wind; and this is the first great fact of all spherical ballooning. Infinitely gentle is this unfelt movement forward and upward. The illusion is complete: it seems not to be the balloon that moves, but the earth that sinks down and away."

Down below, church bells pealed and dogs barked and children yelled, but Santos-Dumont had prepared a special treat for the occasion: a gourmet lunch in cloudland—hard-boiled eggs, cold roast beef, chicken, cheese, ice cream, fruits and cakes, champagne, coffee and chartreuse. White snowflakes formed inside his chilled glass. He was in heaven at last.

Delighted with the experience, Santos-Domont immediately ordered a balloon for himself. Christened the *Brazil*, it held 4104 cubic feet within a spherical covering of light Japanese silk. The 135 square yards of material weighted only 8 pounds. He attached a guide-rope that was 100 yards long and had a 6½-pound grappling iron attached to its end.

Santos-Dumont at this time had already made some 25 ascensions in M. Lachambre's balloons in France and Belgium and was familiar with the routine. He weighed only 110 pounds and his light weight was a help in managing small balloons. In Brazil, he carried 66 pounds of ballast. It was his feeling that airship pilots would do well to get experience in balloons "to become familiar with the caprices of the wind" and other atmospheric phenomena.

Ready now to attempt flight in a dirigible. Santos-Dumont purchased two tricycle autos. He removed their single-cylinder engines and bolted them together in tandem to obtain a 2-cylinder motor that weighed only 66 pounds and produced 3½ horsepower. He reinstalled it in a trike car and entered the Paris-to-Amsterdam Grand Prix for a road test. He did not come in first—the winner traveled at an amazing 25 mph average speed—but he did learn the engines's eccentricities so that he could anticipate trouble in the air by the sound of an roughness.

Next, he designed his first dirigible, the *Number 1* around the engine. It was cylindrical in shape with cones at front and rear, 82½ feet in length and 11½ feet in diameter, with a gas capacity of 6354 cubic feet. A silken rudder was added at the stern and a system of shifting weights hung at the end of ropes fore and aft were added to tilt the dirigible up or down. The engine swung a 2-bladed propeller at a sprightly 1200 rpm.

Santos-Dumont made his first ascension in dirigible *Number 1* from the Jardin d'Acclimation, a captive balloon base where he could buy hydrogen gas for only one franc per cubic foot. Hailed as the *Santos-*

Dumont Number 1, the craft rose gracefully on the morning of September 18, 1898, only to slam into a row of trees (Fig. 7-7) downwind from the launch point. Two days later Santes-Dumont had repaired the holes torn by tree branches and was off again.

This time, in his enthusiasm, Santos-Dumont rose to the height of 1300 feet. Expansion of the hydrogen gas over inflated the cylindrical bag and caused it to fold in the middle like a pocket knife. Rushing downward toward a grassy field in Bagatelle, where some boys were kite flying, he shouted for them to grab his guide-rope and run into the wind. The maneuver slowed the rate of fall and Santos-Dumont's life was spared. He

Fig. 7-7. Santos-Dumont's dirigible "No. 1" hit trees on its first flight in 1898.

deflated the bag, packed it into the airship's basket, and hailed a taxi to take him back to Paris.

Shaken by his narrow escape from almost certain death, Santos-Dumont nevertheless felt he had made a great accomplishment. He had ascended and descended, after a fashion, without sacrificing gas. And more important, he had proven his theory that oblique flight was practical.

"It was astonishing to feel the wind in my face,"he wrote."In spherical ballooning we go with the wind and do not feel it . . . As my airship plowed ahead, the wind struck my face and fluttered my coat as on the deck of a transatlantic liner."

He became the first to make a study of the elements of aerial navigation, flying into and against the wind, likening it to riding a boat on a swift river. Traveling at 20 mph into a 10-mile headwind, he concluded his ground speed was 10 mph. While flying at the same airspeed downwind, Santos-Dumont discovered that his ground speed was 30 mph. He was further delighted to discover that he was not prone to airsickness.

Where a fear of heights had gripped him since his first flight in a dirigible. he also felt uneasy sailing across Parisian rooftops with their sharp chimney pots. Contrarily, sailing across the lush forest of the Bois de Boulogne was more pleasant (Fig. 7-8). "Below me, the great ocean for greenery spreads, soft and safe." Oddly, Santos-Dumont felt no fear from possible explosion of the hydrogen gas he frequently used to inflate his dirigibles. He carried his little gasoline motors suspended well below the gas bag. On only one occasion was he threatened by fire. His engine backfired while crossing the Seine to land on the Ile de Puteaux. "I promptly extinguished the flame with my Panama hat, without other incident," he related calmly.

ADDITIONAL AIRSHIPS

His second dirigible, *Santos-Dumont No. 2,* was the same length as the first, but was fatter and held some 7000 cubic feet of gas and gave 144 pounds more ascensive force. In the first airship he had used an air pump to inflate a bladder inside to help the exterior bag hold its shape, while in the second he used an aluminum rotary fan driven by the motor to keep inflated a bladder at the bottom.

On May 11, 1899, the second airship was ready for a trial flight—but a rainstorm blew in. Rather than empty the airship of its expensive hydrogen, he decided to go up anyway. Again the cylindrical-shaped gas bag shrunk, heavy with rain, and collapsed into the treetops. he immediately began work on dirigible *No. 3*. This one was a lemon-shaped affair 66 feet long by 25 feet thick at the middle and held far more gas: 17,650 cubic feet—three times that of Airship *No. 1*. However, he decided to switch from hydrogen to illuminating (coal) gas, far cheaper and more readily available, though with only half the lifting power.

With no cylindrical shape to worry about Santos-Dumont eliminated the air pump and interior air sack and relied on a 33-foot bamboo pole slung

Fig. 7-8. Santos-Dumont's "No. 5" over Bois de Boulogne.

beneath the gas bag for rigidity. His "pole-keel" worked fine, supporting the passenger basket and guide rope. On November 13, 1899, he made a highly successful ascent from Vaugirard and proceeded directly to the Champ de Mars. He spent the day practicing climbs, dives, and turns—using the weight-shift technique to advantage.

In the distance he spotted the Eiffel Tower, and on a spur of the moment decision headed for it, circling around it several times and then heading straight for the Parc des Princes. It was the same route he would fly two years later to win the Deutsch Prize. His airspeed was 15 mph and he felt he was on the verge of achieving practical air navigation for everyone.

"When, in the future, airships became as common as automobiles," he said, "spacious public and private landing-stages will have to be built for them in every part of the capital!"

Santos-Dumont now moved his operation to Saint Cloud where the French Areo Club had established itself (Fig. 7-9). There he built a large shed which he called his aerodrome. It was 100 by 23 feet and 36 feet high. He used it to house his *No. 4* dirigible which was completed on August 1, 1900, and which would become a familar sight to Parisians as he made frequent sallies along the boulevards—dragging his guide rope.

This airship carried a new 7-horsepower motor that drove a 2-bladed propeller. Each blade was 13 feet long. He rode on a bicycle seat—steering the rudder from the handlebars. The engine controls were foot-operated. The 2-cylinder motor turned at 100 rpm and, mounted forward, developed 66 pounds of tractive thrust.

Santos-Dumont was up daily in this craft. On September 19, 1900, he made a demonstration flight before members of the International Congress of Aeronautics, which included the noted American aeronautical enthusiast, Professor Samuel P. Langley.

This airship was soon cut in half and lengthened with an insert to 109 feet. In addition, the powerplant was uprated, to 4 cylinders. He found it necessary to enlarge his aerodrome to take the longer gas bag. The new engine, which developed 12 horsepower, was mounted at the center of gravity and drove the propeller through a long, hollow steel shaft. Water ballast was substituted for sand for the first time.

THE DEUTSCH PRIZE

Santos-Dumont now felt ready to try for the Deutsch Prize of 100,000 francs. The course from the Aero Club's Parc d'Aerostation to the Eiffel Tower and return was roughly 7 miles and had to be covered in 30 minutes—including the radius of the turn. At 4:30 a.m. on July 12, 1901, Santos-Dumont lifted off from the Aero Club grounds at Saint Cloud, crossed over Longchamps race track, and began searching for the Eiffel Tower through the morning mists. One of the steering ropes broke and the aeronaut was forced to land and make a quick repair. He finally completed the course, but well past the required 30 minutes. His time was one hour 6 minutes.

Fig. 7-9. "No. 6" at the Aero Club.

At 6:41 the next morning, Santos-Dumont was off again in his airship—now called *No. 5* due to design changes over *No. 4*. This flight ended in a near disaster when his engine quit. He landed in a tall chestnut tree near the home of the Princess Isabel, Comtesse d'Eu and the daughter of Dom Pedro, the ruler of Brazil. The princess sent up a lunch for a treetop snack with an invitation to visit her. He did, and she presented him with a medal of St. Benedict to wear in protection against further accidents.

Again the intrepid aeronaut set off on the Deutsch Prize course at 6:30 on the morning of August 8, but as he neared the Eiffel Tower an automatic gas valve he had installed malfunctioned. The Balloon sagged and a suspension wire snagged in the propeller. Santos-Dumont quickly stopped the engine. But the balloon was losing gas rapidly and drifting closer and closer to the Eiffel Tower. Suddenly, it plunged into the courtyard of a hotel near the Trocadero. There the aeronaut was rescued by firemen with tall ladders.

Santos-Dumont quickly began building dirigible *No. 6* in the shape of an elongated ellipsoid. It was 100 feet long by 20 feet thick and with the ends cone-shaped. He installed a larger compensation balloon (2118 cubic feet) inside the gas bag with a connecting tube to draw air from the propeller blast. Three automatic valves were added to keep the gas bag from exploding.

On October 19, 1901, the Santos-Dumont *No. 6* (Fig. 7-10) was ready for another try at the Deutsch Prize. So confident was the aeronaut this time he rejected a dawn starting time and rose at 2:42 p.m. into a brisk crosswind. As he neared the Eiffel Tower, he cautiously rose well above it—remembering the close call he had in *No. 5*. At 2:51 p. m., *No. 6* gracefully make its turn at a good 1500 feet clear of the spiked lightning rod atop the tower. Only nine minutes, including the turning time, had elapsed.

Headed down the back stretch, Santos-Dumont felt like crying—his engine was sputtering badly. He quickly abandoned his steering wheel to fiddle with the carburetor control until he finally got it running smoothly again. Over Autiel racetrack his engine again threatened to quit. This brought cries of alarm from the crowd below. He once more got the balky engine running smoothly, but in doing so allowed the dirigible to climb steeply to an altitude of almost 500 feet. He disregarded his fear of height and plunged on. Finally, he crossed the judge's stand at the Aero Club grounds 29 minutes and 30 seconds after departing. There was just half a minute to spare! See Fig. 7-11.

Santos-Dumont refused to keep the 100,000 franc prize money. He donated 75,000 francs to the Parisian prefect of police to distribute to the poor and split the rest among his workers. Yet another reward was to come—one hundred contos, roughly 25,000 francs, from the government of Brazil, along with a gold medal.

Fig. 7-10. The first flight of Santos-Dumont's "No. 6" airship.

THE PRINCE

Winter was approaching and at the invitation of the Prince of Monaco Santos-Dumont shifted his base of aerial operations to the shores of the blue Mediterranian where the Prince had erected a large hangar for him near the beach of La Condamine. On January 29, 1902, he made his first flight over water. On return he made a perfect approach and sailed right into the open door of the dirigible shed.

A second flight was made on February 12. The Prince followed in his steam yacht. Again the flight was successful as Santos-Dumont cruised down the coast toward the Italian border. On his return, the Prince was waiting in the harbor to grab the guide-rope and help him in. He missed and the rope knocked him off his feet—much to everyones embarrassment. Two days later, the Santos-Dumont *No. 6* was destroyed in the Bay of Monaco due to a combination of high winds and under-inflation. Santos-Dumont said farewell to the Prince and returned to Paris.

A RACING DIRIGIBLE

In Paris, he busied himself building *No. 7*, a racing dirigible, in the event he could find someone to race against—which he did not. Dirigible *No. 7* carried a 60-horsepower motor that swung two propellers (one at each end) that were 16½ feet in diameter. Its speed was reported at close to 50 mph.

Santos-Dumont felt he needed more space and moved his base of operations from the Aero Club grounds to an open area of the Bois de Boulogne. There he ordered a huge hangar built with a row of stalls, like a cow barn, each 165 feet long by 31 feet wide and 44½ feet high. Again he went abroad, to America, and on return in the spring of 1903 found three dirigibles safely housed there.

First was his racing dirigible, *No. 7*. It was 45,000 cubic feet in size and cost more than 3,000 francs to fill with hydrogen. Next was his little runabout, *No. 9*, and beside that was *No. 10*, which he called his *Omnibus*. Omnibus was 80,000 cubic feet in size and able to carry a number of baskets with four passengers each. Or "war munitions, were the sudden need of a belligerent character to arise," he wrote.

No. 9 was the aeronaut's favorite. He enjoyed sailing it along the streets of Paris and stopping now and then for a glass of champagne or a lunch of escargot, his favorite delicacy, a sidewalk cafes.

THE PAX

During his career as a dirigible pilot, Santos-Dumont battled a fear of height. This fear was underscored for him on the early morning of May 12, 1902. A rival Brazilian balloonist, Auguste Servo, accompanied by his mechanic, M. Sachet, lifted off from Paris in a dirigible, named the *PAX*, that had been designed by Severo. They encountered a disaster.

Fig. 7-11. Santos-Dumont wins the Deutsch prize.

115

Fig. 7-12. The Pax.

Severo had developed a new type of dirigible in which the axis of the screw propeller was placed directly on the axis of the balloon itself. He constructed a large bamboo framework and encased it with a spindle-shaped fabric covering provided with slits, 90 feet in length and holding 2334 cubic meters of gas. The car was carried close to the balloon.

Inside the outer envelope were two ballonets holding one-tenth the capacity of the outer balloon. In place of rudders, Severo fitted a pair of screw-propellers—one at each end of the car. These worked opposite to, or at right angles to, the main propeller shaft which swung propeller blades at bow and stern. It was Severo's concept that the forward propeller would diminish the head air resistance, while the rear propeller drove the craft forward. Power was supplied by two Buchet motors. The forward motor had 12 horsepower and the aft one had 24 horsepower.

Severo and Sachet launched their craft, to a height estimated at twice that of the Eiffel Tower. Then an explosion occurred. Horrified witnesses saw the *Pax* fall for eight long seconds. The crash took both lives and might have been the reason Santos-Dumont finally abandoned his peripatetic dirigible cruises over the streets of Paris (Fig. 7-12).

THE DEUTSCH-ARCHDEACON PRIZE

But something else was on the horizon for the adventurous Brazilian playboy. In late 1903, even as he was demonstrating his runabout to the French Minister of War as a future weapon of war, Orville and Wilbur Wright were readying their little Kitty Hawk biplane for historic flights in North Carolina.

Quite naturally, Santos-Dumont abandoned airships for heavier-than-air machines. In 1906 he won the Deutsch-Archdeacon Prize craft that resembled a powered boxkite. Perhaps, he is best remembered for his tiny monoplane, the famous *Demoiselle* of 1909, which was a forerunner of today's light plane. In 1928, Santos-Dumont left Paris for the last time. He returned to his native Brazil where he died in 1932.

Chapter 8

To The Pole!

Ever since Edmond Charles Genet in 1826 sought government funds to launch an expedition to the Arctic in his horse-powered balloon, the dream of polar conquest by dirigible had been foremost in the minds of adventurers seeking to explore the frontier to the north. The dream was elusive and an airplane, not a dirigible, would be first to reach the North Pole exactly 100 years after Citizen Genet had proposed his flight. On May 9, 1926, Commander Richard E. Byrd and his pilot, Floyd Bennett, flew from Spitzbergen to the pole and back in 16 hours. Two days later, Roald Amundsen, Lincoln Ellsworth, and Umberto Nobile started from the same base in their Italian dirigible *Norge*. They crossed the North Pole and landed 71 hours later at Teller, Alaska—3391 miles distant.

WALTER WELLMAN

But the man who tried hardest to reach the North Pole by air was a colorful American newspaperman named Walter Wellman (Fig. 8-1). Born in 1858 the son of an Ohio farmer, young Walter was only 14 when he started a weekly newspaper in Sutton, Nebraska. At the age of 21, he founded the Cincinatti *Evening Post*. In 1884, he joined the Chicago *Record-Herald* and headed for the nation's capital.

From 1894 to 1910 Wellman made four attempts to reach the top of the world, risking life and limb, but always coming back with a top newspaper exclusive for the *Record-Herald*. He wrote: "To reach the North Pole has been the ambition of man through the centuries—the last really great thing to be done in working out the destiny of man to explore, conquer, and know all of the earth that was given to him to live upon and to rule."

Attempt One

Financed by some wealthy Washington friends, in April 1894, Wellman chartered the Norwegian icebreaker *Ragnvald Jarl* and established a supply depot on a sandbar at Smeerenburg in northern Spitzbergen (Fig. 8-2). The base was once used by Dutch whalers. The icebreaker was wrecked punching into the Arctic ice pack. However, the crew managed to save most of Wellman's supplies—including his tuxedo which he had brought with him for testimonial dinners he expected to attend as guest of honor after his venture. But after weeks of struggle against the forbidding ice pack, Wellman gave up and turned back.

Fig. 8-1. Walter Wellman.

Fig. 8-2. A view of Camp Wellman, Spitzbergen. The balloon house is in the foreground.

Failure of the surface expedition turned Wellman's eyes skyward. He wrote: "Often I looked up into the air and wished I had some means of traveling that royal road, where there were no ice hummocks, no leads of open water, no obstacles to rapid progress." Wellman had in mind traveling by free balloon, but the disastrous Andree expedition (See Chapter 7) cooled his enthusiasm.

Fig. 8-3. Wellman's dirigible America at Spitzbergen in 1909.

Attempt Two

From 1894 to 1898, Wellman stayed in Washington to cover the presidential elections. As a result of his favorable reporting, President William McKinley and others financed a second attempt to reach the North Pole by the surface route. On February 18, 1899, Wellman's second dash for the pole by dogslead began. But after an arduous effort, on March 22 the party was forced back when the ice pack opened up and nearly engulfed them.

In the fall of 1905, while covering the Russo-Japanese peace conference at Portsmouth. Wellman read of the successful flight of the Lebaudy dirigible built for the French government and the old dream of flying to the pole returned. This time his bosses at the Chicago *Record-Herald*, seeing the makings of another exciting series of stories, shelled out $250,000 to cover expenses.

On January 1, 1906, Wellman arrived in Paris to talk with balloonists Louis Godard and Alberto Santos-Dumont about his next project. Plans were drawn up for the world's second largest airship (the German Zeppelin was the largest) a 165-footer called the *America*. He set plans for a summer expedition by chartering the *Frithjof* and loading it with hydrogen generators from Paris, 110 tons of sulphuric acid from Hamburg, and 70 tons of iron turnings from Norway.

Attempt Three

Again he established a base (Fig. 8-3) at Virgo Bay near Smeerenburg, and set about erecting a dirigible shed 210 feet long—which quickly collapsed. The National Geographic Society got into the act of officially endorsing the effort. But the 1906 expedition never got off the ground. A 60-horsepower Clement engine for the *America* broke down, and Wellman returned to Paris to have the *America* enlarged for a new attempt in 1907.

Attempt Four

Things now looked promising. A new 80-horsepower, 4-cylinder Lorraine-Dietrich auto engine was installed to drive a pair of 11-foot steel propellers. A 5-horsepower auxiliary engine was added to keep the ballonet inflated. A 115-foot steel car was suspended beneath the gas bag, was an 18-inch pipe held 1200 gallons of gasoline (Fig. 8-4), and the car held the engines, crew, boats, sleds, 10 dogs and provisions for 10 months.

Wellmen added something new—his famous "equilibrator"—to serve as a guide rope to maintain altitude without discharging ballast or gas. The equilibrator was 120 feet long and weighed 500 pounds and was designed to float on the water or drag over the ice. Inside the leather equilibrator (8 inches in diameter) was reserve supplies of food carried in 30 compartments. Overlapping steel scales would protect it from damage—he hoped. A second novelty was a "retarder"—another leather snake stuffed with

Fig. 8-4. Wellman's America carried fuel in an 18-inch pipe.

extra food and covered with thousands of sharp nails to dig into the snow and slow the airship down if it got going too fast.

On September 2, 1907, the *America* was taken from its shed for a maiden flight. Wellman reported in his paper: "With a thrill of joy the three of us of the crew felt her moving through the air. The engine was started and the *America* leaped forward. We could see the equilibrator swimming along in the water like a great sea serpent."

Two hours out, Wellman ran into stiff headwinds that slowed progress almost to a halt. Encountering a high glacier, the crew was forced to pull their knives and slit the gas bag open so it would collapse where they could get it out. They salvaged what they could, and again Wellmen headed back to Paris.

1908 was an election year in America, and Wellman had to cover the Washington beat. It was not until August 15, 1909, that he could start off again with the *America* for the North Pole. With him went Melvin Vaniman, his engineer, and a Russian named Nicholas Popoff—who would die two years later in a balloon accident.

The start was auspicious. A strong tailwind blew, but soon Wellman heard something splash into the sea. The leather equilibrator had rotted in the past two years and simply collapsed. With 1200 pounds of ballast gone, the *America* shot skyward at an alarming pace. With the reserve supply of food in the equilibrator gone, they lowered the retarder, valved off some hydrogen and headed back for Spitzbergen. Over open water they sailed above a Norwegian government vessel named the *Farm*. They tossed them a line and were secured (Figs. 8-5 and 8-6).

As the *Farm's* crew started to haul the *America* in they were shocked to see Wellman light a big cigar—right in the face of the discharging hydrogen gas. By a miracle nothing happened, but two hours later a gust of wind blew the *America* off and it suddenly rose and exploded above its pressure altitude.

On his way home, Wellman received news by radio that Dr. Frederick A. Cook (the great arctic impostor) was claiming he had reached the North Pole on foot. Later Wellman learned that Commander Robert Peary, not Cook, was the first man to set foot atop the world. Wellman did the gentlemanly thing and cabled congratulations to Peary.

A Transatlantic Try

Wellman figured the Arctic story no longer had news value, now that man had walked to the Pole, and he immediately set his sights on a new record—to be the first man to pilot a dirigible across the Atlantic. He had the *America* rebuilt once more, but it ended up overweight and low on fuel. It could only carry 5500 gallons of gas instead of 9000 gallons—much of it inside the equilibrator.

The *America's* rebuilding was completed on October 12. On October 15, without even a test hop, Wellman set off from Atlantic City, New

Fig. 8-5. Attaching a tow line to the America.

Jersey where thousands of curious people had paid $1 each to inspect the airship in its hangar.

A crew of 60 workers carried the equibrator to a pier and tossed it into the water. At the last minute, the navigator, Murray Simon, arrived with a pet cat in a bag. Vaniman refused to go unless the cat was left behind, but the guide rope was already cast free and they sailed off, cat and all. Also aboard with Wellman, Simon, and Vaniman was an assistant engineer, Louis Loud, and Jack Irwin, wireless operator.

Troubles began at once with the Lorraine-Dietrich engine. It ran only four hours out of the first 10 hours aloft. By nightfall, they were sighted 80 miles out of Atlantic City instead of 200 as planned. With the equilibrator dragging heavily in the sea, they had to dump precious fuel to stay aloft. The first night out was a humdinger. Wellman reported:

"Such a night it was! Soon the exhaust pipe heated red hot and began to belch sparks—not an occasional flash of fire, but thick showers flying aft along the varnished cotton enclosure of the steel car, up against the under part of the balloon itself, against the canvas rudder, and the ship's colors floating above the helm.

"Nor were these mere evanescent flashes of filmy flame, but great constellations of living coals, many of them glowing for a few seconds after they had fallen into the sea. It seemed only a question of time until one of these fiery, incandescent masses would lodge in some nook or cranny, set fire to the canvas, and bring our little world to an end.

"For some minutes, half scared, half fascinated, I watched these aerial fireworks, trying to figure out the percentage of chances in one hundred we had to escape being blown to kingdom come by the combination of 345,000 cubic feet of hydrogen, tons of volatine gasoline, half an acre of cotton, and the whole deluged with almost constant eruptions of flying fireballs . . . But before I could determine whether we had ten chances or only five in the hundred of escaping one grand, conclusive explosion, my nerves gave way.

" 'Vaniman!' I cried, 'you must stop that motor at once!"

"He stopped it and called down to me, in the lifeboat, 'What's the matter?'

" 'Nothing but hellfire,' I replied. 'We can't stand this! It's only a question of time when we blow up!' "

The *America* was running low and at one point almost collided with a steamer named the *Bullard*. They survived the next day and night by dismantling the auxiliary motor and throwing it overboard in order to stay afloat.

Wellman knew that they would never make it to Europe. The best that they could now hope for was to drift to the Azores. However, a wind shift dashed that hope. Now Wellman fixed his hopes on reaching Bermuda, or possibly Florida. But the hot sun of the next day brought a new problem. The gas overheated and the *America* began a steady climb. He ordered Vaniman to open the gas valve. By mistake, Vaniman yanked the air valve

Fig. 8-6. The Norwegian steamer Farm rescuing the America.

open, dumping several thousand cubic feet of air from the ballonet. Up she went again—this time to 3000 feet.

More hydrogen now had to be valved off to bring the *America* back down to cruising level near the water where the equilibrator could function. Wellman knew that, with the coming of the next nightfall, the cooling effect would force them into the sea. They could launch their lifeboat, at the risk of having it capsize, but they hesitated.

At 4:30 the next morning, they saw the lights of a ship. Vaniman quickly soaked some rags in gasoline, lighted them, and dropped them overboard. The ship saw the signal and changed course. The ship turned out to be the *Trent*, a steamer from Bermuda. Making radio contact, they arranged history's first rescue of a dirigible by a steamship (Figs. 8-7 and 8-8).

Excited passengers crowded the *Trent's* deck to watch the thrilling rescue. Expertly, Wellman directed the *America* to be cut loose at the precise moment their lifeboat struck the water. As the *America* drifted off, a tear was seen in Wellman's eye as he waved farewell to his airship.

Back home, he nevertheless won a ticker-tape parade down Broadway in New York. But he never again set foot in either an airship or airplane. He figured his luck had just about run out.

UMBERTO NOBILE

On July 30, 1978, General Umberto Nobile, Italian aeronautical engineer, explorer and pioneer of Arctic flying, died in Rome at the age of 93 after one of the most controversial careers of any airman. Born at Lauro, near Naples, on January 24, 1885, Nobile did much pioneering in aircraft construction for Italy during and after World War I. Italian designers had led in the development of semirigid airships which dated back to Renard and Krebs and Lebaudy types. After the war, Nobile was approached by Giovanni Agnelli, a member of the Italian Senate, to promote an airship line linking Rome and Buenos Aires.

Nobile gave the idea serious thought and reported that an airship of 3,000,000 cubic feet would be required. That was far larger than the state of the art would permit at the that time. However, a Milanese industrialist, Usuelli, previously had built some small airships and he proposed building a small dirigible. This became the ill-fated *Roma* (Fig. 8-9). It was the first semirigid craft with a rigid nose cap. The *Roma* crashed and burned in America in 1922, killing 34 persons. Nobile was a member of the *Roma's* design time.

A Secret Conference

On July 15, 1925, Nobile received a telegram from Roald Amundsen, the famous Arctic explorer, asking him to meet with him in Rome "for an important, secret conference." Amundsen, a few months earlier, had returned from an Arctic expedition in which he had tried unsuccessfully to

Fig. 8-7. Wallman's America crew was rescued in the Mid-Atlantic.

129

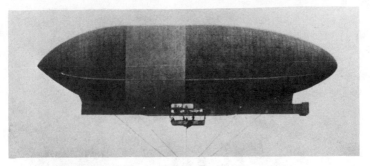

Fig. 8-8. The America as seen from the Trent.

reach the North Pole with two Dornier Wal seaplanes. When one was damaged, both landed on the ice floe north of Spitzbergen. Twenty-five days later, abandoning the wrecked seaplane, Amundsen and his five companions all crowded into the other craft and flew back to King's Bay.

It was obvious to Amundsen that an airship was the only way to fly to the pole. The same idea had occurred earlier to Nobile when he was in charge of the military factory of Aeronautical Constructions in Rome. There Nobile had built the world's smallest semirigid airship which he named the *Mr*. Nobile enjoyed taking off and landing in a courtyard of the barracks beside the workshops. Next, he developed the *N-1* as a prototype airship for the Italian Navy.

Nobile got a second wire from Amundsen, asking him to come to Oslo, since he could not get away. Nobile complied, and Amundsen sketched a plan to cross the North Pole from Spitzbergen to Point Barrow, Alaska, with a refueling base at King's Bay at 79 degrees north latitude. Nobile agreed to use the *N-1* (which would be renamed the *Norge*) in an effort to beat out a German expedition planned to fly over the same route using a Zeppelin of 4,768,000 cubic feet—seven times larger than the *Norge*.

The Aeroclub of Norway agreed to underwrite the cost of the expedition, along with $120,000 pledged by an American, Lincoln Ellsworth. The Aeroclub would supply Arctic clothing, provisions and such gear as tents, knapsacks, skis, and firearms. The agreement was signed by Benito Mussolini as his first act as Minister of Aviation. The *Norge* was rebuilt and lightened by 3500 pounds.

Over the Top

On May 11, 1926, the *Norge* left Spitzbergen carrying, among others, Nobile, Amundsen and Ellsworth. It passed over the top of the world (Figs. 8-10 and 8-11) the next day to continue its 3000-mile flight to Teller, Alaska—where it was dismantled. Total personnel aboard during this trip included six Italians, eight Norwegians, an American and a Swede— making it truly an international affair. The flight to the tiny Eskimo village took 169 hours and revealed that the top of the world was covered by a frozen sea, not land.

Discovery of the Arctic Sea added new knowledge to the geography of the world. And in 1959, the American submarine *Nautilus*, propelled by atomic power, crossed the Pole under the icepack along the same route as the *Norge*. The *Nautilus'* commander, Captain William R. Anderson, wrote to Nobile: "From your courageous flight over the polar ice pack in 1926, it was established that there was no land between Alaska and Spitzbergen. Without this knowledge, found by you and confirmed by the aerial expeditions that followed you, we would not have known enough to undertake our voyage."

In recent years, doubt has been expressed about the validity of Commander Richard Byrd's claim to have flown over the North Pole with Floyd Bennett a few days prior to the *Norge's* flight. These doubts were expressed in a necrology of General Nobile published in the newsletter of the Lighter-Than-Air Society, of Akron, Ohio, by A. D. Topping.

As a matter of historical record, however, Byrd was careful to verify his position on the flight over the Pole. The flight began at 12:37 a.m. on May 9, with Bennett at the controls. Byrd used the new sun compass and a bubble sextant to check his position over the trackless wasteland of ice and snow. When his calculations showed that they were at the top of the world, their Fokker trimotor, the *Josephine Ford*, angled and circled for 13 minutes while they checked bearings to make sure.

In the following year, Nobile traveled to Japan as a technical advisor for the *N-3* (third of the Nobile N-series of dirigibles) which Japan had purchased. The career of the *N-3* (third of the Nobile N-series of dirigibles) which Japan had purchased. The career of the *N-3* was short-lived. During naval maneuvers in October, 1927, it was destroyed at sea.

A Hazardous Expedition

Nobile, promoted to the rank of general by Mussolini, now set out to returned to the North Pole with a purely scientific expedition in the *N-2* (christened the *Italia* (Fig. 8-12) sister-ship to the *Norge*. Nobile recall:

Fig. 8-9. The Roma.

Fig. 8-10. Nobile, Amundsen and Ellsworth reached the North Pole in the Norge in 1926.

"The *Italia*, after a hazardous flight across Europe, arrived at King's Bay in the Spitzbergen Islands and there began a series of exploring flights in regions hitherto unknown to man. In one of these, a nonstop voyage lasting three days, we explored the region of Severnaya Zemblya. A third and last flight was made across the unexplored district east of Spitzbergen and north of Greenland. Having reached the Pole by this novel route, the *Italia* started to return to its base, still over unknown ground between the 25th and 40th meridians of longitude east of Greenwich. For 30 hours the airship struggled against a persistent storm. Suddenly, when it was in its 131st flying hour of exploration and only an hour or two away from its base, a catastrophe occurred—the *Italia*, probably because of very sudden ice formation, crashed on the pack . . .

"There was a fearful impact. Something hit me on the head, then I was caught and crushed. Clearly, without any pain, I felt some of my limbs snap. It was 10:33 on May 25th . . . When I opened my eyes I found myself lying on the ice, in the midst of an appalling pack. I realized at once that others had fallen with me.

"I looked up to the sky. Toward my left the dirigible, nose in the air, was drifting away before the wind. It was terribly lacerated around the pilot-cabin. Upon the side of the crippled, mutilated ship stood out the black letters ITALIA. My eyes remained fixed on them, as if fascinated, until the dirigible merged in the fog and was lost to sight."

Nobile took stock of the situation. His right leg and arm were broken. Around him were all but six of his scientific crewmen, who drifted off in the *Italia*, never to be heard from again—Dr. Aldo Pontremoli, a scientist from Milan; Ugo Lago, a 28-year-old reporter; and crewmen Ettore Arduino, Attilio Caratti, Renato Alessandrini, and Calisto Ciocca.

Of those thrown out, one person was killed—Vincenzo Pomella, a mechanic. Natale Cecioni, chief technician, had a leg broken in two places. Dr. Finn Malmgren, from the University of Uppsala, suffered a shoulder injury. However, the rest escaped with slight injuries: three Navy officers: Filippo Zappi, Adalberto Mariano, and Lieutenant Commander Alfredo

Fig. 8-11. The Norge.

133

Viglieri; Dr. Francis Behounek, Felice Trojani, and Giuseppe Biagi, the wireless operator.

By sheer luck, the emergency field transmitter was found in the snow and Biagi improvised an antenna from scraps of broken metal. He immediately began sending out SOS messages, but was not heard. The survivors gathered up sufficient food to last them for 25 days with rationing. A reindeer-skin sleeping bag and a small tent with double ways were also recovered. A pistol was found and with it Malmgren later shot a polar bear.

For a month, the men survived extreme hardships and Biagi patiently sent out daily signals with his field set. On June 6, an amateur radio operator (ham) named Nicholas Schmidt picked up a signal at Archangel, Russia. Biagi confirmed this by tuning in a broadcasting station in Rome that flashed the news. Nobile ordered their tent streaked with red aniline dye.

Search planes combed the ice pack for days, but not until June 20 did an Italian pilot, Major Maddalena, locate the red tent. He dropped batteries for the radio, provisions and rifles. Four days later, a small Fokker skiplane piloted by Lieutenant Einar-Paal Lundborg landed. Over his objections, Nobile was loaded aboard the small ski plane and flown out to a Swedish base search camp. He would regret the move to his dying day. World criticism made him out as a coward for accepting the ride and leaving his companions behind. A Russian icebreaker, the *Krassin*, picked up the remaining survivors 19 days later.

Court of Inquiry

Nobile was taken before an Italian court of inquiry and was held responsible for the accident and the ensuing fatalities. He resigned his commission in anger rather than accept the verdict and the forced retirement with pension that went with it. In 1931, Nobile was invited to visit Russia to participate in an arctic voyage by the surface ship *Malygin* to Novaya Zembla and Franz Josef Land. He accepted the invitation.

In Moscow, Nobile was offered a position as deputy director of the Soviet airship agency Dirigiblestroi following his return from the *Malygin* voyage. He assisted the development of a second five-year plan to establish airship operations over civil air routes within the U.S.S.R. Several small-pressure airships were built in Russia under Nobile's guidance. In 1933, plans were announced to lay down a 1,304,620 cubic foot commercial dirigible at Dolgo Prutnaja near Moscow and a smaller airship of 705,200 cubic feet at Leningrad.

Nobile stayed on in Russia until 1936 when work began on the 882,829 cubic foot semirigid *DP-9* and the 650,000 cubic foot semirigid *V-6*. In September of that year, the *V-6* set a record for endurance of 130 hours 27 minutes which would stand still until November 1946 when it was broken by the U.S. Navy blimp *XM-1*.

Fig. 8-12. Nobile's airship Italia crashed on ice.

The *V-6* was destroyed with a loss of 13 lives in 1938 when it crashed into a mountain while participating in rescue operations to assist Soviet scientists marooned on a drifting polar ice floe. Other Russian airship activities included the trials of *V-10* in May, 1938, and another, the *V-8*, was then reportedly under construction for a proposed civil air link between Moscow and Leningrad. In 1945, a small airship, the *Victory*, made an 80-hour flight over the Black Sea. And in 1946, a 150-foot long craft, the *Patriot*, was reported flying—using helium instead of hydrogen. Helium resources had been discovered in Soviet oilfields.

With the rise of the Fascists in Italy in 1939, Nobile moved to the United States. In 1940-41, he gave a lecture series at Notre Dame University on aeronautics. He returned to Italy in 1942. After World War II, he was able to clear his name in the *Italia* affair and was restored to rank—with a promotion to major general in the Italian Air Force.

Chapter 9

Uncle Tom's Rubber Cows

Professional balloonist Thomas Scott Baldwin, better known to his admiring public as Captain Baldwin or to his intimates as Uncle Tom (Fig. 9-1), was already a veteran of more than 5,000 balloon ascensions when he opened the paper in the fall of 1901 and read startling news. Alberto Santos-Dumont, the daring Brazilian aeronaut, had sailed a "rubber cow" around the Eiffel Tower in Paris and had won worldwide notoriety. Here was a new way to turn a fast buck at circuses and carnivals—driving a balloon around the sky and coming back to land where you started!

Aside from a few earlier experimenters like Carl and Carlotta Myers, Charlie Ritchel and Solomon Andrews, lighter-than-air pilots in the United States simply rode the winds in pear-shaped aerostats. Dirigibles were something new worth looking into.

At 37, Uncle Tom Baldwin already had a variety of experiences. Piloting a dirigible just might be a real money-maker, he decided. Born in Marion County, Missouri, he paid his way through life working as a newsboy, a lamp-lighter, a messanger boy, a printer's devil, a type setter, and a train candy butcher. He eventually joined a circus as an acrobat and won fame as the only man ever to walk blindfolded on a slackwire from Seal Rock to Cliff House (near San Francisco).

PARACHUTE JUMPS

In 1887, he developed a modern style parachute and launched a new career making drops from his balloons at county fairs. He charged a dollar a foot. Baldwin's balloons, which he constructed himself, were rotund caricatures of his own portly shape. The balloons were varnished tight and covered with netting from which the basket was suspended.

When Baldwin heard about the Santos-Dumont's achievements in Paris, he decided to make his own dirigible, install an engine, and reap a fortune in America. Baldwin left a record of successes as a jumper. His first leap was on January 30, 1887 before a throng of 30,000 people gathered at Golden Gate Park in San Francisco.

Baldwin moved east to Chicago, but nervous city fathers hastily passed an ordinance banning parachute jumps as hazardous and foolhardy stunts.

Captain Tom even traveled abroad with his parachutes to perform leaps before the crown heads of nations. The Prince of Wales gave him a seal ring as a token of appreciation following a jump in England.

THE CALIFORNIA ARROW

Back home in California in 1903, Baldwin settled down in Los Angeles to build his first dirigible. It was called the *California Arrow* and was almost a direct copy of the Santos-Dumont *Number 6* machine. However, Baldwin lacked one thing—a dependable motor. The engines available, developed largely for early autos, were overweight, underpowered and asthmatic. He was about to abandon on the whole project when his ears caught the pleasant sound of a smooth-running motorcycle engine chugging down the street outside his shop.

Baldwin ran outside and chased the motorcycle rider a few blocks. After, finally overtaking him, Baldwin introduced himself, exchanged pleasantries, then asked the rider where he got the motorcycle. The youth pointed to the name on the gas tank: HERCULES.

"Dunno," he told Baldwin. "I bought her second hand."

But then he remembered something in his pocket—a pamphlet with directions on how to start and stop the cycle engine. He pulled it out and handed it to the balloonist, who read: G. H. CURTISS MANUFACTURING CO., HAMMONDSPORT, N.Y.

Baldwin thanked the lad and hurried home to write a letter to Hammondsport. He asked for prices and specifications for a light and strong engine suitable for use in a flying machine. A reply came in a few weeks and Baldwin placed an order for immediate delivery.

Impatient when weeks and months passed and no engine was forthcoming, Captain Tom made a decision. He bought a railroad ticket to Hammondsport and headed East himself to find out what was wrong. He left his balloon factory in charge of his young assistants, 17-year-old Lincoln Beachey and Roy Knabenshue, only slightly older.

At Hammondsport, Uncle Tom sized things up quickly. The Curtiss plant was small, with only a single lathe and drill press. Glenn Curtiss, a motorcycle racer who built and sold bike engines, appeared particularly unbusinesslike. Finally they had a heart-to-heart talk. Curtiss explained that he had expected a down payment on the engine and Baldwin explained that there was a tremendous future in aeronatuics. Curtiss engines might even power heavier-than-air flying machines, not only rubber cows! The two got along famously, and soon Captain Tom returned to California with his brand new HERCULES engine.

Fig. 9-1. "Uncle Tom" Baldwin.

Back home, Baldwin, Beachey and Knabenshue got busy working the engine over for installation in in the *California Arrow*. It was a tough job. The air-cooled cylinders had been designed to cool the 2-cylinder engine running in a motorcycle at from 30 to 60 mph. However, dirigibles poked along at perhaps 10 to 15 mph. Baldwin solved the cooling problem by properly ducting the airflow from the engine's propeller over the cooling fins to keep the engine from overheating during short exhibition flights.

At Oakland one August day in 1904, Uncle Tom became the first American to fly a dirigible in a complete 360 degree turn. His *California Arrow* upstaged a new competitor on the scene from nearby San Francisco—Dr. August Greth, who made his first flight in a craft similar to the *California Arrow*. The engine on his craft was geared to turn twin propellers. Dr. Greth repeated his flights during the week of April 23-28, 1904.

Although the Wright Brothers had introduced heavier-than-air flight at Kitty Hawk the year before, there were those who still maintained that Uncle Tom's rubber cows were the only way to fly. His *California Arrow*, displayed at the Louisiana Purchase Exposition in St. Louis in 1904, drew admiration from the crowds who examined the little 2-cylinder, 5-horsepower Curtiss engine.

America's leadership in the skies already was at stake. Europeans already were forging ahead with experimental dirigibles such as the semi-rigid craft build by the Lebaudy Brothers. Two years before, they had built and flown an earlier dirigible, the *Jaune*, but it had met with disaster in November that year returning to its hangar at Chalais-Meudon, near Paris, following its 29th successful flight. The engine was installed in its successor, the *Lebaudy*, launched in June, 1904. With a pointy nose and rounded stern, fitted with rounded horizontal and vertical vanes, it cost $60,000 to build. In addition, another half million dollars was spent on development. In its second year (1905) the *Lebaudy* made 76 successful flights and was taken over by the French Ministry of War as France's first government airship.

The German Army was not far behind in aviation development. Major August von Parseval, a Bavarian officer, designed and built *Parseval I* in 1906 on order from Emperor Wilhelm. It was a curious "pressure" airship that resembled nothing more than a Polish sausage with tail fins and a crude car hung underneath. More than twenty *Parsevals* were built for the German Army between 1906-1914 and a number also saw service with the German Admiralty. One, the non-rigid *PL-6*, had been a familiar sight to prewar Berliners as a flying billboard advertising the Stollwerck Chocolate Company. The *Persevals* were used primarily as trainers.

THE CITY OF PORTLAND

With worldwide interest in dirigibles mounting, Uncle Tom pushed ahead with his rubber cows. He ordered a 7-horsepower engine for his next airship, the *City of Portland*. Linc Beachey, who would later become famous as a stunt pilot flying Curtiss pusher aircraft, put the *City of Portland* through its paces at the Lewis and Clark Exposition in 1904. He won headlines by landing the dirigible atop the Portland Chamber of Commerce building and then 20 minutes later returning to his starting point.

Uncle Tom's rubber cows now were in great demand at carnivals and county fairs. He soon ordered a new engine from Curtiss to be built with double the number of cylinders, arranged in a V shape and capable of producing 18 horsepower. This engine worked so well that Curtiss received orders from other aviators for both heavier-than-air and lighter-than-air powerplants. The V-engine was the forerunner of Curtiss' famed Model 0 and its successor, the Model 0+, that accidentally became designed as the Model OX when a draftsman tilted the + onto its side.

A disastrous fire in Captain Baldwin's dirigible plant early in 1906 destroyed the original *California Arrow*, the *City of Portland*, and his entire stock of tools and parts. Only a newer ship, the second *California Arrow* which had been shipped to Hammondsport for an engine installation, remained. Uncle Tom moved east to join other aeronauts who had pitched their tents at Watkins Glen to be safe from summer storms.

Clara Studer, in her biography of Glen Curtiss, *Sky Storming Yankee* (Stackpole Sons, New York, 1937), relates: "Curtiss, as head of the Hammondsport plant, was surrounded by eccentric individuals from all over the country who had heard of his knack for creating power. They came worrying him with schemes for rotary valves, sleeved valves, radial engines, for the most fantastic balloons. And Curtiss welcomed particularly the airmen among them. 'Why wouldn't I?' he shrugged. 'I get twice as much money for my motors from those aviation cranks!'"

At the St. Louis Aero Club air meet of October, 1907, Uncle Tom sent two of his rubber cows to compete. Linc Beachey easily nosed out

Fig. 9-2. Roy Knabenshue flew "rubber cows" at air shows.

Baldwin's other pilot, Roy Knabenshue. Meanwhile, Glenn Curtiss was busily developing more efficient propellers for the dirigible pilots. These propellers were mounted on a simple 3-wheeled wind-wagon for test runs.

The following year, Uncle Tom was distressed to hear of a dirigible disaster in San Francisco. An inventor, J. A. Morrell, had built a huge dirigible 450 feet long. On the initial test flight May 23, 1908, the gas bag exploded and collasped at an altitude of some 300 feet before a throng of thousands of watchers. Fifteen passengers, including Morrell, were seriously injured.

Another dirigible pilot who hung around the Curtiss plant at Hammondsport wasn't so lucky. Charles O. Jones was killed in a crash during an exhibition flight in Maine. But Uncle Tom restored public confidence in rubber cows in 1909 during the Hudson-Fulton Celebration in New York City by being one of two dirigible pilots to fly around the Statue of Liberty. The other dirigible pilot was Dr. George N. Tomlinson.

On June, 27, 1907, Uncle Tom's latest airship was ready for flight testing. It had a new Curtiss air-cooled engine that drove twin propellers in opposite direction to neutralize the effect of torque—a phenomenon today called P-factor. After an initial flight around Pleasant Valley, he landed to discuss a center of gravity problem with Curtiss.

"If you can trust me with that thing for a few minutes, Uncle Tom, maybe I can get a better idea of the problem," Curtiss offered. Baldwin shrugged. "Go ahead, Sonny," he said, using his favorite nickname for Curtiss.

With factory hands jogging along beneath him, Curtiss sailed up and over the treetops in Uncle Tom's airship, circled the valley, returned and made a perfect landing. "Not bad," he grinned, "but there's no place to go!" It was his first and last dirigible ride. He would stick with motorcycle racing for a while and build more powerful engines for those crazy new heavier-than-air flying machines that were all the rage.

Meanwhile, Linc Beachey and Roy Knabenshue (Fig. 9-2) set off on airshow careers of their own (Fig. 9-3). Beachey gained fame by looping the loop over the White House in Washington D.C. in a Curtiss Pusher, while Roy stuck primarily with rubber cows. Later on he became advance man and manager for the Wright brothers exhibition team.

THE SIGNAL CORPS I

Uncle Tom's last big success was to sell a dirigible to the United States Army on August 18, 1908. It was named the *Signal Corps I* and sold for $10,000. The price was set by the United States Government for a "practicable military means of dirigible aerial navigation." Uncle Tom flew it over a straightaway course at Fort Myer, Virginia, at speeds up to 30 mph. Measuring 96 feet in length, it carried a Curtiss engine of 20 horsepower and was America's first government airship.

Fig. 9-3. Roy Kanabenshue (right, in car) barnstormed the nation in the 1900s.

PROFESSORS OF THE AIR

Uncle Tom's protege Roy Knabenshue, was actually an old hand at ballooning. In 1881, at the State House grounds at Columbus, Ohio, he first witnessed a gas balloon ascension by Professor E. D. Hogan. Hogan was the balloonist who later would be lost at sea in 1889 while flying Peter Campbell's patented airship over New York.

It was 11 years before Roy saw another balloonist perform (at Toledo, Ohio). This time it was an aeronaut who called himself Professor Don Carlos. He would later admit: "I made it my business to be on hand every day of the week's engagement, and incidentally I made the acquaintance of the Professor, and learned that his real name was Flynn. My parents were properly shocked when they learned of my intention to become a professional aeronaut. Father's arguments were most impressive, having occurred in the woodshed."

In 1897, Roy again disobeyed parental authority and visited with another professional aeronaut in Detroit. "Unfortunately," he remembered, "the aeronaut was killed in a fall from his balloon, his body crashing through a plank sidewalk. My ambition suffered a relapse, and for some time nothing was said further about the matter."

This tragedy did not deter Knabenshue long. When a new balloonist appeared at the Toledo fair grounds with a tethered hydrogen aerostat in the summer of 1899 and begain earning a small fortune taking up passengers 500 feet for a dollar, Knabenshue knew his future lay in the sky. When the fair ended, Roy made a deal with the balloonist to buy his equipment. The next summer, he hit the road with his new balloon and a new name. He became Professor Don Carlos—borrowing the name of the performer he'd meet 19 years earlier at Columbus, Ohio.

There was a good reason for Roy to change his name. His father was the editor of the Toledo *Blade* and it would not do to have it known the son was a balloonatic. It was just as well. A week after starting operations he sent the balloon up on its tether in the teeth of a gale. The balloon was dashed wildly about and finally came down when a lightning rod atop a nearby barn punctured it.

When a second similar near-disaster occurred a few weeks later, Roy gave up captive balloons and built himself a pair of 5000-cubic foot balloons 23 feet in diameter and hit the road as a free balloonist. He contracted for 10 engagements at $500 per day.

Roy manufactured his own hydrogen gas by filling four wooden casks with iron nails, horseshoes, and filings—then adding water and sulphuric acid. On his first free ascent, he was carried rapidly up to an altitude of 3000 feet. He pulled on the valve rope and descended. He then hitched a ride back to the fair grounds on a farmer's wagon.

The next venture aloft was more exciting. At 1500 feet the wind was so strong and gusty he valved off gas and came down. This time he landed on a barn roof and a lightning rod tore the bag open. Roy was spilled out of the basket and tumbled headlong to the ground. He fortunately (or unfortunately?) landed in a manure pile.

Another time Roy encountered a thunderstorm and found his balloon alive with St. Elmo's fire. Fearing a gas explosion, he dumped all remaining ballast in an effort to rise above the towering cumulonimbus cloud— with no luck. He was so unnerved by the time he got back that he gave up free ballooning for good and decided on starting a new career as a dirigible pilot under the tutelage of Uncle Tom Baldwin.

On October 25, 1904, Roy had the ride of his life in Uncle Tom's *California Arrow* at the Louisiana Purchase Exposition in St. Louis (Figs. 9-4 and 9-5). Baldwin, who weighed 230 pounds, found the dirigible wouldn't lift him satisfactorily along with the 10-horsepower Curtiss engine. Roy recalled later: "The motor was missing and shaking the frame so much I thought it was going to bounce me off. I yelled: 'Turn it off!' but the ground crew thought I said "Let her go!" Then I was in the air heading for a 30-foot fence. I had to learn to fly that thing and do it pronto.

"I nearly hit the dome of the Brazilian Building but I finally figured out how to handle it, and took it around the Ferris wheel. Then, for no apparent reason, the motor stopped. With all that noise gone I could hear the folks below yelling at me. I hit some bad air currents and the people watching

Fig. 9-4. Knabensue's dirigible at St. Louis, Missouri (1905).

145

Fig. 9-5. Lincoln Beachey's Number 2 dirigible at the St. Louis Exposition in 1905. A gasoline powered motor drove the propeller at the front. The aeronaut steered with a crude rudder. The craft went up or down with a shift in the weight along the catwalk.

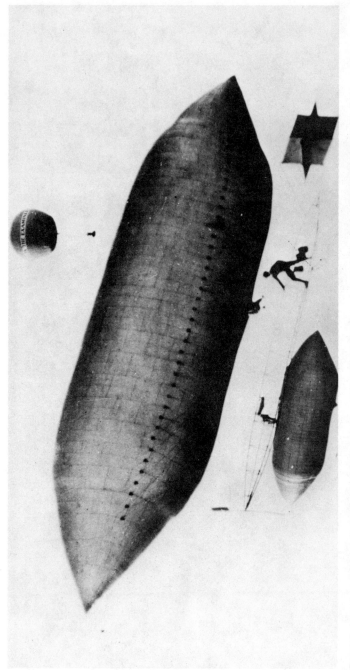

Fig. 9-6. Near Los Angeles in 1910, Lincoln Beachey and Roy Knabenshue race dirigibles at a Dominguez Field air meet.

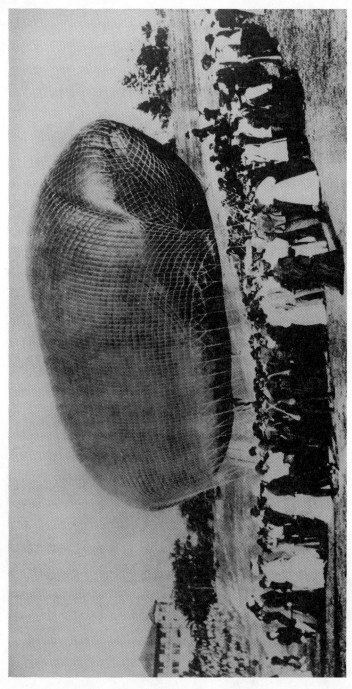

Fig. 9-7. Knabenshue landing on the grounds of the Raymond Hotel in Pasadena.

later said they were amazed at how I maneuvered. I wasn't maneuvering—I was just hanging on!" Roy drifted across the Mississippi River and landed on a farm in Illinois, returning to the fair grounds later in the day aboard a farmer's hayrack.

His reputation now made as a daring aerobat, Roy came up with a new stunt—a dirigible race with Linc Beachey flying a second Baldwin airship (Fig. 9-6). Some times Roy would win and other times Linc was the victor, but the sight of the two giant rubber cows struggling along overhead pleased the crowds during thier tour of the nation. At Los Angeles on December 26, 1904, Roy set a distance record of fifteen miles with and against the wind in the *California Arrow*. On New Year's Day 1905, he was the star of the first moving picture ever shot in Hollywood—flying from Los Angeles' Chute Park.

Fig. 9-8. Knabenshue tries his silken oars.

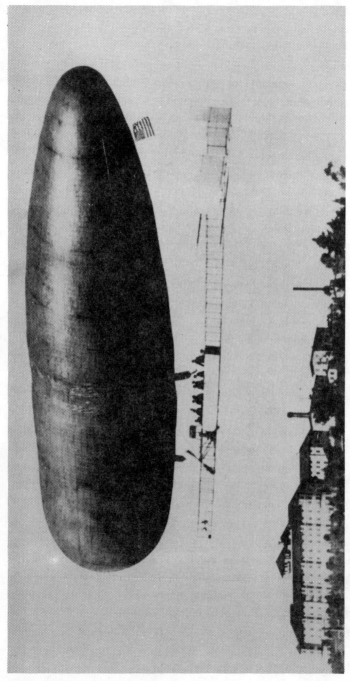

Fig. 9-9. Knabenshue carries a dozen passengers over Pasadena, California.

Fig. 9-10. Knabenshue flies the Toledo II from the rooftops.

151

In New York the following August 22, Roy made a dirigible flight from 62nd Street and Central Park West, following Broadway south to Second Avenue. Along the route he scattered coupons that could be cashed in for amounts up to $100 at the New York *American* newspaper office as a promotional stunt designed to arouse America to the potential of air travel.

A small, dapper man with a broad Irish grin who wore a bowler hat as a trademark, Knabenshue thrilled crowds from coast to coast (Fig. 9-7). In Los Angeles on December 17, 1908, the fifth anniversary of the first Wright flight at Kitty Hawk, Roy made the first night dirigible flight in America from Chute Park. Later he sailed over nearby Pasadena, and tried out a pair of silken oars for propulsion in place of a motor (Figs. 9-8 and 9-9).

Fig. 9-11. A pilot's-eye view from Knabenshue's dirigible.

Fig. 9-12. Guiding planes helped Knabenshue's dirigible climb and descent.

On April 18 1910, Knabenshue made his final dirigible flight, over Pasadena, Leaving LTA craft to take over management of the Wright brothers exhibition team. During World War I, Roy manufactured observation balloons for the U.S. Army. A member of the Early Birds, pioneer airmen who had flown before the war, Roy Knabenshue is still remembered by old timers for his daring feats in the *California Arrow* and another dirigible of his own design, the *Toledo II* (Fig. 9-10), in which he hopped passengers from the rooftops of office buildings in numerous cities (Figs. 9-11 and 9-12). He died in 1959 at 83.

Chapter 10

The American Way

Promoters of the 1904 Louisiana Purchase Exposition in St. Louis had been shrewdly aware of the commercial potential of aeronautics. Commercialization was a theme that pervaded aviation from the start. It was consistent with the get-rich-quick philosophy of flying that the fair officials would post a prize of $100,000 for the "airship which should make the best record over a prescribed course, marked by captive balloons, at a speed of *not less than twenty miles an hour*." The Wrights had retired to Dayton to improve their flying boxkite, and John J. Montgomery's glider had no engine, so they felt the prize money was reasonably safe. However, scores of other inventors worked feverishly to complete all manners of flying machines in time for St. Louis races and public interest ran high.

"At one time," observed a contemporary chronicler, "announcement was made that no less than 92 contestants had filed their application of entry, but as it came to be known that the requirements were less experimental than practical, and that the governing rules made it necessary that, to win the prizes contensants must sail over a prescribed course, execute certain movements, and return to the starting point within a specified time, the list of entries diminished so rapidly that when the date set for the flight arrived, not a single inventor had fulfilled the conditions necessary for eligibility to compete for the prizes."

Of the airships that appeared at St. Louis in 1904, only two were able to leave the ground in any sort of free flight—Uncle Tom Baldwin's *California Arrow* and a 74-foot dirigible constructed at the Carl Myers Balloon Farm in Frankfort, New York for Thomas C. Benbow of Absarokee, Montana.

Benbow was sure he had a winner. His craft employed a novel propulsion system which he patented the same year. Four side-wheel propellers, each containing four blades, were operated by a 10-horsepower gasoline engine in a manner that, by an ingenious mechanical movement, remained open just long enough to strike the air in a predetermined direction to cause the craft either to ascend, descend, move forward or back up. Benbow actually did make two short flights, but neither of which proved of any value in qualifying for the 1904 air races.

All in all, besided Roy Knabenshue's drifting flight in the *California Arrow*, the Louisiana Purchase Exposition failed to give the impression that America had done much in the way of conquering the air. Perhaps the expostion's greatest contribution to the American way of life was its introduction of the ice cream cone.

One other dirigible might have won the $100,000 prize money for an unforeseen disaster. Alberto Santos-Dumont sailed to America from Paris with a specially constructed dirigible. But an unidentified vandal broke into the hangar shortly before the races were scheduled to start and so badly slashed the gas bag that Santos-Dumont returned home in disgust.

AERIAL ADVERTISING

One thing the 1904 St. Louis "air races" did for America was to suggest the inauguration of the first reliably recorded use of aerial advertising in the world. The scheme was conceived in the fertile mind of Charles B. Knox, a wealthy gelatine manufacturer from Johnstown, New

Fig. 10-1. The Gelatine was the first "flying billboard."

York, who had been impressed with Knabenshue's flight in the *California Arrow*.

Knox returned home to Johnstown with an idea he quickly confided to George T. Tomlinson, a balloonist from nearby Syracuse. Work was immediately begun on a dirigible closely resembling Baldwin's *California Arrow*. On May 26, 1905, the *Retail Grocers Advocate* announced that "the ship now being built by the famous aeronaut, George T. Tomlinson of Syracuse, will be completed in about six weeks. Mr. Knox told a reporter that while he expected to derive some benefits from the advertising the ship would give his business, his prime object in having it built was the pleasure he would get from starting it in the great races that are soon to be inaugurated."

The potentials of aerial advertising were quickly recognized by the press and many remarks, not all complimentary, were printed regarding Knox's ingenious scheme. Commented the *Newport Herald*: "Imagine the furor this ship will create: some beautiful morning, it will be sighted in one of the cities of Arizona, a strange aerial object, gracefully floating to the westward. All the citizens will gather on the plaza; gradually the ship will descend, soon will be discerned the name '*Gelatine*' on the helm; the natural cry will be, 'Whose Gelatine?' when the ship comes within speaking distance. The cry will be heard by the pilot, and from aloft will come the answering cry: 'Knox's!' Isn't it splendid?"

A man of vision, Knox saw in his flying *Gelatine* (Fig. 10-1) more than an advertising medium or a rich sportsman's toy. He joined the ranks of those pioneers who believed aircraft would become engines of destruction with eventual superiority over surface ships of war.

"Every detail of war in the skies has been considered by Knox and the inventor, George T. Tomlinson," commented the San Francisco *Chronicle* on January 31, 1906, following the dirigible's arrival on the West Coast. "They are both convinced that they can build an air ship that can with safety to itself hurl down swift destruction on ships that merely sail on the water.

"The *Gelatine* will naturally be built for offensive operations, rather than for defense. To save itself it must kill or fly. But it will be able to do both, and do them quickly. It will be fitted with torpedo tubes, which can be depressed to any angle. The mode of attack will be to take a position in the air directly over an enemy's ship. There it will be out of reach of any guns with which the navies of the world are now armed. Ship's guns were not built to kill birds, and they cannot be elevated to hit an object directly overhead. Thus, with the enemy at a disadvantage, the *Gelatine* will be able to quickly drop a torpedo on the deck of a water ship, over which it will poise like a gull over a ferry boat."

Opening of the Lewis and Clark Exposition in Portland, Oregon in 1905 gave Knox a splendid opportunity to publicly demonstrate the flying *Gelatine* dirigible. Tomlinson, the pilot, was greeted with considerable advance publicity. The year before he had set an American record for duration of flight at the St. Louis Exposition by staying aloft in a balloon 23 hours 37 minutes.

Friendly competitors at the Lewis and Clark Exposition were Captain Tom Baldwin and Linc Beachey. They had brought along a new dirigible named the *Angelus*. The gas bag on the *Angelus* began leaking, so Knox generously offered to merge their two craft, suspending the *Angelus* framework from the netting and gas bag of the *Gelatine*. Of course, Knox was well aware that he had the advantage of advertising his product. The name was emblazoned on the sides of the gas bag. Wherever Knox went his aerial billboard was sure to attract interest. As a historical commentary, it is interesting to know that the Johnstown dessert king, first to adopt the technique of aerial advertising, was also first to send an automobile through New York State on an advertising mission.

THE ARKANSAS TRAVELERS

We now come to the story of the Arkansas travelers—Rice & Riggs—whose strained business relationship during construction of the

Fig. 10-2. The American Eagle.

Fig. 10-3. Rice with the American Eagle.

nation's then largest dirigible, the *American Eagle* (Fig. 10-2), would have been ludicrous had it not ended tragically. As it was, the bitter feeling that existed between these two airship pioneers provided a Gilbert-and-Sullivan touch to their venture.

Long before their feud started, Joel Trout Rice (Fig. 10-3) had been an inventor of flying machines. In 1897, he thought up a humdinger in which a balloon lifted an open car fitted with wing-like propeller blades at the ends of long shafts. Springs were attached to the bottom of the airship "to let the passengers down easy." At the stern hung a parachute, "for safety." All in all, it was not a very revolutionary invention, yet Rice succeeded in

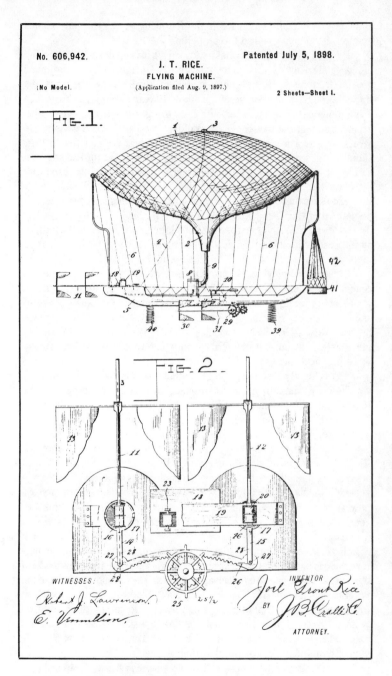

Fig. 10-4. A patent held by Rice.

obtaining patent protection for it the following year. The only claims granted, however, covered the propelling mechanism.

By 1901 Rice had somewhat improved his airship design by attaching the propeller blades in a more conventional manner. Ideas continued pouring from his fertile imagination and early in 1908 he was granted a third United States patent see Figs. 10-4, 10-5 and 10-6). The basic idea was a unique arrangement for detaching the gas bag in the event of an accident so that the passenger car could be used as a boat if catastrophe struck at sea. The bottom half of the gas bag was constructed so that, should the gas suddenly escape, it could fold up inside the top half and form a rude parachute canopy. The forward end of the gas bag was covered with a streamlined stiffener to retain its shape during forward flight.

Rice's partner was John A. Riggs, a well-to-do businessman of Rice's hometown of Hot Springs, Arkansas. Born in Illinois in 1867, Riggs had drifted West. In Wichita he rose to control the Lopez Medicine Company, an interest he held until his death. The home office of the Lopez patent medicine concern later moved to Hot Springs.

Soon after applying for his third patent, inventor Rice made the rounds of Hot Springs' financial district seeking a backer for construction of one of his patented dirigibles. John Riggs thought Rice knew his stuff, and launched The Hot Springs Airship Company. The directors consisted of Rice, Riggs, Dr. W. H. Connell and a Dr. Westmoreland. Work was immediately begun, but materials with which to construct their airship were hard to come by.

Dr. Connell subsequently told me that "barrels and barrels of nails" were dissolved in sulphuric acid to produce the necessary hydrogen gas for their airship. But it was discovered, too late, that Rice had miscalculated. The gas bag was too small to lift their craft more than a few feet. Therefore, The Hot Springs Airship Company was soon disbanded.

However, this did not discourage Riggs. He was firm in his belief that Rice's design could be made practical. And like Charles B. Knox, he saw an advertising potential in the dirigible. Riggs leased the Rice patent for two years and in July, 1909 left for New York City to supervise construction of a new airship—putting up the required capital as well. Rice and his two sons, Roy and Alphonso, went along to help construct the dirigible's framework.

In New York, Riggs and Rice began shopping for someone to manufacture the gas bag for their new airship. It was at this time that New Yorkers began calling the pair the Arkansas travelers. They stopped off to see the veteran dirigible maker, Captain Tom Scott Baldwin, but eventually let the contract to a competitor, A. Leo Stevens. Recalling their previous failure, Riggs and Rice instructed Stevens to make the gas bag 125 feet long and 25 feet in diameter at the widest part. It was the largest dirigible ever attempted in America at that time.

Patriotically christening the dirigible *American Eagle*, Riggs and Rice planned a great promotional tour of the country. Riggs was to personally

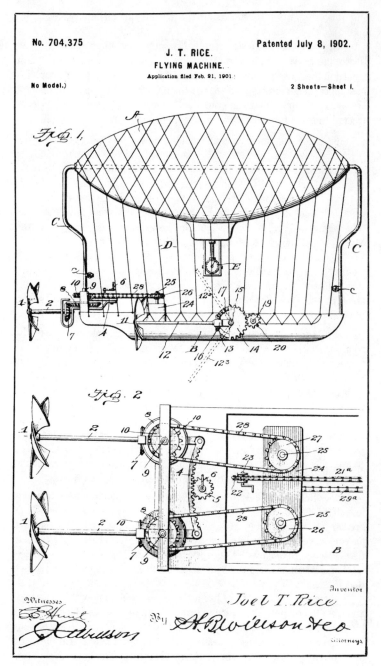

Fig. 10-5. A patent held by Rice.

pilot it nonstop from Hot Springs to the forthcoming dirigible races at St. Louis.

On August 5, 1909, Riggs applied for and was granted membership in the exclusive Aeronautic Society of New York in order to erect a giant tent hangar at the Society's Morris Park Race Track grounds. Stevens got busy making the huge gas bag, while the firm of C. & A. Witteman, builders of an unusual heavier-than-air craft they called the *Cycloplane*, was contracted to make the necessary castings, couplings and other metalwork.

It was at this juncture that trouble bagan developing between the Arkansas travelers. The elder Rice and his sons were quick to find fault with construction details and time and again delayed work on the *American Eagle*. Not until October 4 did Stevens complete the gas bag and inflate it to test its lifting capacity. He found it to be roughly 1500 pounds. In three days, less than 10 percent of the hydrogen gas had escaped, which Stevens told them was acceptable. On the 7th, the gas bag was taken out to the Morris Park hangar where further troubles developed.

The bone of contention was a huge sign Riggs had painted on both sides of the gas bag in block letters: LOPEZ. After all, it was Lopez money that built the airship and Riggs, like Knox, saw no reason to be modest about it. But Rice did. He threatened to destroy the dirigible unless the offensive word was removed.

In alarm, Riggs sent for his brothers, Steve and Frank, and his son, E. Marion, to post a 24-hour watch over the airship. Roy Rice, son of the temperamental inventor, pleaded with Riggs to remove the name for fear his father would carry out his threat. Finally, to avoid further trouble, Riggs decided that it was best to forego his advertising campaign for the moment. He drove out to Morris Park, but was infuriated to discover that Rice had beaten him there. The inventor had somehow crashed the Riggs guard and stricken out the name LOPEZ with indignant strokes of a paintbrush dipped in ordinary house paint. Riggs took one look and wanted to cry. The paint had caused the balloon fabric to shrink and crack and the *American Eagle* had to be returned to Stevens' shop for repairs.

Back in shape, the *American Eagle* finally managed to make its initial test flight on November 16. The flight, though successful, widened the breach between the two Arkansas travelers. Convinced now that his patents were of great value, Rice became foolhardy and attempted to sell them elsewhere in New York despite the fact that Riggs held a valid lease on them. When interviewed by reporters, Rice failed to mention the fact that Riggs was his partner.

Riggs quickly decided he had had enough squabbling with his partner and traveled to New York City to bring back a prospective buyer and rid himself of the whole enterprise. He warned Rice not to touch the airship while he was away, but the inventor could not restrain himself at the sight of his brain-child tugging its moorings inside the canvas hangar. A contemporary newspaper reported:

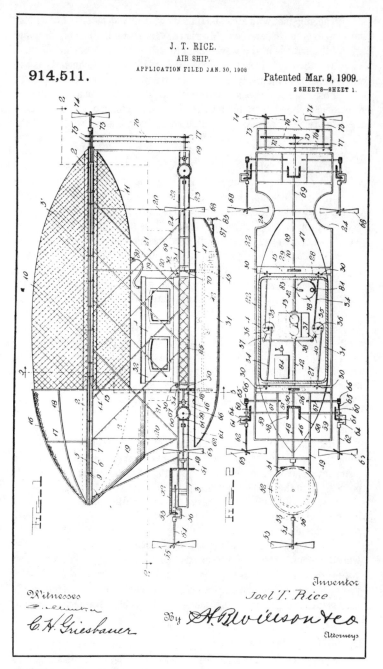

Fig. 10-6. A patent held by Rice.

"The ship met with almost a tragedy when it was taken out of its big, canvas-covered aerodrome at Morris Park for its flight. The big dirigible ship is the largest in the world, next to that built by Count Zeppelin.

"Mr. Rice and his son, Roy, were in the car of the elongated gas bag when they found themselves helpless in the air with a broken propeller.

"Fortunately, the long drag-ropes were still trailing on the ground and the crowd grabbed them, towing the balloon to earth, and the aeronauts to their safety. The damage was to be repaired in a short while, and the dirigible was to be made ready for a flight over the city and perhaps for a cross-country run to Texas.

"When the big ship was towed out of the aerodrome, about fifty men were hanging onto the ropes. When they let go, the big ship soared majestically into the upper air, but in lowering his horizontal plane in front, to give the nose of the airship an upward lift, Mr. Rice brought it in contact with the propellers which were smashed. This left him helpless to direct the course of the machine and a still wind was blowing. The drag-rope still reached the ground, however, and the big balloon was drawn back to earth, stern first, and secured in its tent."

That same night, adding to the damage, a thunderstorm struck Morris Park with full fury and so badly damaged the *American Eagle* that Riggs stored the remains of the airship and returned to Hot Springs in disgust. He had spent nearly $50,000 on the venture and for his trouble and money drew only a headache.

To top off his difficulties with the inventor, Rice and his sons were reported to have made off with all the tools, the engine, the framework and other parts of the *American Eagle* before it could be removed from Morris Park. Later the inventor maintained he had only intended to hold those parts to force Riggs to pay him for the interest he claimed to hold in the venture.

In the fall of 1910, Riggs brought two law suits against Rice—one to compel the inventor to assign his patents to the Hot Springs Airship Company as he had contracted to do and the other to compel Rice to yield possession of the airship parts he had removed from Morris Park. Riggs won the first suit, but he did not press the second. He had spent a good deal of time and money and did not consider it worth his while to attempt to rebuild the airship.

This ended the story of the Arkansas travelers—a pair of visionaries whose temperaments were unsuited to each other, but who nevertheless got into the air America's largest dirigible airship for its time. In later years, Riggs encouraged a little neighborhood girl to take an interest in aeronautics. She became world famous as the aviatrix Katherine Stinson.

THE GOODYEAR BLIMPS

Where Charles Knox and the Arkansas travelers had pioneered the art of aerial advertising with dirigibles, it remained for the Goodyear Tire

Fig. 10-7. The Goodyear blimp America.

& Rubber Company of Akron, Ohio to illuminate the night with sophisticated messages of commerce.

The stimulus of World War I launched Goodyear in the lighter-than-air business, thanks to the foresightedness of P. W. Litchfield, a company production wizard who later would become chairman of the board of the rubber firm. Litchfield had witnessed a balloon race in France in 1910 and was determined that Goodyear should become a major part of the infant aviation industry.

Goodyear built its first airship envelope in 1911 for a wealthy LTA enthusiast, Melvin Vaniman, who dreamed of becoming the first to cross the Atlantic after an unsuccessful attempt by a daring newspaper reporter, Walter Wellman, had failed. Vaniman, Wellman's chief engineer, and a crew of four other men had set out with Wellman from Atlantic City on October 10, 1910. But they were forced to ditch off New England when they encountered bad weather.

Vaniman persuaded Goodyear to finance construction of a semi-rigid airship with a hull 285 feet long. Its fabric was coated with a special process invented by the North British Rubber Company. This Scottish firm granted Goodyear American rights in return for certain benefits. Vaniman's airship, the first *Akron*, carried three motors driving three propellers. On July 2, 1912, the *Akron* departed Atlantic City, Wellman's departure point, with three others aboard. Only 15 minutes outbound, a spark ignited the *Akron's* hydrogen gas; there was a brilliant explosion and the *Akron* dropped writhing into the sea. All four men perished.

Loss of the 40,000 cubic foot *Akron* did not dampen Litchfield's enthusiasm for LTAs. During World War II, Goodyear produced more than one thousand balloons and roughly 100 non-rigid airships for the Allies. Since 1911, Goodyear has produced a total of 327 airships. That total is more than any other organization in the world.

Early on, Goodyear adopted the aerial advertising stuntsmanship that had carried the names GELATINE and LOPEZ to an uncertain fame. One of Goodyear's early blimps took to the air with the company's name and trademark (a wingfoot) emblazoned on its sides. The first improvement on the painted "billboards" came when the airships began towing trailing banners carrying advertising messages and slogans, some of the banners were 200 feet in length.

For a time in the 1930s, sound was added to get folks to turn their heads heavenward. Loudspeakers blared out commercials, but they couldn't be turned off like a radio or TV set and the obnoxious "voice in the sky" concept was quickly dropped.

NIGHT MESSAGES

The late 1930s saw inauguration of the first illuminated night signs on Goodyear blimps. Specially designed lightweight frames carrying white neon tubing were strapped on their sides. Called the "Neon-O-Gram", this sign utilized neon tubing bent in such shapes that they could permit formation of varying numbers or letters—each sign containing 10 frames.

Fig. 10-8. The Goodyear airship Columbia.

Neon-O-Grams were used widely until World War II broke out and the Goodyear blimp fleet was drafted into service with the U.S. Navy. Following the war, Goodyear engineers came up with a new whizzer that used incandescent lamps in place of the neon tubes. Ten frames each contained 182 individual lamp bulbs. Only one color was possible (white) and messages were limited to words or phrases of only 10 spaces.

In the late 1940s, one Goodyear airship was outfitted with an unusual type of running-copy illuminated sign. It was an aerial copy of the famed Times Squares sign in New York called the Trans-Lux sign. It was bulky and heavy and was tried out for one year aboard a 250-foot long K-type blimp Goodyear purchased as a war surplus item. It proved too costly to be worth while to operate.

Then Robert H. Lane, Goodyear's public relations boss, happened to see another running-copy sign on a building in Brussels, Belgium—with color and animation yet! He fired off a note to upstairs and thus was born Goodyear's fancy "Skytacular" animated flying billboard. It was first installed in 1966 on the former *Mayflower* and in 1968 it was transferred to the newer, larger *Mayflower*. The *Mayflower* Skytacular measured 105 feet long, 14½ feet high and contained a total of 3080 lamps, on both sides of the blimp.

I well remember encountering a Postwar Goodyear blimp flying billboard one dark and stormy night in 1948, while making an instrument approach into Burbank Airport near Los Angeles. I was groping my way down the glideslope in my BT-13 through a deep stratus deck. Suddenly the approach controller's voice crackled in my headset: "LOOK OUT FOR THE HORSE!"

I was startled and looking up from my panel I gasped to see a huge Pegasus flying horse making its way through the cloud across my flight path. I pulled up and over to narrowly avoid a midair collission with a blimp carrying the animated logo of an oil company. The controller could not have been more succinct with his warning—for which I am forever grateful.

Today Goodyear has topped itself with their new Super Skytacular billboards fitted to three of their public relations blimps—the *America* (Fig. 10-7), *Columbia*, (Fig. 10-8) and *Mayflower* (Fig. 10-9). Red, blue, green, and yellow lights—3780 on each side of the airships—animate the new Super Skytaculars in cartoons and messages 24½ feet high and 105 feet long. The lights are controlled individually or in intricate combinations using some 80 miles of wiring. Cartoons and messages are intermingled and moved left to right, right to left, or up and down (Fig. 10-10).

Animation includes a golfer driving a ball toward the green, then putting the final distance to the hole; a game of tennis; a basketball player sinking a foul shot and a long field goal; and a baseball player hitting a line drive. Special animated messages are used during holiday seasons. Santa, his sleigh and reindeer, flash across Yuletide skies and the Magi and their

Fig. 10-9. The Goodyear blimp Mayflower.

Fig. 10-10. A Goodyear blimp with an illuminated night sign.

camels follow the star of Bethlehem. A Thanksgiving turkey runs to escape his executioner and a youngster lights a Fourth of July firecracker which explodes to form an American flag.

The majority of messages run on the Super Skytacular are public service statements for nonprofit charities and service organizations. All these fancy messages and animated cartoons originate in an electronic laboratory where a technician, using a light gun, "draws" the cartoon by outlining it on an electronic screen that simulates the Super Skytacular's lamp positions. Then, frame by frame, the animation sequence is fed into a computer memory storage unit and then onto magnetic tapes. A typical 6-minute tape will contain 40,000,000 bits of information. Aboard the blimp, the tapes are decoded and fed into four lamp driver units—one for each color.

These blimps tour the nation's skies six months a year and log about 180,000 miles of travel. The other six months of the year the blimps operate near their winter bases—the *America* in Houston, the *Columbia* in Los Angeles and the *Mayflower* in Miami. A fourth Goodyear blimp, *Europa*, tours Western Europe during the spring and summer months from a base at Capena, Italy, 18 miles north of Rome. At one point, *Europa* was the first airship seen over Great Britain in more than 20 years.

Charles Knox and the Arkansas travelers would be impressed with what the world's skies have come to as far as selling goods. And they would be relieved to know that the Goodyear blimps all carry non-inflammable helium.

Chapter 11

Zeppelin

Air battles over the Western Front were hot and heavy that March day in 1917 when news reached America that Count Ferdinand von Zeppelin (Figs. 11-1 and 11-2) had died on March 8 at Charlottenburg, Germany. Rather than rejoicing, there was sorrow at the passing of the giant of dirigible designers whose creations had spread terror and death over Paris and London. Typical was the obituary that appeared in the *Aerial Age Weekly* ten days later:

"Count Zeppelin is dead. Count Zeppelin is dead, with the dream of his life unfulfilled. It was always claimed by those close to the Count that his ambitions for his aircraft lay not in destroying life, but in linking the new world closely with the old, bringing communication between the two a matter of hours, rather than days or weeks.

"The name of Count von Zeppelin will always be indelibly linked with the development of those giant machines to the evolution of which he devoted the best efforts of his long life. He had reached almost the years of an octogenarian, and yet he was seventy years old before he gained any appreciable success in his efforts to perfect a practicable lighter-than-air machine.

"Germany stood sponsor for the dream, for the creation that grew out of it and for Count von Zeppelin himself. That some of these giant warcraft have played their part during the present war in the scheme of Prussian frightfulness is well known. They have crossed the Channel. They have dropped explosives upon London and Paris and have killed scores of inoffensive non-combatants, including women and children. The ranking strategists and tacticians of the Entente Allies, however, contend that as a potential factor among war making forces their influence has been well neigh negligible. They have succumbed above the land to the attack of swooping aeroplanes and the aircraft gun, while above both land and sea they have more than once surrendered to the stress of the elements.

"Though he was a German of the Germans, it chanced to be in the United States that Count Zeppelin made his first balloon ascension. That

Fig. 11-1. Count Ferdinand von Zeppelin in 1900.

Fig. 11-2. Count Ferdinand von Zeppelin.

occurred when he was attached to the command of General Carl Schurz, in the Civil War, in the capacity of a German Army military observer. A captive balloon in use for military observation by the Union troops greatly interested the young German officer, and he was taken up in it in 1863."

It was President Abraham Lincoln who had accredited the 25-year-old Prussian to pass freely along the Union lines (Figs. 11-3 and 11-4). On May 28, 1863, he joined the headquarters of the Army of the Potomac on the Rappahannock, where Schurz was a division commander with the 11th Corps. At the time, the Rebel Army of Northern Virginia was rapidly advancing up the Shenandoah Valley under Robert E. Lee. Zeppelin was involved in a cavalry skirmish with Jeb Stuart's troopers and barely managed to gallop away to avoid capture.

Fig. 11-3. Count von Zeppelin (in felt hat) visited America during the Civil War.

With the decisive Battle of Gettysburg only a few days off, Count Zeppelin left the Northern army on June 22 and headed west for Detroit. He followed a pair of half-breed guides in an effort to find the source of the Mississippi, according to German biographers. However, Douglas H. Robinson, noted British airship historian, rather believes he simply wanted to see the "Wild West."

THE INTREPID

Following the frontier rivers via Crow Wing and Fort Ripley, Zeppelin's party arrived at St. Paul on August 17. German born aeronaut John Steiner was there operating a coal-gas observation balloon of 41,000 cubic feet capacity. Steiner had been one of Professor Thaddeus S. C. Lowe's assistants when he joined the chief of the Union Army's Balloon Corps in December, 1861, operating the captive balloon *Intrepid* with Brigadier General Charles P. Stone's Observation Corps on the upper Potomac. Two months later, Steiner was transferred to the Western Department of the Army for service along the Mississippi. There he won some fame by directing mortar fire of Commodore Andrew H. Foote's mortar scows against Island Number Ten with effectiveness.

Steiner, who had had his troubles with Professor Lowe, also found difficulty working with the army in the West. They simply ignored him and his German brusqueness. Shortly after arriving at Cairo Steiner wrote to Lowe:

"I can not git eny ascistence here. Thay say thay know nothing about my balloon business they even laugh ad me . . . let me hear from you as soon as possible and give me a paper from Headquarters to show theas blockheads hoo I am." Later Steiner expressed his opinion that "all the officers hear are as dum as a set of asses."

Steiner's difficulty led him further to report: "I am here like a dog wisout a tail and I dond know ware I will be abel to draw my pay for no one seams to know eny thing about this thing . . ." He complained that "I am treeded wis contempt and if I had the means to return to Washington I wold start today . . . now that I can git no pay out here." In fact Steiner was unable to obtain compensation for his military services for more than three months after arriving in the West.

Obviously glad to see a fellow German in St. Paul, Steiner welcomed Count Zeppelin who had taken a room in a hotel across the street from where he operated his *Intrepid* captive balloon. Steiner invited Zeppelin to join him in an ascent to more than a mile altitude. Zeppelin returned home impressed with the independence of the American military citizen-soldiers. It was something he would carry with him the rest of his life.

WEALTHY SCION

Zeppelin had been born to the purple in Constance, Baden, on July 8, 1838. He was the scion of a wealthy family of ancient lineage. His child-

Fig. 11-4. Count von Zeppelin in 1862.

hood home on Lake Constance near Friedrichshafen would become the scene of successful dirigible flights in later years.

As a youth, Zeppelin came into close contact with King Karl of Wurttemberg, his sovereign. In 1866, after returning home from America's frontier, Zeppelin fought in the war in which his native state sided with Austria. They suffered defeat by the Prussians. He fought again in the war of 1870-71 with France.

In 1885, Zeppelin entered the diplomatic service as Wurttemberg's plenipotentiary in Berlin. Two years later he was named Ambassador Extraordinary and Minister Plenipotentiary to the Prussian court. Later he commanded a Prussian cavalry brigade in Saarburg and during the Franco-Prussian War his troop was surrounded and captured in a farmyard. Only Zeppelin managed to escape.

Zeppelin first became intrigued with the idea of building an airship in 1874 when he read a speech delivered by Heinrich von Stephan, founder of the World Postal Union, predicting that mail one day would be carried around the world by air. He knew that the existing airships would not do. The French dirigible *La France* was far too small. Yet when it did fly in 1884 as a military reconnaissance craft, Zeppelin felt it his duty to warn his sovereign, the King of Wurttemberg, that Germany had best get moving on development of a military dirigible.

Zeppelin was further concerned with an Austrian lumberman turned inventor, David Schwartz, who built an all-metal aluminum dirigible at Templehoff airfield near Berlin between 1895 and 1897. Schwartz already had built a similar aircraft at St. Petersburg, Russia in 1893, but it had collapsed during inflation when interior bracing wires snapped.

The Schwartz airship was elliptical in cross-section, 46 feet high, 39 feet wide and its length was nearly 156 feet. An aluminum framework was covered with .008 inch thick aluminum skin that enclosed a single gas compartment of 130,600 cubic feet. A Daimler motor delivered 12 horsepower at 480 rpm to drive three airscrews. Schwartz never lived to see his all-metal dirigible fly. He died before the initial test flight could take place. However, his widow and partners carried on and on November 1, 1897 inflation began.

Two days later the Schwartz dirigible was raised at the end of a tether. But when it was flown free by an inexperienced pilot, a mechanical failure caused the propeller's drive belts to slip off and a rising wind forced it toward a row of nearby buildings. The pilot panicked, opened the gas valve wide and jumped free as the ship crashed to earth. Coincidentally, in the 1920's two more all-metal airships were built and flown. They were the U.S. Navy's *ZMC-2* and Thomas B. Slate's unusual *City of Glendale*.

If the Schwartz airship was a failure, it revealed to Zeppelin that aluminum might be the answer to the problem of constructing a rigid airship sufficiently light and strong to lift its own weight plus an acceptable payload. Production of aluminum had been possible on a commercial scale since 1886 and the Count knew he had the means of building his dream ship.

Heinrich von Stephan's lecture had set his mind thinking along specific lines for an airship built similar to an ocean liner. It would have movable elevator planes to steer it up and down and the whole craft would be just bouyant enough to remain floating at a standstill. Individual gas cells would be used to adjust the lifting force. The entire ship, of more than 700,000 cubic feet displacement, would carry 20 passengers plus mail and cargo. Zeppelin would abandon the idea of using lifting planes for dynamic climb or descent, but his other concepts would find their way into general use in 20th Century airships.

THE FLYING TRAIN

As early as 1891, Zeppelin began a systematic examination of the problems to be faced. Two years later he submitted a design to the Prussian military for an airship built in sections. It had a forward "locomotive" that would tow passenger and freight "cars" behind it. He was assisted in this design by his chief engineer, Theodor Kober.

The Zeppelin "flying train" was to be built in three sections. The first section was to be 385 feet in length with the front end rounded. And have a volume of 336,000 cubic feet. Hopefully, that would be enough to lift a payload of 880 pounds. The second unit would lift a 1320-pound payload and the third 4400 pounds.

On August 31, 1895, Zeppelin obtained a patent on his "express train" airship design and a model was exhibited at the Zeppelin Museum in Friedrichshafen for years afterward (Fig. 11-6). The proposal had been studied carefully by a commission of experts who finally shook their heads and turned it down in a report to the War Ministry in July 1894.

While Zeppelin had followed the work of David Schwartz' "tin can" airship project closely, he never considered going that route. He stuck with his idea of containing the lifting gas in unpressurized fabric cells spread along the length of the craft. When Major H. Gross of the Prussian Airship Battalion publicly charged that Zeppelin had appropriated the Schwartz patents and paid off his widow, Zeppelin angrily responded with a challenge to a duel. Intervention by Kaiser Wilhelm II averted the confrontation.

Zeppelin finally got things moving in May 1898 by founding a Joint Stock Company for Promotion of Airship Travel. He personally subscribed 300,000 of the total capitalization of 800,000 marks. His friend, Carl Berg, took 100,000 and other businessmen advanced smaller amounts. A giant floating shed was built on Zeppelin's native *Bodensee*. It could be swung around with the wind for easier access and egress and Zeppelin felt a dirigible could land more safely on flat water that on land.

LZ-1

Work on his first ship, *LZ-1*, began in June 1898. The hull was designed to be 420 feet long and 38½ feet in diameter with sixteen

Fig. 11-5. Ludwig Durr was the chief constructor of Zeppelins.

24-sided polygons for bulkheads spaced along 24 longitudinal aluminum stringers.

LZ-1's hull was divided into 17 compartments. All but two of the compartments contained individual gas bags of rubberized cotton. Each had an automatic relief valve at the bottom and five had maneuvering valves at the top that could be opened from the forward car to alter the craft's trim. The two open boat-shaped gondolas were suspended closely below the hull, built from aluminum sheets over aluminum framework and

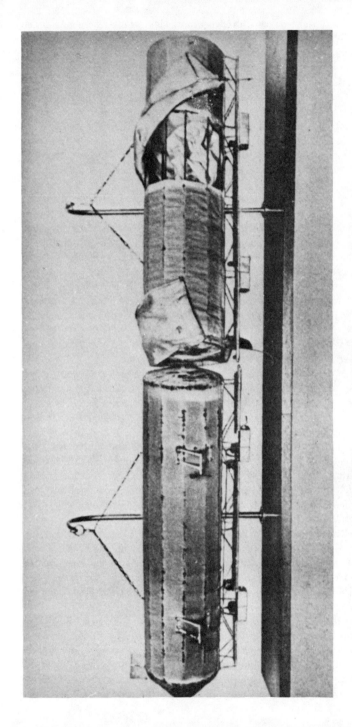

Fig. 11-6. A model of Zeppelin's "Express Train" dirigible in a museum at Friedrichshafen. It was patented in 1895.

made watertight to float with a wheel at the bottom of each for landings on land. Water ballast was contained in a double bottom of the cars and there was more water ballast inside the hull. Each gondola also carried a 14.2-horsepower Daimler 4-cylinder water-cooled engine weighing 850 pounds, a fuel tank, and a driveshaft geared to a pair of 4-foot propellers.

Gottlieb Daimlier, four years older than Count von Zeppelin, figured largely in the success of the Zeppelin story because of his genius in developing light and powerful engines. Born at Schorndorf in Wurttemberg in 1834, he attended Polytechnic School in Stuttgart and worked in England and Germany prior to becoming director for the Gasmotorenfabrik Deutz in Cologne. There he developed a high-speed, 4-cycle powerplant.

At Reutlingen, Daimler founded a vocational school for orphans. One of the orphans was a studious young man named Wilhelm Maybach. Daimler and Mayback perfected a version of the Otto internal combustion gas engine with a new ignition system consisting of a thin-walled tube, closed at one end and heated by a bunsen burner, which Daimler patented on December 16, 1883.

In 1888, Daimler read of a balloonist named Karl Woelfert of Leipzig and invited him to bring his balloon to Kannstatt a suburb of Stuttgart, where he and Maybach were experimenting with engines. On August 2, 1888, Daimler and Woelfert ascended from a hilltop at nearby Seelberg and landed 2½ miles away. The Daimler 2-horsepower engine drove two propellers—one for lift and one for forward propulsion.

In 1897, Woelfert and mechanic Robert Knabe attempted to fly a larger airship with a similar petrol engine at the Prussian Army Battalion field at Templehof. At 3000 feet, the burner flame ignited hydrogen escaping from the gas bag and the blazing wreckage crashed to earth. Both occupants were killed.

In later years, both Daimler and Maybach built successful powerplants for the wartime Zeppelins. Daimler adapted the British Roots Blower to his powerful 500 and 600 horsepower engines. He supercharged them to permit efficient operation at high altitudes. These were the famed "Height Climber" Zeppelins of World War I that raided England from the substratosphere.

The maiden flight of Zeppelin's first airship, *LZ-1*, was made on July 2, 1900 (Fig. 11-7). Five men were aboard, including the Count. Towed from the floating hangar (Figs. 11-8 and 11-9) by a steam launch, it rose smoothly to a height of 1000 feet and landed safely 18 minutes later. Difficulty was experienced with the longitudinal trim, after a sliding-weight mechanism caused the frame to buckle slightly.

With the framework strengthened, *LZ-1* made a second flight of 80 minutes on October 17. The flight was witnessed by Hugo Eckener, a young reporter for the *Frankfurter Zeitung*. His report was not too favorable—*LZ-1* could only make a headway of 16 mph in calm air, he reported. After a third hop, the stock company folded for lack of funds and *LZ-1* was dismantled after barely two hours of flight time.

Fig. 11-7. On July 2, 1900, the first rigid Zeppelin flew.

A NEW HERO

The German public had a new hero in Count Zeppelin, however, and a state lottery was held to raise funds for a second dirigible. Designed by a young engineer named Ludwig Durr (Fig. 11-5), *LZ-2* was slightly smaller than its predecessor. It was 414 feet in length and had 336,200 cubic feet of gas displacement in 16 cells. Stronger, lighter aluminum girders were used and more powerful Daimler 85-horsepower engines, both weighing 425 pounds, were installed to swing bigger propellers.

Construction began in April 1905, in the rebuilt floating hangar that now rested on pilings at the water's edge. *LZ-2* was accidentally damaged while being towed from the shed on November 30, 1905. On January 17 the following year, Count Zeppelin and six others finally got airborne. They rose sharply to 1500 feet when too much ballast was dumped and a stiff southwester baffeted her hull. Engine failure knocked out both powerplants and *LZ-2* was driven some 20 miles cross country to where an emergency landing was made. During the night, a severe storm came up and virtually wrecked the aircraft.

Hugo Eckener, the *Frankfurter Zeitung* reporter, was more sympathetic this time and Zeppelin personally looked him up to thank him for his objectivity. Their association would last a long time and Eckener would eventually become world famous as a Zeppelin driver.

The Count went heavily into debt to build *LZ-3*. The craft covered 60 miles in a round-robin flight on October 9, 1906. It stayed aloft more than two hours. The following September it remained aloft for more than eight hours and a gratified German public subscribed more than half a million marks for Count Zeppelin to build a new rigid airship of 500,000 cubic feet displacement and a length of 450 feet. It carried two 105-horsepower Daimlers. The ship, *LZ-4*, was highly successful and on July 1, 1908 covered nearly 200 miles in 12 hours.

On the acceptance flight for the military, Zeppelin took it up on August 4 to attempt a qualifying flight of 450 miles in 24 hours. With a dozen passengers aboard, it left Friedrichshafen for Basle and then down the Rhine to Mainz and back. All went well for 11 hours until the forward engine quit and a forced landing was made to repair the engine. Off again, the trouble recurred and a second landing was made near Stuttgart. There a storm tore the craft apart and it collapsed—a burned out wreck.

Again the German people rallied. They subscribed 6,000,000 marks for Count Zeppelin to continue his great work. By now the giant airships had become symbolic of Teutonic pride. With this money, Zeppelin formed a new company to build airships, a second to manufacture aircraft engines designed by Maybach and a third to supply support equipment. In 1909, he formed a fourth firm named Deutsche Luftschiffarts-Aktien-Gesellschaft (DELAG) to operate commercial dirigible flights. At this time, Hugo Eckener gave up his newspaper career to work for the Count on a full time basis.

Fig. 11-8. The LZ-1 in a floating hangar.

185

A new dirigible, *LZ-5*, was quickly completed. In July 1909, the rebuilt *LZ-3* was taken over by the military and renamed *Z-1* to be used as a training craft. *LZ-5* got into the air on May 26 and flew a record 600 miles in under 38 hours. It then joined *Z-1* as the German army dirigible *Z-2*.

Next came *LZ-6*. But the German army refused to take the *LZ-6* since it was switching to smaller pressure airships being built by Major von Gross. Zeppelin concentrated on his DELAG operations. In May, 1910, he completed *LZ-10* for DELAG and christened it the *Deutschland*. After several successful flights, the *Deutschland* was wrecked during an emergency landing in the Teotoberg Forest after an engine quit.

Zeppelin, angry with the pilot, called on his friend Hugo Eckener to learn to fly and assume command of a new ship, *LZ-8*, which became the *Deutschland II*. After several flights, it was damaged while being taken from its shed in a stiff crosswind. Eckener determined then and there not to endanger his aircraft to accomodate passengers. He established a weather forecasting department to predict and avoid such problems.

Another 17 airships were completed prior to the outbreak of World War I. Four of these were for DELAG: the *Schwaben, Viktoria-Luise, Hansa* and *Sachsen*. Another ship, *LZ-14*, became the German Navy's first dirigible, *L-1*. In September 1913, it participated in naval maneuvers off the German North Sea coast. There it encountered a severe storm, was wrecked at sea and broke in two. Fourteen members of the crew of 20 drowned. Investigation showed that gas vented from under the hull had been ignited by the forward engine.

Although the *Schwaben* was lost on June 28, 1912, when it broke up in a gale and caught fire, not one of DELAG's 10,000 passengers suffered any injury during some 1600 flights between 1910 and 1914.

COMPETITION

The German War Office introduced competition for Count Zeppelin in 1909 by backing a new company, Schutte-Lanz, that proposed building dirigibles using plywood instead of aluminum in the framework. The first airship was designed by Dr. Johann Schute, Professor of Naval Architecture at the University of Danzig and designated *SL-1*. The first flight was made in 1911. It carried 750,000 cubic feet of hydrogen in its hull, which was 420 feet in length. The firm continued building airships as late as 1918.

Across the Channel, England was alarmed at the growing German fleet of Zeppelins. In 1909, His Majesty's *Airship No. 1*, a 512-foot long dirigible, was laid down in a floating shed built at Barrow-in-Furness. It was to be powered with two 160-horsepower Wolseley engines. It proved to be grossly overweight and on September 24, 1911, it was mysteriously wrecked just prior to a scheduled maiden flight. It had been built by the firm of Vickers Ltd. from plans supplied by the Director of Naval Construction. The accident report was suppressed by Winston Churchill, First Lord of the Admiralty. As a result of this accident, Germany alone possessed a

Fig. 11-9. Tail planes of a Zeppelin airship on Lake Constance.

187

fleet of Zeppelin-type airships when war was declared. Seven German dirigibles were operational. Others were later requisitioned from DE-LAG.

The Zeppelins proved to be highly vulnerable to anti-aircraft fire at the start. On August 6, 1914, *Z-6* was sent out to attack the Belgian fortress at Liege. It was hit by artillery fire on its return and crashed. A fortnight later, *Z-7* and *Z-8* were similarly destroyed in one day. *Z-5*, operating on the Eastern Front, was hit by artillery fire on August 28 and landed behind Russian lines. The commander was killed and the crew surrendered. *Z-9* was destroyed on October 8 when British naval aircraft bombed its shed at Dusseldorf. Earlier, *Z-9* had killed or injured 26 people in a raid on Antwerp.

The French and Italians briefly used pressure airships starting in 1915 and another two were bought from France by Russia for ground support along the Eastern Front. England began the war with seven airships assigned to the Royal Naval Air Service. Later a fleet of small, low-powered airships were employed for ASW patrol duty in the English Channel and the North Sea. They were known as Sea Scouts or Blimps.

Count von Zeppelin had not initially intended his dirigibles to be used in offensive warfare. He once said: "I intend to build a vessel which will be able to travel to places which cannot be approached by other means of transportation, and for observations of hostile fleets and armies but not for active participation in actual warfare."

Nevertheless, the Imperial German Navy placed a large order with Zeppelin before the War Office could grab the total output. Between September 1, 1914 and the end of 1915, the Navy commissioned half a dozen Zeppelins of the L-3 Class. Another seven airships were lost in active service, accidentally destroyed or damaged beyond repair. The German Army in the same period commissioned 19 new airships while writing off nine for various reasons.

BOMBING RUNS OVER ENGLAND

The German Navy Zeppelins originally were intended for use in scouting enemy forces for the High Seas Fleet, but soon their goals became targets in England (Fig. 11-10). It was half a year before Kaiser Wilhelm II could be persuaded to attack the British homeland, and then only with the proviso that the bombing crews would avoid hitting historic buildings and private property—specifically in the city of London. Dockyards and military installations were to be the prime targets. The Zepps were to cross the North Sea in daylight, strike at dusk and return under cover of nightfall.

During World War I, 88 Zeppelins were built at four separate fabrication plants. During this period, the Zepps underwent a remarkable improvement under pressure of demands for greater range and larger bomb loads, higher airspeeds and higher operational altitudes. By 1918, the size had grown to 2,400,000 cubic feet, speed was up to 80 mph, useful load was up to 50 tons and ceilings were above 20,000 feet. Some carried machine guns in their cars for defensive use against attacking airplanes and a subcloud car in which an observer could be lowered at the end of a cable for more than a mile to navigate or direct bombing by intercom while the airship remained hidden above.

Two weeks after the loss of the *L-1*, Gervany's Naval Airship Division was taken over the energetic and capable officer Korvettenkapitan Peter Strasser. Strasser had learned to handle an airship under Captain

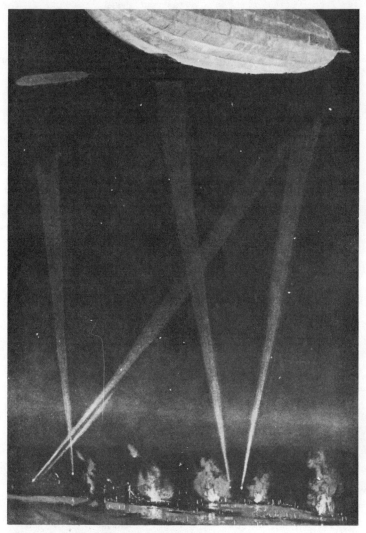

Fig. 11-10. A Zeppelin raid over London, England.

Ernest A. Lehmann of the DELAG's *Sachsen*. But it was not Strasser who led the first attempt by naval airships to attack targets in Britain. On January 13, 1915, Kapitanleutnant Heinrich Mathy, aboard the Zeppelin *L-5*, led a flight of four airships—the *L-3*, *L-4*, *L-5*, and *L-6*—from their bases at Fuhlsbuttel and Nordholz toward the Thames Estuary. Encountering heavy rain off the British coast, Mathy ordered the formation to turn back at 2:54 p.m.

Five days later, the weather improved enough for Strasser to order two Zeppelins, the *L-3* and the *L-4*, to go out again and attempt to attack the River Humber region. The *L-6* was sent to raid the Thames.

Strasser was aboard the *L-6*. He felt his heart sink when the crankshaft of the port engine snapped while still 90 miles from the coast of England and ordered the craft turned back. Steering a compass over the open North Sea, Kapitanleutnant Hans Fritz in *L-3* dumped a third of his ballast to climb to 3300 feet and by 6:30 p.m. ran into a wind shift of 15 knots on the nose. Deciding to steer for Norfolk, closer than the Humber, he reached the coastline at 8:50 p.m. to become the first Zeppelin commander over England. Over Great Yarmouth, he dropped his bomb load from 5000 feet, destroying a few cottages and killing two elderly persons. *L-4*, with Kapitanleutnant Magnus Graf von Platen-Hallermund in comman, bombed Sheringham and Hunstanton, then dumped the rest of the bomb load over King's Lynn, killing a woman and a boy.

The raids over England continued into the Spring, but Strasser finally ordered all raids held up until the newer larger airships ordered at the war's outbreak could be delivered. The first of these, *L-10* (Fig. 11-11), was commissioned on May 13. On June 4, it was sent off to strike London under the command of Kapitanleutnant Klaus Hirsch. He missed the target badly and bombed Gravesend instead.

Kaiser Wilhelm II, distressed at first, finally authorized vigorous attacks on London—but only on Saturdays and Sundays when most people would be out of town for the weekends.

While the German Navy was claiming great victories on their bombing raids over England, the Army Zepps were having their own problems (Fig. 11-12). On June 6, Army Zepps *LZ-37, 38* and *39* headed for London. Passing over Brussels, the *LZ-38* experienced engine trouble and turned back to its base at Evere. The other ships continued on, but soon they also turned back. On the homeward flight, *LZ-37* was spotted by Flight Sub-Lieutenant R. A. J. Warneford. Warneford was flying a bombing mission in his Morane monoplane headed for the airship sheds in Belgium.

Warnerford turned and followed the *LZ-37*, slowly climbed above her and released his bombs. The dirigible burst into flames and crashed near Ghent. On the same day, the *LZ-38* was destroyed by bombs dropped on its shed by British Navy pilots, Flight Lieutenant J. P. Wilson and Flight Sub-Lieutenant J. S. Mills. Warneford had to make an emergency landing to repair a broken fuel line behind enemy lines, but managed to fix the

Fig. 11-11. The Zeppelin L-19 was lost at sea on a raid on England in 1916.

Fig. 11-12. The wreckage of a World War I Zeppelin shot down over England.

break and get off again for home. He was killed ten days later when his plane crashed near Paris.

The mounting ferocity of the Zeppelin raids on England finally resulted in the formation of a stronger civil defense network and improved fighter opposition. This forced the German Zeppelin pilots to limit their raiding to nights when the moon was down.

With Germany on the verge of defeat, Strasser ordered what would be the last raid on Britain of World War I. On the afternoon of August 5, 1918, *L-53, 56, 63*, and *65* headed for the heartland of England with instruction not to bomb London without specific orders. Strasser flew aboard *L-70*, a new Zepp commissioned on July 8, 694 feet in length with a capacity of more than 2,000,000 cubic feet and able to hit 81 mph. Strasser was convinced it could outclimb and outdistance any British interceptor plane. It was under the command of Kapitanleutnant Johann von Lossnitzer, who was Strasser's former adjutant.

Approaching the British coast, the formation broke radio silence as Strasner ordered all ships to attack according to a prearranged secret plan. Despite a low stratus deck heavy with rain, the sky above was clear where a DH.4 2-seater was on coastal patrol. Major Egbert Cadbury was piloting and Captain R. Leckie was in the observer's seat. The DH.4 had a cruise speed of 120 mph and a service ceiling of 22,000 feet.

Shortly after 9 p.m., *L-70* was slighted slowly flying westward at 17,000 feet. Major Cadbury swung onto her tail. Captain Leckie fired a quick burst of incendiary bullets. In second, flames erupted from the rear gas bags and spread along the full hull. Two minutes later the craft plunged into the sea in a blazing wreck. Cadbury then attacked the *L-65*, but Leckie's guns jammed. The remaining Zeppelins headed for home as fast as they could go.

Peter Strasser's death in action was the end of an offensive which he had personally guided. German naval airships had made more than 40 raids over the British Isles dropping some 200 tons of bombs and killing or injuring close to 2000 citizens. The Zeppelin crews would forever be remembered as the "baby-killers."

Chapter 12

The Graf and the Hindenburg

I was a boy of 15, sitting before the family Atwater-Kent superheterodyne radio set listening intently to reports of a missing dirigible somewhere out over the Atlantic: the giant new *Graf Zeppelin*. The Graf had left Friedrichshafen for America, at 7:55 a.m. on October 11, 1928. Aboard was the crew of 43 and 20 passengers. They were on the world's first commercial transatlantic flight and they were in trouble. At mid-ocean, Dr. Hugo Eckener (Fig. 12-1), the *Graf's* commander, squinted his eyes to make out a band of castle-like cloud fortresses stretching from horizon to horizon. A fast-moving cold front was blocking their passage. Lightning stabbed the sky and sudden turbulence gripped the monster airship.

The *Graf's* 776-foot long hull pitched upward as it plunged headlong into the storm. Startled passengers in the dining salon grabbed for dishes as they slid into their laps. At the stern, fabric ripped away from the port stabilizer fin. Dr. Eckener sent his son, Knut, and other crewmen aft to check and repair the damage. He was not unduly alarmed, but safety of his passengers was uppermost in his mind. He turned to Lieutenant Commander Charles Emery Rosendahl. Rosendahl was the U. S. Navy observer on the flight and skipper of the *USS Los Angeles* which Dr. Eckener had ferried to Lakehurst NAS four years earlier (Fig. 12-2).

"Commander," he said, "please advise your people of our situation."

Rosendahl hastily wrote out his dispatch and handed it to the radioman who tapped out in Morse code their position—*Lat 32N Long 42W*, half way to America. Then a request for a surface ship to stand by.

I heard that message repeated from radio station WOR and I prayed they'd make it through the storm the way I'd prayed the year before, sitting before the same radio, listening to reports of Charles A. Lindbergh's lonely west-to-east flight over the same ocean.

Fig. 12-1. Dr. Hugo Eckener.

The *Graf*, of course, made it. Expertly, Dr. Eckener guided his airship through the cold front. He was astutely aware of the micrometeorology factors of temperature, pressure, wind, and humidity that added up to the weather picture. It was the kind of awareness that distinguishes the true airman who is at home in the sky.

That night I piled into the back seat of the family Dodge touring car and huddled under a blanket with my sister Phoebe. Mother and dad sat up front with Bob Hamilton, of the New Jersey State Police, a close friend of the family. From suburban Plainfield, we drove south through the night and covered the 50 miles to Lakehurst over back roads Hamilton knew

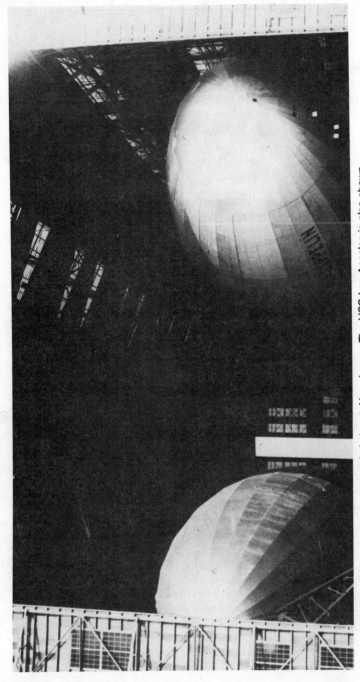

Fig. 12-2. The Graf Zeppelin in a hangar at Lakehurst, New Jersey. The USS Los Angeles is also shown.

well. Outside the gates, thousands of other cars blocked the way in one of history's biggest traffic jams. We spent the night in a motel listening to the radio reports of the *Graf's* progress.

On Monday came news that the *Graf* had beaten the storm and crossed the coastline of Virginia near Cape Charles. From there, Dr. Eckener swung north to fly low over Washington. A score of planes, military and civilian, buzzed her and causing the skipper to order the 200-foot trailing antenna reeled in for safety.

We cheered when the radio announcer, H. V. Kaltenborn, reported that President Calvin Coolidge had run out onto the White House lawn to wave at the *Graf*. From there, it swung north again to pay respects to New York City before heading for Lakehurst NAS. In the dusk, we could see the silver shape coming lower and lower and then passing overhead to land in the early winter darkness.

Landing lines were dropped to the ground crew. To lighten the *Graf's* bow, 500 pounds of water ballast was dumped overboard—directly onto

Fig. 12-3. The Graf under construction.

the head of Rear Admiral Moffett, chief of the U. S. Navy's Bureau of Aeronautics.

Under the skilled piloting of Hugo Eckener, the *Graf* completed nine years of successful, continuous passenger service (See Figs. 12-3, 12-4, 12-5, 12-6, 12-7, 12-8, 12-9, 12-10 and 12-11). When finally decommissioned in 1937, it had made a total of 590 flights. Included were 144 ocean crossings, flying 1,053,391 miles, carrying 235,300 pounds of mail and freight, and 13,110 passengers, without a single injury.

Dr. Eckener knew well the advantages of publicity in selling commercial air travel to the world. His hope was to form an American Zeppelin corporation that could cooperate with the parent German firm to establish a regular transatlantic air service. From the first crossing came formation of the International Zeppelin Company. This was an American corporation backed by Goodyear, United Aircraft, and other industrial and banking groups. Colonel E. A. Deeds was chairman, Goodyear's Paul W. Litchfield was president and J. C. Hunsaker was vice president.

ATLANTIC CROSSING

At the request of Litchfield and Goodyear's public relations boss, Hugh Allen, press relations for the first Atlantic crossing were handled by Harry Bruno. Bruno was veteran publicist and a founder of the exclusive airman's fraternity, the Quiet Birdmen. Bruno had his hands full "selling" papers on the comfort and safety of dirigible flying after the *Graf*, on her return flight from Lakehurst, encountered another severe cold front that had not appeared on the synoptic charts.

Blown far off course to the north, the *Graf* ran into winds of hurricane force from the southeast that gave the 64 persons aboard a rough time. Again the craft came through, however, and Bruno got his story. A stowaway, 19-year-old Clarence Terhune, became the hero of the flight and grabbed most of the headlines in the world's press. Bruno didn't mind—it was great human interest stuff.

AROUND THE WORLD

It was Bruno who came up with the brilliant idea for a world flight (Fig. 12-12)—"Not as a dangerous stunt," he reminded Litchfield, "but as a routine review of things to come, with the ship carrying passengers, mail, and only her regular crew."

Newspapers bid for exclusive rights to the story and William Randolph Hearst was highest bidder. For Bruno, there was another story bonus. Leaving the big hangar at Friedrichsafen for Lakehurst, the starting point of the global trip, Dr. Eckener was informed he had another stowaway aboard. An 18-year-old lad had leaped from the roof of the giant shed onto the airship as it was being undocked.

Landing at Lakehurst again (Fig. 12-13), there was more for reporters to write about. Susie, a trained gorilla, was led off the *Graf* munching a

Fig. 12-4. The interior of the Graf Zeppelin (looking aft).

Fig. 12-5. The Graf Zeppelin.

Fig. 12-6. The control room of the Graff.

banana. When the airship was provisioned and loaded for the world flight, among the cargo were 600 canaries, frozen lamb chops, a live alligator and a Boston terrier. The world flight was a huge success. The *Graf* sailed from country to country with no problems to speak of. The planned route took the airship from Lakehurst to Friechshafen to Tokyo to San Francisco and back to Lakehurst.

Over Russia, Dr. Eckener incurred the displeasure of the Soviet observer aboard in bypassing Moscow to catch favorable winds further north. Such a furor was raised that Eckener made a special flight over Moscow the following year in appeasement.

Among the reporters aboard on the world flight was Karl von Wiegand, who had persuaded Hearst to finance the trip, and Lady Drummond Hay, who, would write glowlingly of the luxury of such travel. Sir Hubert Wilkins also was along.

Approaching America, Eckener expressed concern that the trip from Los Angeles to Lakehurst was fraught with problems presented by crossing the hot Western deserts. Bruno solved that problem by having 20 crewmen off-loaded at Los Angeles and flown to Lakehurst by two Transcontinental Air Transport DC-3s chartered for the mission. Later he explained to the press at Lakehurst that the men were simply sent ahead to assist the Navy ground crew at the landing of the *Graf*.

Fig. 12-7. The dining salon of the Graf.

THE HINDENBURG

Due to the stock market crash in October 1929, delays in the program set for inaugurating regular ocean flights held off formation the American Zeppelin Corporation until May of 1936. By then the monster new Zeppelin, *Hindenburg*, 803 feet length and able to carry 72 passengers, had been built.

Bruno, who also represented the new dirigible, was highly skeptical of its real purpose since the *Hindenburg* never flew the same route twice on westbound flights. His suspicions were aroused that Germany was carefully mapping the North American continent on the eve of World War II.

On October 9, 1936, Bruno and his wife made their first flight in a dirigible aboard the *Hindenburg* on her return flight to Germany. As a heavier-than-air pilot himself, Bruno was curious to know whether the *Hindenburg* lived up to all the superlatives he'd been writing. They found the accomodations equal to those of a Pullman compartment.

On the second day out, they were invited by the skipper, Captain Lehmann, to visit the control room. Dr. Eckener was sitting in his comfortable wicker chair directing the flight over Nova Scotia. Bruno would later relate:

"We climbed a little ladder to the catwalk which ran the entire length of the giant airship. We followed this toward the nose and there, after passing through a door with a lock on it, we found ourselves in a hidden observation post with two seats, one on each side of the catwalk.

"Below us were two windows with cleverly concealed covers, so that from the ground they looked just like part of the fabric. We were way out in the nose of the airship over the North Atlantic, looking down on a very rough sea. Two whales broke the surface, blew water, and dove again.

"I said, 'Well, so this is where you lads do all your aerial mapping?' Lehmann laughed and said, 'You're too observant, Harry!' I had hit the nail on the head—on every flight the Germans were mapping and checking the country over which they flew, and all this, obviously, for military purposes.

"Perhaps my questions were reported to the Nazi secret agent on the airship. He was just a member of the crew, but he; carried the power of the German secret service behind him and particularly was watching Dr. Eckener, who was not too friendly with the Hitler regime. The identity of this secret agent was known to our government, as were many other things that the Germans thought they were getting away with."

The *Hindenburg* landed at Frankfurt at 10 a.m. on Monday, October 12, "after an air voyage as motionless and luxurious as if we had been carried through space on a magic carpet," Bruno reported.

Fig. 12-8. The salon and dining room of the Graf.

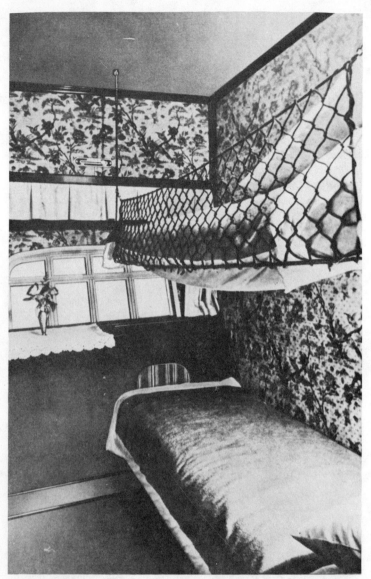

Fig. 12-9. A passenger compartment of the Graf made up for night.

The giant airship was special. Of conventional Zeppelin design and listed as the *LZ-129*, it had 36 longitudinal girders and 15 wire-braced main transverse frames a gondola (Fig. 12-14), It was powered with four 1100-horsepower Mercedes Benz diesel engines that gave it a speed of 84 mph maximum and a cruising speed of 78 pmh. It had a range of 8750 miles and carried 50 passengers in her sumptuous staterooms inside the hull.

Commercial Service

In 1936, the *Hindenburg* operated the first commercial service across the North Atlantic by carrying 1002 passengers on 10 scheduled round trip flights between Germany and the United States. The eastbound flights, with prevailing tailwinds, took an average of 65 hours. The westbound flights averaged only 52 hours due to Dr. Eckener's skill in pioneering the method of pressure flying around the counterclockwise flow.

Fig. 12-10. A passenger compartment of the Graf made up for daytime.

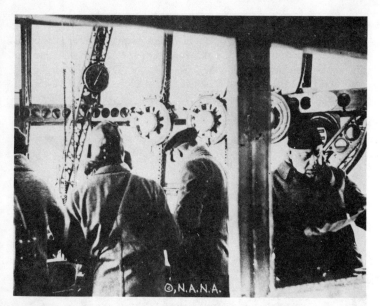

Fig. 12-11. Crewmen of the Graf Zeppelin over the Atlantic.

American Airlines (Fig. 12-15) joined the action early in 1937 by announcing inauguration of "an exclusive air service between New York and Lakehurst, N. J., with giant Douglas DC-3 Flagships, connecting with all trips of the airship *Hindenburg*," (Fig. 12-16) in addition to nonstop Chicago-to-New York hops and overnight service from the West Coast on their low-level Southern Transcontinental Route. The fare from New York to Lakehurst was $6 and from there to Europe only $400. There were 18 scheduled sailings to Frankfurt planned (Fig. 12-17). They advertised!

NOW FLY TO EUROPE IN 2 DAYS!

"There are accomodations for 70 passengers in two-berth staterooms. All comforts are provided: hot and cold running water, downy beds, steward service, shower baths. Meal service equal to that in the finest restaurant.

"Recreation facilities are ample—there is a Reading and Writing Room, a Lounge, cozy Smoking Room and Bar, besides a Gallery and Promenade Deck on either side."

That was flying in style. It was the dream come true of dirigible men for more than a century.

Then Came Disaster

On May 6, 1937, on the first of the 1937 season of North Atlantic crossings to pick up passengers in America for Coronation Year ceremonies in England and a Year of Pageants in Germany, the *Hindenburg*, delayed by storms, drifted over Lakehurst (Fig. 12-18) at 6 o'clock in the evening.

A weather report from the base at 7 p.m. advised there was an overcast, light rain, with lightning to the west, ceiling 2000 feet, visibility improving, wind southwest at 4 knots, gusting to 10. Altimeter setting two niner seven zero.

Maneuvering to land, hydrogen was valved off to lighten the forward cells, while 2500 pounds of water ballast was dumped from the stern. At 7:21, hanging virtually motionless 200 feet above the ground in air highly charged with static electricity, orders were called to drop the forward lines.

Reporters, photographers and radiomen were waiting for the landing. Ansel Talbert, a cub reporter for the *New York Herald Tribune*, arrived late due to the usual traffic jam that accompanied every such dirigible landing. Talbert hurried to the Operations office to notify his city desk that he had arrived. As he started to speak, he glanced out the window and choked.

Fig. 12-12. The route for an around the world trip of the Graf Zeppelin.

Fig. 12-13. The Graf at Lakehurst.

In the *Hindenburg*, Captain Max Preuss, had started to wave to Commander Lehmann and Harry Bruno standing just below. Bruno recalled: "Then came that loud pop, like the explosion of a paper bag, and from the tail a long streamer of yellow flame shot across the sky (Figs. 12-19 and 12-20).

"Several explosions followed and the ship became a flaming torch, falling to earth. Commander Rosendahl and I had the instinct of airmen, and ran into the wind. That saved our lives—the *Hindenburg* dropped exactly where we had been standing."

He continued: "Out of the flames came one man without a stitch of clothing on, and burned almost to a crisp. He staggered a few feet and died

Fig. 12-14. The Hindenburg's rear gondola had a 530-hp Maybach engine.

209

Fig. 12-15. The only way to fly to Europe—1937.

by my side. Then I saw a short, stocky figure come out of the flames, and a sailor and I ran to him. It was Captain Lehmann. He was unhurt."

Bruno concluded: "In my opinion, there were one or two causes for the disaster. One may have been a static spark that flew up the landing rope at the time when the ship was possibly valving hydrogen. The second, and perhaps the more logical theory, is that both rear engines were throttled down and a flying spark may have ignited a hydrogen leak."

There was talk of sabotage, but that was later ruled out. Dr. Eckener reported: "The *Hindenburg* was obviously tail heavy during the landing. And it remained so, despite all efforts to ballast and trim it. Unquestionably, there must have been a hydrogen leak. This is substantiated by the

Fig. 12-16. A Douglas Dolphin greets the Hindenburg at Lakehurst NAS.

Fig. 12-17. The Hindenburg.

fluttering of the fabric and by the fact that one of the crew stated that a cell near the tail looked quite empty just before the explosion.

"The ship made a fast, sharp turn during its landing approach. I believe that a bracing wire gave way during this maneuver. And that the end of the wire whipped about and tore a large gash in one of the cells. Hydrogen then began to escape. It rose and collected just under the cover near the upper fin. Finally a spark, generated by the heavily electrified atmosphere, touched it off."

Dr. Eckener was interviewed later by a former U. S. Navy LTA man, J. Gorden Vaeth, who relates the incident in his excellent book, *GRAF ZEPPELIN*, published by Harper & Brothers, New York in 1958.

Fig. 12-18. The Hindenburg over the Lakehurst mast.

And what about cub reporter Ansel Talbert? Already on the telephone to his city desk when the tragedy struck, he was the first newspaperman to flash word of the awful disaster to a shocked world.

The Aftermath

At the time of the Hindenburg tragedy, the *Graf Zeppelin* was over the South Atlantic and headed home from Rio de Janiero to Germany. It was now the sole remaining Zeppelin. A radio dispatch reported that the *Hindenburg* had exploded and killed all crew and passengers. The Commander, Hans von Schiller, decided to withold the awful news from the passengers until they could land, only then did they learn that the death toll actually was 35.

Of those who died, only 13 were passengers. They were the first and the only passengers to die in the whole history of hydrogen-inflated Zeppelin operations. Often I have flown through electrically charged clouds and looked in awe at the shimmering St. Elmo's fire dancing on the wings of my metal aircraft and spilling off from the propeller disc like a Fourth of July pinwheel. At such times I remember the *Hindenburg* and wonder what the future of airships might bring.

According to a recent study by the Naval Research Laboratory, "the safety record of commercial airship operations is remarkable. Excluding Soviet operations, for which statistics seem not readily available, commercial airship operations carried 354,265 passengers for 4,412,672 miles in flight time of 91,452 hours. The total passenger fatalities were 13, all on *Hindenburg*, and crew fatalities 29, 22 of them on *Hindenburg*.

"In all military and experimental operations, including World War I, 762 were killed. The automobile can match this in the United States alone with one good three-day weekend. Of the 158 rigid airships which have existed, only 12 were built after World War I and two of these were basically of wartime design."

The NRL report continued: "It is evident that the later airships were strong enough structurally to withstand winds, storms, and what have you, or certainly very close to it. There is no doubt that with modern materials and techniques they could be made stronger, and lighter as well.

"There is probably no such thing as a foolproof or completely indestructible structure, nor is there need for one. There is not more a legitimate cause for condemnation of airships than the fact that surface ships are occasionally lost would justify their abandonment at sea."

There was one more Zeppelin after the *LZ-129 Hindenburg*. The *LZ-130* bore the name *Graf Zeppelin II* and was completed and tested in September 1938. It was designed for helium operation and built for transatlantic commercial service. But World War II was brewing and Secretary of the Interior Harold Ickes refused to permit shipment of helium overseas.

Inflated with hydrogen instead, *LZ-130* made a few exhibition flights over Germany. On one of its last flights *LZ-130* cruised off the coast of

Fig. 12-19. The Hindenburg afire at Lakehurst Naval Air Station, N.J. on May 6, 1937. Note the falling water ballast tanks.

215

Fig. 12-20. Headline news on May 7, 1937.

England loaded with secret electronics gear seeking information on tne new British radar defenses which had been established prior to World War II. Herman Goering ordered it dismantled, along with the original *Graf*, to provide duraluniun and steel for his Luftwaffe fighters. In July 1944, Allied bombers destroyed what was left of the old Zeppelin works.

Chapter 13

Challenging The Atlantic

At 2:42 a.m. on the foggy night of July 2, 1919, the slender silver hull of British dirigible *R-34* lifted off from the East Fortune air station near Edinburgh, Scotland. In moment it was engulfed in mists at barely 100 feet altitude. The ground party that had launched the craft waved and cheered in farewell with the sound of the bugle call signalling "All Clear!" still echoing in their ears.

R-34 was off on an exciting adventure. This was an attempt to become the first aircraft in the world to make a round trip crossing of the North Atlantic and prove to skeptics that LTA's were up to the challenge of global commercial air travel.

The crew of 30 settled down to the rigors of the flight under the able command of Major G. H. Scott of the Royal Air Force. Scott was a highly motivated officer whose dedication to airships would one day cost him his life. The entire crew were RAF men although the British Air Ministry had assigned responsibility for *R-34's* design and construction to the Admiralty.

Three special duty officers were aboard. They were Air Commodore Edward Maitland-Maitland, the Air Ministry's Director of Airships; Major J.E.M. Pritchard, O.B.E., who would be the first man to land in America after the flight—by parachute; and Lieutenant Commander Zachary Lansdowne (Figs. 13-1 and 13-2), liaison officer for the United States Naval Aircraft Service and a leading LTA commander himself.

Unknown to the crew, there was a stowaway hiding inside the *R-34's* hull between two gas bags. Rigger William Ballantyne, a former crew member who had been ordered off as a supernumerary to save weight, had climbed back aboard during preflight preparations.

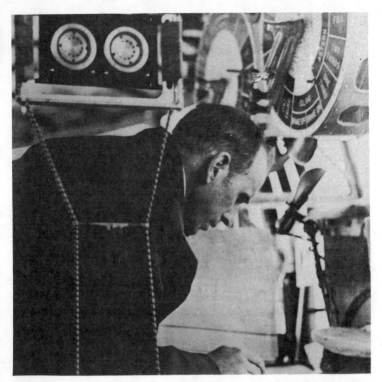

Fig. 13-1. Lt. Cmdr. Zachary Lansdowne, USN, laying out the course for his airship.

As the giant ship rose into the black night, Major Scott ordered a ringthrough to the engine gondolas to increase engine speed to higher rpms from the *R-34's* five Sunbeam Maori-4 engines. Soon the ship nosed through the cloud top at 1500 feet, with clear sky above, to set course for the Firth of Forth, the first checkpoint on its long voyage.

R-34 was not the first aircraft to cross the Atlantic nonstop. Barely two weeks earlier, Captain J. Alcock and Lieutenant A. Whitten Brown touched down their Vickers-Vimy landplane at Clifden, Ireland after covering 1890 miles in 16 hours 28 minutes. The month before, Lieutenant-Commander A. C. Read's *NC-4* flying boat had crossed the Atlantic by way of Azores. It covered 2400 miles in 25 hours and 1 minute. It had been Maitland's hope to save England's airship program from collapse by bringing off a successful long range voyage to launch a postwar commercial LTA passenger and cargo program.

SUPER-ZEPPELIN

The *R-34* was almost a direct copy of a German super-zeppelin, *L-33*, that had fallen into British hands toward the close of the war. On the night of September 23, 1916, *L-33* commanded by Kapitanleutnant der Reserve alois Bocker crossed the Channel from the Belgian coastline, flew up the Thames Estuary and shortly after midnight dropped a bomb load on the heart of London. Among the casualties were four patrons of the Black Swan pub, who died clutching their mugs of beer.

Bocker's raid was spectacular and successful but ended disastrously for the *L-33*. The craft climbed well above artillery range to 13,000 feet. However, a lucky shot lodged a shell inside cell 14 of *L-33* over Bromley. In its death-run for the open sea, hydrogen gas streamed out. Sailmakers rushed to patch the tear, but a new menace suddenly appeared. BFC pilot Lieutenant A. de B. Brandon was bearing down in his 90-horsepower fighter!

Brandon had attacked Zepps before. Once he flew above the *L-15* and attempted to bring it down by dropping a box of incendiary darts into the

Fig. 13-2. Lt. Cmdr. Zachary Landsdowne, USN.

null. They failed to ignite. For 20 minutes, he chased the *L-33*, but his guns jammed. Finally he lost it in the clouds. Bocker reached the seacoast in his deflating dirigible, but stalled and dropped into a marsh. After setting the craft on fire with a signal flare, he and his men ran for the coast. They hoped to seize a boat and escape across the North Sea. However, they were captured.

L-33 was not sufficiently damaged to prevent a team of Admiralty experts from camping out for several weeks near the wreckage and making detailed drawings of its construction. All prior British dirigible plans were scrapped and in November 1916, production was authorized of two carbon copies—*R-33* and *R-34*. Curiously, these were armed with a battery of anti-aircraft guns with which to attack the higher climbing Zeppelins. There were plans to inflate them with American helium after the United States entered the war in April, 1917. The code name for helium was "C-Gas."

Construction of the *R-34* was assigned to the firm of William Beardmore & Co., Ltd. of Glasgow, and it was laid down on December 9, 1917. With a gas capacity of 2,000,000 cubic feet in 19 gas bags, it measured 650 feet in length and 80 feet in diameter. Gross lift when filled with 95 percent pure hydrogen at 15°C and 760 mm barometric pressure was 68 tons with disposable lift of 25 tons.

Total horsepower of 1375 would give it a maximum speed of 75 mph and its ceiling was 14,000 feet. The engines were manufactured by the Sunbeam Motor Car Company and were specially designed for airship use with 12 cylinders each in two rows of six set in a 60-degree V. Cylinders were of 110 mm bore and 135 mm stroke. Each had four overhead valves actuated by two camshafts for each row of cylinders.

The Sunbeam Maori-4 engines were designed to operate at 2100 rpm cruising and delivered 175 brake horsepower. Four Claudel Hobson B.Z.S. 38 carburetors were fitted outside the V with gasoline fed either by gravity or pressure. A special large water pump and governor were fitted so that when the rpm hit 2500, or when oil pressure fell below 20 psi, the ignition would cut off automatically to avoid overspeed. Both a hand starter and compressed air starter were provided and the exhaust stacks were fitted with water jackets for cooling. The huge propellers were 19½ feet in length.

R-34's hull framework consisted largely of longitudinal and transverse lattice girders of duralumin. They were built up of three corner rails and X-shaped webs, with the girders crossing one another at right angles and the bays forming trussed with wire stays. In the bottom of the hull, a triangular A-shaped keel ran the length of the ship, providing passageway between the cars, with ladders leading to platforms atop the hull.

The keel held 81 gasoline tanks (each of 71 gallons capacity) plus storage space for oil, water ballast, food and drinking water, plus living quarters for the crew. Each man could log "sack time" in his own hammock slung from the keel's main ridge girder.

The hull was braced by radial wire trusses, at the transverse frames, forming partitions separating the 19 gas bags from one another. The gas bags were made of balloon fabric lined with goldbeater's skin and the outer cover was of doped, waterproof fabric laced to the hull in sections.

R-34's tail planes consisted of horizontal and vertical fins with hinged control surfaces and trussed with wire stays. Four cars were suspended from the hull by streamlined struts. The forward gondola, largest of all, contained a navigation room, radio cabin and forward engine room. The navigation room held elevating and steering wheels, navigation and engine gauges and engine telegraphs. Amidship were two wing cars (Fig. 13-3) serving as engine gondolas. At the stern, another engine gondola carried two Sunbeam Maori-4 engines hooked up in tandem through a clutch arrangement to permit either or both engine to swing the big 19½-foot propeller.

THE DELIVERY FLIGHT

The delivery flight of *R-34* on March 24, 1919, from its construction site at Inchinnan to East Fortune got off to a bad start. An elevator jammed and sent the dirigible skyrocketing at a steep angle from 300 to 7800 feet and ripped loose a number of gas tanks in the keel. One slammed down into the aft gondola, but there was no fire.

The first major flight was a propaganda run along the coast of Germany. The craft cruised for 56 hours low enough to impress ground watchers used to seeing giant Zepps outbound to attack England. After the signing of the Versailles Treaty on June 28, 1919, a greater opportunity presented itself for the *R-34* to grab worldwide publicity—the east-to-west Atlantic crossing and return flight.

The flight was planned in response to an invitation from the Aero Club of America, a prestigious aeronautical society with headquarters at 297 Madison Avenue, New York, to attend their annual meeting. Aero Club members included Thomas Scott Baldwin, who on August 14, 1908, set an

Fig. 13-3. The forward gondola and "wing cars" of the R-34 dirigible.

American dirigible speed record of 19.61 mph piloting the airship U.S. Signal Corps *Number 1* from Fort Myer to Cherrydale and return. The *R-34* crew missed the Aero Club's board meeting, but quickly the project won official sanction of the British Air Ministry and American services.

A Thrilling Flight

From the start, the flight was a thriller. Initially, *R-34* had to rise through a 1500-foot overcast and then clear surrounding hills at 3000 feet. It carried 15.8 tons of gasoline (4900 gallons) and other payload distributed along the keel that totaled 24.32 tons. Orographic turbulence made the start of the trip severely bumpy. Over the Firth of Forth, things got better with a following wind of 25 mph giving a ground speed of 66 mph.

Major Scott was in command in the forward control car with two non-coms handling the huge control wheels. One crew member operated *R-34's* elevators and the other operated the rudder surfaces. At 3:15 a.m. the morning sun appeared, warming the countryside and producing strong thermal updrafts that sent the ship careening skyward at an angle of 23 degrees and forced the crew members to hang on. Inside the hull, stowaway Ballantyne clutched a girder in fright as Lieutenant Guy Harris, the meteorological officer, climbed up a ladder 100 feet to the topside to take observations. Ballantyne was not discovered, but he was becoming ill.

The sea between Scotland and Ireland was calm and at 4:30 a.m. Rathlin Head, on Ireland's northeast coast, was raised. A thick ground fog covered Ireland, but by 8 a.m. *R-34* was making headway over the Atlantic at 56 mph on four engines. The forward Sunbeam Maori-4 was resting. At 140 miles out from Ireland, a thick fogbank was encountered with heavy rain from a second cloud deck above. Major G. G. H. Cooke, the navigation officer, ordered the dirigible to drop lower in hope of finding visual flying conditions near the water. Flying through the clouds worked to *R-34's* advantage as the sun rose. The lower temperature prevented loss of gas by expansion.

During the day, Lieutenant R. D. Durant, the wireless officer, kept in constant contact with stations on the Azores, in Great Britain and even Newfoundland. The crew stood 4-hour watches and during rest periods exercised by strolling along the 600-foot keel from bow to stern, listening to gramaphone music, eating, and resting in their hammocks.

The comfort of airship travel was in sharp contrast to the rigors of airplane flight in the NC-4s and Vickers-Vimy types. As *R-34* bored on, by 11:30 a.m. it reached a point 200 miles west of Ireland's coast. It was at this moment that the crew was startled to see a human form emerge from the airship above them—Rigger Ballantyne, severely nauseated, had revealed himself. He soon recovered and was put to work. Later he was courtmartialled.

At mealtimes, when 15 crew members sat down to dine in the forward end of the keel, *R-34* became so nose-heavy that half the group was sent aft to finish their meals. No further inconvenience marred the flight through the rest of the first day and the first night at sea. At dawn they had reached the midpoint on their great circle route to America. Nothing unusual occurred until early afternoon when Second Lieutenant J. D. Shotter, the engineer officer, spotted a cracked cylinder jacket on the starboard engine amidship. He saved the day by raiding the ship's supply of chewing gum and with the aid of two other officers masticated enough to plug the leak.

Late afternoon brought more fog as they crossed the cold ocean currents from Labrador and a low pressure area appeared from the south. The counterclockwise circulation around the low provided a good tailwind from the south-southeast. However, by 8 p.m. they were able to climb through heavy rain to 8000 feet and a clear sky. The moon rose to brighten their second night at sea.

At 59 hours out, *R-34* raised the coast of Newfoundland at Trinity Bay. After crossing a large ice field and approaching St. John's, a wireless message was received with information that they would be greeted in flight by the British airplane pilot F. P. Raynham in his Martinsyde biplane *Raymor*. Raynham and his navigator, Captain W. Morgan, had crashed earlier attempting to take off in a crosswind heavily loaded in an abortive effort to win the L10,000 Daily Mail prize for the first Englishmen to fly the Atlantic. Lieutenant Durrant, at Major Scott's order, rapidly fired back a warning not to approach *R-34* too close because of their long trailing antenna astern.

R-34 still had roughly 1000 more miles to fly to reach the mainland. Around midnight, they reached Nova Scotia and turned inland to avoid a storm to the southwest. The dirigible dropped low over the wooded countryside and the crew enjoyed inhaling the scent of the vast pine forest below.

By noon, with New York 500 miles distant, Major Scott estimated they could make it on two engines running at best cruise speed if the weather held. But at the suggestion of the American officer aboard Lieutenant Commander Lansdowne, a wireless appeal was sent to U.S. naval authorities for a destroyer to stand by to tow in case they ran out of gas. The message caused considerable undue alarm when it was read as a message of distress rather than of precaution.

Rough Weather

Suddenly, dead ahead, a violent summer electrical storm appeared with flashing lightning bolts and peals of thunder echoing ominously across the water. Major Scott hesitated. To fly around the storm would cost them precious fuel, but to plunge through would expose them to the hazard of fire by lightning strike. He chose the former course, wisely, and soon a wireless message came that American destroyers would be standing by off Cape Cod.

The weather worsened and became hazardous with severe turbulence that rocked *R-34* heavily and forced crew members not on duty to seek

Fig. 13-4. The British dirigible R-34 lands in America.

refuge in their swinging hammocks. Lieutenant Shotter, the engineer officer, barely escaped being hurled overboard by grabbing a girder as he fell through a hatch. Now the dirigible was weaving crazily through violent storm cells to avoid the worst of them. The trailing antennae were reeled in since they gathered electrical charges that sent heavy discharges to the wireless operators. Looking back from the control car, Major Scott was startled to see the tail section bend under the severe gust loads. He quickly ordered full speed ahead on all five engines to escape the turbulence.

Ground crews and fuel supplies were ordered stationed at Chatham and at Montauk Point. It was from there that the *C-5* had begun its journey to St. John's a few weeks earlier. Shortly before 5 a.m., Major Scott decided they would land at Montauk Point rather than chance pushing on to New York. This was a bitter disappointment to the crew.

With American destroyers standing by in case of an emergency landing at sea, *R-34* moved slowly ahead and at 7:20 a.m. reached Montauk Point at the tip of Long Island. Now Major Scott changed his mind once more and decided to press on for Roosevelt Field at Mineola—their intended goal. Flying low along the shoreline, the crew was treated to a travelogue by Lieutenant Commander Lansdowne who pointed out places of interest.

When *R-34* sailed over Mineola, executive officer Major J. E. M. Pritchard chuted up in a Guardian Angel parachute, stepped over the side of his gondola and yanked the ripcord. His canopy blossomed and he floated gently down to become the first person to land in America from Europe by air. He quickly directed the waiting ground crew of American sailors and soldiers in bringing *R-34* to earth (Fig. 13-4).

The official log of the flight showed the time elapsed in the crossing to be 108 hours and 12 minutes for a total distance nonstop of 3559.5 statute miles. There was still fuel left aboard for another two hours flight at maximum speed.

R-34 was moored for three days while the crew accepted congratulations and enjoyed the hospitality of a New York City welcome. Shortly before midnight on July 9, R-34 rose into a gusting southwester of 26 knots and circled over the bright lights of Broadway.

An approaching low pressure system from the Great Lakes provided a 35-mph tailwind that gave *R-34* a groundspeed of 83 mph as they headed homeward. This time Major Scott flew over the open sea to avoid turbulence from the coastal route.

THE RETURN TRIP

The trip home was relatively uneventful with the exception of a breakdown of one of the Sunbeam engines in the aft car that threw a connecting rod through the crankcase. By flying the pressure pattern to take advantage of circulatory tailwinds, they made good time flying much of the time in weather. Navigation was by dead reckoning using calcium flares dropped astern to estimate groundspeed.

Crossing Belfast, Ireland they received instructions from the Air Ministry to change course and land at the Pulham airfield in Norfolk rather than at East Fortune. After 75 hours and 3 minutes of flight time, *R-34* nosed down smoothly into the arms of the ground crew with some 1000 gallons fo fuel remaining (Figs. 13-5 and 13-6).

No further Atlantic crossings were made for five years until in 1924 the German rigid airship *ZR-3* crossed to America for delivery under the Reparations arrangement. With a capacity of some 2,500,00 cubic feet of hydrogen, *ZR-3* was in the command of Dr. Hugo Eckener as it rose from the Zeppelin company's station at Friedrichshafen, Germany at 6 a.m. on a Sunday, October 12, 1924. A military band played *Deutshland uber Alles*. It circled Lake Constance, then crossed the Rhine Valley, France and Spain to take the southerly route to America.

Fig. 13-5. The R-34 returns to England after its first Atlantic crossing.

Fig. 13-6. The R-34 crossed the Atlantic.

A storm system forced Dr. Eckener to swing north from the Azores toward Cape Sable, Nova Scotia, rather than across Bermuda and then down the coast as *R-34* had flown to Cape Cod.

Passing the Statue of Liberty, *ZR-3* circled New York City for an hour before swinging south to land at Lakehurst Naval Air Station after an uneventful 5000-mile flight of 80 hours 45 minutes. Atlantic airship crossings had truly become old hat.

Chapter 14

The British Experience

Great Britain launched into the construction of rigid airships as early as 1911 with the 660,000 cubic foot *Mayfly*. It was a direct copy of the German Zeppelin type. Hopes were high for success, but were quickly dashed on the very day the craft was first brought from her shed at Barrow. It was caught in gusty winds, broke in two and collapsed. Rigids were abandoned for three years and not resumed until 1914 when work began on the *R-9*.

In the meantime, England forged ahead with development of nonrigids. The first was laid down in 1907 and from that date to the beginning of hostilities in 1914, eight British pressure airships were built. Five more were purchased from France and Germany.

WORLD WAR I DIRIGIBLES

During the war years, from 1914 and 1918, seven nonrigids types were developed for ASW work and coastal patrol duties. They ranged in size from the 60,000 cubic foot S.S. type to the 360,000 cubic foot North Sea class. *NS-11* made a 101-hour endurance flight in 1919. A total of 207 nonrigids were flown by Great Britain during World War I and more than 9000 patrol and 2200 escort missions were flown. A total of 49 U-boats were sighted.

The first S.S. type was constructed by hanging a B.E. airplane, stripped of wings and tail, beneath a suitable envelope. A larger type then emerged—called the Astra class—the first of which used the gas bag obtained from a ship built before the war for a Belgian millionaire as a flying yacht. This type was modified in 1918 to become the C Class, or Coastal Star dirigible.

Construction on *R-9* began in 1914 and was completed three years later as England's first rigid airship after the *Mayfly*. Half a dozen rigids of the R-23 type were next laid down, followed by *R-31* and *R-32* which were of wooden construction. All these rigids were inferior to the German Zeppelins. When the German *L-33* was shot down in good condition over Essex in 1916, it served as a model for the next British rigids—*R-33* and *R-34* completed in 1919. The latter made history with a round trip crossing of the Atlantic—the first transatlantic airship flight in history.

Two more British rigids, *R-80* and *R-36*, were launched in 1920 and 1921 and followed by the ill-fated *R-38*. It was a giant dirigible of 2,700,000 cubic feet, designed and built by a staff of government bureaucrats attached to the Air Ministry.

R-38, also designated *ZR-2*, was a carbon copy of the crashed and captured Zeppelin *L-33*. It was a high-altitude type that featured lighter than normal construction. On its third flight, a structural weakness was spotted but forgotten. On the next flight the craft was put through unusual maneuvers, making tight turns over the Humber, in perfect weather. The craft suddenly broke in two, with the forward section catching fire and plunging into the river. Fourty-four lives were lost.

Nevil Shute Norway, an engineer-novelist who was assigned the task of heading a staff of calculators for the future *R-100* British rigid, was aghast when he studied the accident report of *R-38*. He reported: "The officials responsible had made no calculations whatsoever of the aerodynamic forces acting on the ship in flight." In his autobiography, *Slide Rule* (William Morrow & Co., New York, 1924), Norway wrote that he was "inexpressibly shocked" that the same design team from *R-38* was entrusted with building still another rigid, *R-101*, for the Air Ministry in competition with *R-100*, to be built by the Airship Guarantee Company, a subsidiary of Vickers, Ltd.

LINKING THE EMPIRE

In 1923, before the *R-100* and *R-101* projects got under way, Vickers and Sir Dennis Burney, England's leading airship enthusiast, proposed building a fleet of six rigids to link the far-flung British Empire by commercial dirigibles (See Fig. 14-1, 14-2, 14-3, 14-4, 14-5, and 14-6).

A key witness at the Air Conference held by Parliament on February 7-8, 1922, to hear this proposal was Major G. H. Scott. Scott had commanded the transatlantic crossing of *R-34* in 1919 and had warned that England was in danger of falling behind other powers of the world in airship activities. He told Parliament that in America the United States Navy had made a deal for construction by the Zeppelin Works in Germany of a giant airship as part of America's share of war preparations. The airship was due to fly within 12 months. The U.S. Navy also had *ZR-1* under construction at Philadelphia. This ship was later christened the *Shenandoah*.

The National Advisory Committe for Aeronautics, Scott pointed out, had stressed in 1921 that: "attention now being given to the development

Fig. 14-1. During initial trials, R-101 was found to be much too heavy. A 45-foot section was added to the middle, but this measure proved to be inadequate (courtesy of British Air Ministry).

of types of airships to realize fully the advantages which the use of helium would afford should be continued. Such development would give America advantages for purposes either of war or commerce with which no other nation could successfully compete."

In France, three large airship sheds were being rebuilt from wartime bases, near Paris, Marseilles and in Algiers. Two other huge sheds existed at Maubeuge and Marseilles that were perfect for France's future airship program.

In Germany, Scott said, technical LTA staffs were being held together and a deal was cooking with Spain to establish a commercial airship line between Spain and Argentine.

Italy recently had completed a 1,240,000 cubic foot semi-rigid airship for the United States. *Roma* was the largest airship of its type ever constructed. Measuring 410 feet in length, it had been fitted with Liberty engines. On February 22, just two weeks after Major Scott's testimony before the British Parliament, the *Roma* left Langley Field on its fourth flight in America. There were 45 persons aboard. Then, 49 minutes later, a rudder cable snapped and the craft went into a steep dive and crashed with a brilliant explosion. It had struck a row of high tension wires attempting an emergency landing at Langley. Only 11 men survived the tragedy. If nothing else, it ended the day of hydrogen airships in America. Helium, a nonflammable gas, would be used in the United States.

Italy also had taken over three German Zeppelins in 1920-21 as a war reparations payoff. The Italians managed to wreck two of them in the first year. Major Scott revealed that Italy also had "under consideration a commercial airship service from Rome to her North African colony, Tripoli."

What Major Scott wanted for Great Britain was a rigid airship of 2,500,000 cubic feet with a gross lift of 75 tons and a 12-ton payload for freight hauls up to 2500 miles nonstop or for carrying 35 passengers and seven tons of mail and goods nonstop from London to Cairo—completing the trip in 50 hours at 50 mph.

He further envisioned extending the airline from Cairo to Port Said, Bombay, Rangoon and Singapore—with refueling bases and mooring masts at each stop.

Major Scott saw a great failure in diesel engines primarily because they were more efficient than petrol engines and reduced the fire hazard of carrying flammable gasoline. He emphasized the hope of switching from hydrogen to helium for safety or else employing an outer envelope of non flammable gas to protect the hydrogen from lightning strikes.

Such an air service could, Scott said, reduce the travel time from England to India from 15 to 5 days, or to Australia in 10-12 days instead of 35 by ship. He also drew an exciting picture of utilizing dirigibles as airborne aircraft carriers to carry numbers of fighter planes for offensive or defensive use.

Fig. 14-2. In 1930, Britain's R-101 was the world's largest and most luxurious airship.

The following year, Major Scott's testimony was amplified by Commander C. Dennis Burney who stressed that "the imperial and political advantages accruing from a safe and cheap form of transport by airship travel would provide for the British Empire the equivalent of the through tank railways of America."

He raised an interesting point. "Experiments," he said, "have established beyond dispute that kerosene and hydrogen can be used together as an airship fuel" much in the manner of today's use of gasohol in automobiles. "In consequence," he went on. " the radius of action of a vessel has been increased by 33 percent, and furthermore, owing largely to the very high thermal efficiency obtainable with this fuel, the exhaust temperatures are so reduced that the life of an engine should be increased by 400 percent."

He proposed that the British government underwrite construction of a fleet of dirigibles each of 5,000,000 cubic feet, 760 feet long, able to transport 207 passengers and 10 tons of mail over distances up to 3000 miles nonstop. Used by the military for reconnaissance purposes, passengers and cargo would be replaced by more fuel making it sufficient to obtain a nonstop range of 24,000 miles at 40 mph—virtually clear around the equator!

Used as an airborne aircraft carrier, such as a dirigible, Burney told Parliament, could transport heavier-than-air craft to a scene of action. The aircraft could be launched and attack with torpedoes, bombs or poison gas. Furthermore, they would render a surface Navy obsolete, he went on—perhaps too enthusiastically for a Parliament traditionally used to dependency on the British Navy.

"If the political object—the safe transport of our troops and merchandise—can be obtained without the intervention of a floating navy," he concluded, "then there is no reason for a floating navy at all!"

This last point nearly shot down the whole idea. Parliament refused to go along with his suggestion that a surface Navy was obsolete. However, authorization was granted to press on with two 5,000,000 cubic foot giants. The *R-100* and the *R-101* became England's last venture in the dirigible field.

TWO HUGE DIRIGIBLES

Intense jealousy and competition marked the building of the two huge dirigibles. The *R-100* was built by capitalists and the *R-100* was built by state enterprise. Said Nevil Shute Norway: "In the five years that were to elapse before either ship flew, neighter designer visited the other's works, nor did they meet or correspond upon the common problems that each had to solve."

Work on *R-100* began with a mountain of paperwork in Vickers House in Westminister. This was followed by a year or so of theoretical calculations carried out in a derelict office maintained by the Airship Guarantee Company in the industrial heart of Crayford in Kent. Barnes Wallis,

Fig. 14-3. The R-101 crashed in France en route to India.

Fig. 14-4. The R-101 jettisons water ballast.

designer of *R-100*, was a veteran designer of Vickers airships during the war years. From the first, there was bitter rivalry between Wallis and Lieutenant Colonel Victor Charles Richmond, designer of *R-101*, at the government works at Cardington.

Both ships were to be more than twice the size of any airship that had ever flown before and there was much work to be done developing engines to run on a combination of kerosene and hydrogen drawn from the gas bags. *R-100* was built at Howden in Yorkshire in a derelict aerodrome that had to be completely reconditioned.

Actual design work on R-100 began in the spring of 1926. Part of the staff's duty was to shoot rabbits, partridge, snipe and ducks that frequented the grounds. Wallis finally perfected a method of making the

234

Fig. 14-5. R-100 made a successful crossing of the Atlantic in 1930.

airship's girders from three duralumin tubes rolled up helically from sheet metal and riveted with a helical seam. Next, polygonal girders forming a ring 110 feet in diameter were hoisted into a vertical position, hanging from the shed's roof.

Meanwhile at Cardington, an entire section of *R-101* had been built and scrapped as worthless—at a cost to the taxpayers of 40,000 pounds. Wallis' crew was busily revarnishing all the ship's girders to prevent corrosion. Nearly a ton of extra weight was thereby added to the *R-100*.

Norway was shocked to discover that female "Rosie the Riveters" were behaving in a highly promiscuous manner. Much sexual play was going on in dark corners and slowing production seriously. A matron was brought in to put things right. "The girls were straight off the farms," Norway shuddered. "Most jungly types."

Late in the program it was found that little time was left to further develop the special engines designed to run on kerosene and hydrogen. It was decided to substitute diesels of the type being installed in the *R-101*. Then it was found that the diesels would be grossly overweight. They were in turn, scrapped in favor of six Rolls Royce Condor aeroplane power plants, which worked fine.

With no such things as modern computers then available, engineering calculations were a tedious chore. Stress calculations for each transverse frame required the work of two mathematicians for three months. By the summer of 1929, *R-100*'s 14 gas bags were finally ready for inflation and the six Condor engines, with a total of 1400 horsepower, had to be run up.

R-101's initial flight was made on October 14, 1929. This was some time before *R-100* was completed and Wallis' men were glad to learn that the R-101 was terribly overweight. It had a useful load of only 35 tons compared to *R-100*'s 54 tons. A month's delay of the *R-100*'s first flight, following her completion, was another sore point. The lone mooring mast in the British Isles, at Cardington, was occupied by *R-101* and *R-100* had to wait its turn.

With a length of 709 feet, *R-100* was only 50 feet shorter than the ocean liner *Maurentania* and half again as wide in the beam. Getting *R-100* out of its shed at 3 a.m. on December 16, 1929 required the help of 500 soldiers for a ground crew. Norway admitted taking along a sharp clasp knife, to cut his way free in the event of a crash, but the precaution was unnecessary. With a speed of 81 mph, it was the fastest airship of the day and proved to be all that Wallis had hoped for.

In July 1930, *R-100* made an Atlantic crossing in 78 hours and returned the following month in 58 hours. The overall performance can only be described as completely uneventful. By contrast, *R-101* was doomed to hard luck. In the first place, being overweight, it could not carry sufficient fuel for a planned flight to India. Therefore, it was cut in two and an extra gas bag was inserted in the middle. This increased the payload to 49.3 tons. That was still five tons less than that of *R-100*.

Other technical problems in the *R-101* appeared during early trials.

Norway shook his head when Major Scott was ordered to take the *R-101* on a run to India, despite the fact that shakedown cruises had not been completed. Scott had been in command of *R-100* on a round trip to Canada and Norway remembered that Scott had decided to buck headlong into a dangerous cold front instead of flying around it—jeapordizing the ship and the crew.

Scott was under heavy political pressure to start for India prematurely. England's Secretary of State for Air, Baron Thomson, insisted that they start right away so that he could reach Karachi by October 9 and return to England by October 18 in time for an Imperial Conference. Lord Thomson of Cardington, it was rumored, had been tapped to be the next Viceroy of India.

Fig. 14-6. The R-101 at Cardington, England.

R-101 set off on the flight for India at 6:30 p.m. on October 14, 1930 with Lord Thomson, his valet and four other passengers, plus half a dozen officials of the Royal Airship Works on board. Major Scott glanced at the weather forecast and shrugged. The barometer was falling and so was the ceiling over France. Westerly winds of 30 mph were predicted.

Despite the urgency to begin the trip, *R-101* lazily circled over Bedford for half an hour. Over London, revised forecast warned of a windshift over France—to 50 mph out of the south, directly on their nose. Scott, who had braved a North Atlantic storm and won, decided to plunge on. By 2 a.m., seven hours out of Cardington, *R-101* had covered only 220 miles. The craft was now rolling and pitching in heavy weather over Beauvais, France, at an altitude of 1000 feet above ground level.

Ten minutes later *R-101* entered a long, rather steep dive that threw the engineers off balance. Scott guided the craft to an even keel, but then it again dived. This time the craft thundered into the ground, exploded and burned to a charred wreckage.

A total of 46 persons lost their lives in the *R-101* disaster. The cause was never fully known. However, it was suspected that the fire was caused by ignition of a mixture of hydrogen gas and air escaping from a damaged gas bag and touched off by a spark from a broken wire. With that setback, airship activity in England came to an end. In 1931, the British government scrapped the *R-100*.

Chapter 15

U.S. Navy Blimps in World War I

Lighter-than-air-craft activities of the United States Navy were initiated on April 20, 1915 when the Navy Department contracted with the Connecticut Aircraft Co. of New Haven, Connecticut for one nonrigid airship. According to Commander Jerry Hunsaker of the Navy's Construction Corps, "LTA engineering was a very recent development in the United States and was not taken seriously until December of 1916 when the possibility of the United States becoming involved in submarine warfare began to be feared." (See *Aviation and Aeronautical Engineering*, August 15, 1919.)

Remarking on the 1915 order with the Connecticut firm, Hunsaker recalled that "The Navy Department had always had a mild interest in airships or dirigibles, and placed a contract in 1915 with a firm which had got hold of a German engineer, a German mechanic, and an Austrian airship pilot. This contract called for a training ship of very modest performance but it was not delivered until two years later, and was so much overweight and otherwise so unreliable that after a few short flights it was broken up as useless. This experience was discouraging, as it was hoped from experience with this ship to get some idea of where the Navy ought to use airships."

THE FIRST AIRSHIP FOR THE NAVY

The Navy's first airship, designated *DN-1* (Fig. 15-1), ran its final flight tests at Pensacola Naval Aeronautical Station after preliminary engine and blower tests were completed at the factory. Of the nonrigid type, *DN-1* was 175 feet long, 50 feet high and had a beam of 35 feet. It displaced 115,000 cubic feet and used hydrogen gas. Total lift was approx-

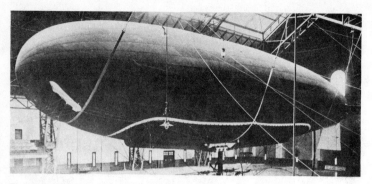
Fig. 15-1. The first U.S. Navy Dirigible—DN-1.

imately 7000 pounds. This was based on the lifting power of hydrogen at .069 lb/cubic foot.

Included were two ballonets. The rear one had 8000 c/f displacement and the forward one had 7000 c/f. They helped maintain the gas bag's shape and assisted in navigation in the pitch plane. The craft's gondola was suspended by cables and ropes from belly bands that distributed the weight evenly.

DN-1's gondola carried an 8-cylinder Sturdevant engine that delivered 140-horsepower at 2100 rpm through a transmission to a pair of 4-bladed propellers. A blower mounted directly over the engine was belt-driven from the main shaft of the engine and was used to keep the ballonets inflated. It was operated by signals from the pilot to the engineer. The engineer shifted T-levers that opened and closed the large air valves. For safety, an auxiliary engine was added to run the blower if the main engine failed. The auxiliary powerplant was a 1½-horsepower, air-cooled, single-cylinder, Indian motorcycle engine connected to the blower by a clutch and chain linkage (Fig. 15-2).

The two Paragon propellers were large and powerful and geared to turn at 80 percent of the main shaft rpm, or 800/1000 rpm, with pitch equal to their eight-foot diameters. Built from white and silver spruce, they were designed to operate at 73 percent efficiency.

DN-1's gas bag was built of two-ply rubberized cotton fabric with a strength of 70 pounds per square inch for both warp and weft and a permeability of 35 cubic feet per 24 hour at two feet water pressure. All seams were double stitched, with the cloth diagonally doubled for strength. The outside ply was on the bias and colored yellow to withstand sunlight deterioration. The inside ply, colored gray, was waterproofed.

Designed to attain speeds from 25 to 30 mph with an endurance at full speed of two hours, it could carry seven men and was supposed to be able to climb or descend at 6 feet per second, or 360 fpm. Gauges included a barometer, barograph, pressure gauges for envelope, ballonets, fuel and water, chronometer, air speed meter, inclinometer, statoscope, and compass. Also included was a signal system of colored lights for communication between pilot and engineer. A first aid kit and food for long trips were provided. But alas, the Navy's first dirigible was a total flop.

DESIGN STUDIES

Set back but not discouraged, the Navy Department turned to their Bureau of Construction and Repair in December 1916 to initiate a design project for an airship to be used for training and coastal patrol. The Navy Department had reports that the British Navy already was employing small airships for *antisubmarine warfare* (ASW), coastal patrol and dropping depth bombs. What the Navy asked for was a top speed of 45 mph, 12-hour endurance at 35 mph, water-landing capability, a crew of three and a wireless set that could reach the amazing distance of 150 miles.

There was little to go on other than the unfortunate experience with the *DN-1*. This was particularly true since the world leader in dirigible work, Germany, still maintained dipolmatic relations with the United States. This made it next to impossible to obtain detailed information legitimately from that source.

To meet the problem, the Navy began a design study later designated as the Type B dirigible. The only reliable engines available were the

Fig. 15-2. This airplane fuselage served as a blimp gondola. The propeller blew air into the vent to keep the tail straight.

100-horsepower 8-cylinder Curtiss OXX-3 powerplant and the four-cylinder Hall-Scott A7A engine of equal power. A research staff assiduously gathered all related materials from the Library of Congress and Smithsonian Institution Shelves—which proved virtually useless. Where theoretical aspects of ballooning were well covered, the theory of airship design had largely been developed under strict governmental secrecy in France (Fig. 15-3) and Germany. The important information was missing since it was highly confidential data.

The only useful data found was a report on inspection of airships made in 1913 in France, England, and Germany—all four years old and outdated. The Navy began running its own basic research investigations. For starters, a series of models was built and analyzed in the Navy's wind tunnel to develop an envelope of low resistance.

These tests revealed that the desired speed of 45 mph was so high that difficulties in steering might be anticipated. Therefore, careful experimental and theoretical studies were undertaken to verify their suspicions. Results were favorable, however—the calculated design features gave ample stability. After pilots became experienced, it was possible to reduce the vertical fin surface.

The car design offered no difficulties. A standard airplane configuration was adopted and mated to a standard aircraft powerplant. But connecting the car to the gas envelope was another matter, since there was no prior data to fall back on. The problem was how to suspend the car and all its heavy payload from the gas bag without causing deformation or undue stress on local areas.

General naval architectural principles were employed in this delicate research, but their calculations fell short of the goal due to the indeterminate nature of the distribution of load between the various suspension cables. The problem was how to keep the envelope safe, yet built from the lightest fabric. Naval engineers based their calculations on methods of computing longitudinal strength of water vessels. To verify them, they decided to run tests on models of the proposed dirigibles.

Turning to a German reference by Haas and Dietzius, *Formanderungen der Hulle von Prall Luftschiffe*, they learned that a one-thirtieth scale model of a fabric airship, filled with water instead of gas and hung upside down, should behave exactly like a full-size ship. This and other design studies satisfied the Navy enough to push ahead using a theoretical ultimate load factor of 9—which turned out to be just what the French used.

The Navy airship design called for a hull length of 160 feet, a diameter of 31½ feet, a height of 50 feet, and an envelope volume of 77,000 cubic feet of hydrogen and a ballonet volume of 19,250 cubic feet. Empty weight was calculated at 3256 pounds and the useful load was 38 percent or 2019 pounds. The empty weight included 100 gallons of gas and a 250-pound radio set—among other things.

On January 27, 1917, The United States Navy and Army approved the

Fig. 15-3. The French
Zodiac dirigible (1909).

plans for a B Class airship. An official announcement was made by Navy Secretary Daniels and Secretary of War Baker:

"A Joint Committee of Army and Navy officers representing the aeronautical branches of both services, the General Staff of the Army and the General Board of the Navy, after a study of the question of rigid airships, has recommended that the construction of a large airship of the general Zeppelin type be undertaken at once under direction of the chief constructor of the Navy . . . with cost of construction borne equally by the Army and the Navy from appropriations made by the Sixty-Fourth Congress. The importance of the rigid airship is fully realized, and it is believed that the problems can be worked out better, more rapidly, and more economically by joint action than if each service took them up separately."

Curiously, this was America's first attempt to merge its military forces in the face of a threat of war. It was a step that would be repeated in World War II with the merging of the Army Air Corps and the Air Force Combat Command in March, 1942 into the combined Army Air Forces. This was a powerful global weapon composed of 16 air forces (12 of them overseas), 243 combat groups, 2,400,000 soldiers and nearly 80,000 aircraft.

RAPID PRODUCTION

The war threat growing in Europe in 1916 acted as a stimulus to the stillborn U.S. dirigible program. Initially, proposals for one, two, four, eight, and then more airships were made to five private firms. According to Commander Hunsaker: "Instead of authorizing one or two units as an experiment to work out the design, the Navy Secretary ordered 16 ships to be produced as rapidly as possible."

"This came as a thunderbolt, and it seemed at first impossible of execution. It was impossible to allow six months to build an experimental airship, develop the proper gas-tight fabric needed, correct defects in design, and then instruct contractors in the manufacture.

"The Chief Constructor, therefore, decided to go ahead with the construction regardless of the unproved nature of the design, and on February 6, 1917, sent copies of the plans and specifications to five firms which had offered their facilities to the Department for war work and which he considered to be in a position to help. Representatives of these five firms met with the Chief Constructor on February 12 to discuss ways and means for getting the sixteen ships built quickly.

"The five firms requested to undertake the work were the Curtiss Aeroplane & Motor Corporation, the Connecticut Aircraft Company, and the three great rubber manufacturers—Goodyear, Goodrich, and U. S. Rubber. The conference resembled a patriotic meeting rather than a gathering of prospective government contractors; but in spite of a very great desire to help the Navy, it was immediately apprarent that not one of them was in a position to handle the work.

"In the first place, they were without experience in airship building, with the exception of the Connecticut Aircraft Company. None of the rubber companies had ever made fabric of the hydrogen-resisting quality and strength required, and it would be necessary not only to develop new processes, but to put in new machinery and special equipment to manufacture it. Supplies of the special fine cloth needed would have to be obtained, and the market for it was in an abnormal condition."

Among the problems faced was a lack of hangar space. None of the five firms had a building large enough to erect an airship. Although the Navy planned to build eight airship sheds at coastal stations, that lay in the distant future. They desperately needed at least one airship for experimental flight testing—now.

The cost-plus method of contracting was then unknown, and a fixed price of roughly $40,000 per airship was agreed upon. Most of the contractors lost money on the effort as they patriotically rushed ahead with no expense spared.

Among the contractors, Goodyear was the most experienced, having already built free balloons for a number of years, and they agreed to erect at their own expense a complete building and testing establishment. This consisted of a field near Akron, Ohio with a large capacity hydrogen generating plant and an airship shed 200 × 100 × 100 feet—complete with barracks for the required field organization. By June 1, 1917, the first airship—a free balloon—was inflated in the new Goodyear Akron hangar.

Of the 16 dirigibles ordered, Goodyear built nine, Goodrich built five and the Connecticut firm built two. The 14 cars and engines for the Goodyear and Goodrich aircraft were built by Curtiss.

Goodrich already had experience building kite balloons and observation craft. While they were committed only to build five B Class dirigibles, they proudly advertised their place in the war effort as producers of "the lion's share of gas masks, rubber boots, truck and pneumatic tires, raincoats and panchos, tubing, insulated wire, mechanical and surgical goods for the lads who wallowed through the muck of the trenches."

Making up for its lack of experience in making dirigible envelopes, Goodrich cabled to France for M. Henri Julliot, a well known engineer at the Lebaudy dirigible plant in Paris, to join them. When the United States declared war on Germany, the U.S. Navy Department was able to arrange for the release from the French Army of M. Julliot's two assistants, M. Bourguignon and M. Gautier. Together with Mme. Bourguignon, a skilled fabric worker, they were a great help in introducing refinements to the manufacturing process.

The U.S. Rubber Co. decided not to attempt to build complete airships, but undertook to supply fabric for the Connecticut Aircraft Company's dirigibles.

Goodyear completed its first airship in May, 1917, even before their shed at Akron was completed. The Goodrich firm meanwhile took over an abandoned shed at the "White City" amusement park in Chicago. There a large supply of hydrogen in flasks was gathered. It was decided to ship the first Goodyear ship to the White City Goodrich shed for initial flight trials for the benefit of all contractors. There a Goodyear engineer, R. H. Upson, took up dirigible *B-1* for a short hop.

Upson was so impressed with its handling that on his second flight, the weather being favorable, he considered there was less danger in trying to fly home to Akron than in attempting to land back at the small Chicago field that was surrounded by buildings and telegraph wires. Accordingly, he set out for Akron at midnight and at noon the next day—Decoration Day, 1917—he landed in a meadow 10 miles from Akron when his engine seized up for lack of oil.

This flight was significant for a number of reasons. It was one of the longest airship flights on record at that time and it was a maiden flight of an untried airship designed from theoretical and experimental data by a designer of no previous experience in airship work. In addition, Upson was not an airship pilot, though as an experienced free balloonist and aeronautical engineer he had a good grasp on how to handle it, proving once and for all that the design was good.

DELIVERY

All 16 dirigibles were delivered to the Navy by September 11, when Goodrich's *B-13* was handed over, and by the year's end they were all in service at the various coastal naval air stations. Goodyear also undertook to train Navy personnel in flying and docking the new blimps, as they were called. The first naval airship detachment, under the command of Commander L. H. Maxfield, was organized and trained at Akron.

These first Navy dirigibles were highly successful in meeting their mission requirements and were at least equal to the foreign craft at that time. All were used on the west side of the Atlantic during the war, yet the 16 B Class airships did train 170 pilots and on coastal patrol flew 13,600 hours covering some 400,000 miles without a fatality. Designed for 16-hour patrol duty, one ship based at Key West was out 40 hours, while another remained in service 15 months with its original envelope. Still another kept one inflation of hydrogen for 9 months and was airborne 743 hours during that time.

It is an old hangar tale, hard to shoot down, that "Blimps" got their name as a contraction of the miiltary designation of World War I British airships known as "Balloon Type *B, limp*." According to an authority, Dr. A. D. Topping, editor and historian of The Lighter-Than-Air Society, the story is so much hot air. He claims the British never had an airship with a "limp" designation, or even a Type B.

Dr. Topping credits Lieutenant (later Air Commodore) A. D. Cunningham of the Royal Navy Air Service with originating the term while serving as commanding officer of the British airship station at Capel. On a Sunday, December 5, 1915, Lt. Cunningham was conducting his weekly inspection of the airship station inside a shed housing His Majesty's

Airship SS-12 (SS for Submarine Scout). The shed was built with a deep recess in the floor to accomodate the airship's car and to permit crewmen to walk along the floor at the same level as the gas bag of the airship.

During this inspection, says Dr. Topping, Lt. Cunningham could not resist thumping the gas bag with his thumb to produce a hollow noise that echoed off the taut fabric. Cunningham reportedly grinned, then orally imitated the sound—*BLIMP*! A young midshipman, who later would become Air Marshall Sir Victory Goddard, repeated the story of the humorous incident to fellow officers in the mess hall and the rest is history.

A series of improvements led to better performance of the B Class dirigibles, which originally cruised at roughly 40 mph. By removing one of the vertical fins to cut drag, and hanging the car closer to the envelope, faster speeds were attained. The envelope itself was further streamlined, the air pipes to the ballonets were placed inside the envelope, with the air scoop modified, increasing the top speed to 48 pmh. All 16 B Class airships met their weight limits, showing a useful lift well in excess of the design load.

If Goodyear outdid its competitor Goodrich in the number of B Class airships built for the Navy, the latter firm's last airship delivered, *B-13*, became the star of the immediate postwar Aeronautical Exposition when it was suspended from the ceiling of the 69th Regiment Armory in New York City. Visitors learned that *B-13* had been accepted by the Navy following a series of top secret tests conducted under cover of darkness over Lake Michigan.

Fig. 15-4. The U.S. Navy's C-1.

Fig. 15-5. The U.S. Navy's C-1 blimp.

Bearing the Goodrich designation *A-247*, this huge blimp remained in active service from September 11, 1917, until February 15, 1919, when the Navy authorized Goodrich to give the public a closeup view of the type of aircraft which had played such a notable role in convoying American troopships through submarine infested waters of the western Atlantic.

Although the original B Class blimps performed their patrol and convoy duties with honor, in the spring of 1918, a larger, faster type of nonrigid airship was designed to carry heavy depth charges for overseas antisubmarine warfare. This new design provided higher speeds to cope with headwinds, greater range to escort convoys and redundant powerplants to lessen the hazard of engine failure at sea. Designated Type C, the design proved highly successful—with speeds up to 60 mph. Contracts were placed with Goodrich and Goodyear for 30 C Class airships to be built in accordance with the Navy design. The cars were all to be manufactured by Curtiss with rudimentary standard airplane fuselages fitted with pontoons for water landings.

The first Class C airship, designated *C-1* (Figs. 15-4, 15-5 and 15-6), was completed in September 1918. On its maiden flight on October 22, it flew nonstop for 400 miles. As a result of the signing of the Armistice, only 10 C Class airships were finished (Figs. 15-7, 15-8 and 15-9). The remaining contracts for 20 more blimps were cancelled. A record flight for nonrigid airships was made by Lt. Commander E. W. Coil on May 15, 1919 in *C-5* (Figs. 15-10, 15-11 and 15-12). He flew nonstop from Montauk to Newfoundland, a distance of 970 nautical miles, in 25 hours and 50 minutes.

This flight was undertaken to prove the radius of action of C Class dirigibles as well as their ability to operate under varying weather conditions (Fig. 15-13). The next goal of the *C-5* was a transatlantic voyage. Taking off from Montauk NAS at 8 a.m. with a moderate tailwind, the *C-5*

Fig. 15-6. A U.S. Navy C-1.

249

Fig. 15-7. The U.S. Navy's C-2 blimp.

shaped a course by way of Cape Cod, Cape Sable, and Cape Breton to St. Johns, Newfoundland.

Throughout the day, the weather was fair and at night a bright moon shone until 10:30 p.m. when a fast-moving cold front was encountered. Through the rest of the night the crew hung on. They fought airsickness as the ship swayed, bucked and wallowed through gale force winds. It rolled so heavily at times that the engines temporarily stopped. Through the intense cold, the airship pressed on until at dawn the storm subsided.

A new menace appeared—an intense fog bank that caused Lt. Cdr. Coil to lose his bearings. Wireless direction-finding efforts were fruitless. But at 10:45 a.m., they contacted the *U.S.S. Chicago* by radiophone and finally landed safely at Pleasantville, near St. Johns. The crew members—Lt. J. B. Lawrence, first assistant pilot; Lt. (j.g.) E. O. Campbell, coxswain; Ensign M. H. Easterly, radio operator, and Chief Machinists Mates G. H. Blackburn and T. L. Mooreman were tired but pleased.

But disaster lay ahead. During the afternoon, a fresh gale struck and the resulting pitching and swaying of the *C-5* badly damaged its envelope. The forward rigging guys finally gave way and it was decided to dump all gas. Lieutenant C. G. Little, USN, of the ground crew, leaped aboard and began pulling on the rip cord to release the hydrogen when a violent gust snapped the remaining mooring guys. Lieutenant Little leaped overboard, spraining his ankle, as the *C-5* shot upward, dropped the car and was swept out to sea by the storm.

A novel means of extending the range of the C Class blimps was a provision to run the engines on a mixture of gasoline and hydrogen. This method was intended to utilize gas valved off for lightening or due to expansion rather than letting it go to waste. The power plants consisted of a pair of vertical 6-cylinder Union engines each able to develop 125 horsepower at 1350 rpm.

Good as they were, the C Class dirigibles (Fig. 15-14) were subject to considerable criticism from the pilots who flew them. Efforts were made to correct the problems in the ensuing D Class ships. Cars of the D Class were fitted with a pair of Union engines mounted close together on

250

Fig. 15-8. The gondola of a C-class airship with a bomb in pack.

Fig. 15-9. A C-3 blimp.

Fig. 15-10. A C-5 dirigible.

outriggers at the stern, placing the crew members ahead of the propeller blast, and the fuel was carried in tanks suspended from the envelope to get them clear of the car where they posed a fire hazard. The envelope was a standard C Class type with a 6-foot section added to the middle to give greater length. The fins were radically different, being long and rather narrow in contrast to the fairly short, wide fins of the C blimps.

While the new car arrangement made the crew positions more comfortable, maintenance was more difficult. The gas tanks on the bag were hard to fill and keep tight and a great amount of tubing was required to connect them to the engines. This further increased the hazard of fuel line leaks. Modifications were made in the car to overcome these difficulties. Five D Class airships were built from the original design. One other was built with the boat-shaped car inclosed and with the fuel inside it.

THE WINGFOOT EXPRESS

In June, 1919, Goodyear, which had accumulated a sizeable design staff, felt the time was ripe to build a commercial blimp. They called it the *Wingfoot Express* and it had 95,000 cubic foot hydrogen inflated envelope. It was powered with a pair of French Gnome Rhone rotary engines suspended from the envelope above and behind the car.

Fig. 15-11. Flight preparation for a C-5.

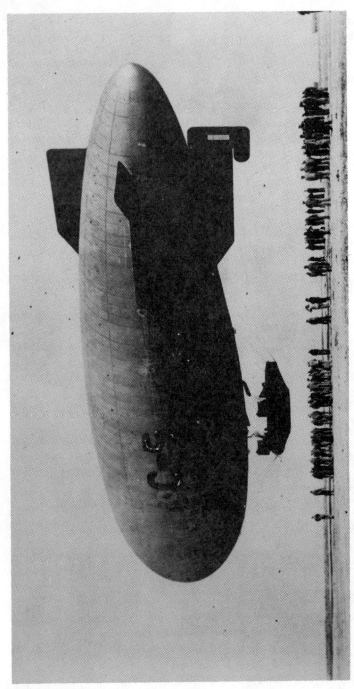

Fig. 15-12. This C-5 airship attempted a transatlantic crossing.

Fig. 15-13. A U.S. Naval airship and a World War I convoy.

Listed in company records as *D-44*, it had the fourty-fourth airship envelope scheduled to be produced by that firm. It was known as the Type FD airship. The name indicated that it was a continuation of the basic design series with began with Types F and FA. These types were (respectively) 77,000 and 84,000 cubic foot Navy B ships.

On July 21, 1919, the *Wingfoot Express* departed its base at the old White City Amusement Park on Chicago's south side, never to return. Somehow, the hydrogen gas was ignited and the airship was lost. This led to Goodyear's pioneering in 1925 of the use of inert helium instead of inflammable hydrogen gas with their blimp *Pilgrim*. In 1919, Goodyear also built a single-engined pusher with an envelope only slightly larger than that of the B ship. The Navy acquired this blimp for evaluation of what was called the E Class dirigible. Another Goodyear blimp, with a slightly different car, also was acquired by the Navy as an F-Class dirigible. The main differences between these two aircraft were in details of the car and the fact that the engine of the *E-1* was fitted with a reduction drive to the propeller.

The Navy bureau next designed a large, nonrigid ship, labeled the G Class, during 1919. However, none was ever constructed since the Navy by then was leaning toward development of rigid airships for large LTA transports. The G Class ship was to have carried a 3-inch gun of the long recoil type, together with a substantial bomb load, and with all this have an endurance of 50 hours at 45 mph, or 25 hours at 60 mph.

It was discovered, however, that a much larger gas bag would be required than anticipated to tote all the extra weight. Fears that the extra

Fig. 15-14. The first trip of a helium filled C-7.

stresses would cause the envelope to deteriorate prematurely resulted in its abandonment.

In 1920, the Navy went to the other extreme with the H Class design, sometimes referred to as an "animated kite balloon," that called for a very small gas bag capable of being towed like a kite balloon yet able to maneuver on its own with the tow cable slipped. A contract for an H ship was let with Goodyear in 1920 and trials were held the following June and July. The H Class envelope was of 43,000 cubic feet displacement and a single 60-horsepower Lawrance air-cooled engine was used. An improved model, the *H-2*, proved entirely successful in its trials.

There was no I Class airship in the Navy's list of nonrigids, due to the letter's similarity to the figure 1. Therefore, the last of the World War I type Navy nonrigid blimps was the *J-1*. Serious efforts were made to correct all the mistakes of the earlier blimps. It passed its trials in the fall of 1922 with flying colors. It was a 174,880-cubic foot blimp, 168 feet long, powered with two Union engines of 145 horsepower each, capable of speeds up to 60 mph and a maximum range of 480 miles at 60 mph or 810 miles at 40 miles.

Chapter 16

Navy Blimps of World War II

Nonrigid blimps of the United States Navy were relegated to a second class status after World War I. There was a shift in emphasis to rigid types. When the Secretary of the Navy on August 9, 1919 approved construction of a copy of the German Zeppelin *L-49*, the blimps were gone, if not entirely forgotten, until the 1940's.

GOODYEAR'S CONTRIBUTION

The airship experience possessed by Goodyear Aircraft Corp., as a result of the firm's blimp fleet operations, was a vital asset of the firm's blimp fleet operations, was a vital asset to the war effort after Pearl Harbor. There was a seasoned nucleus of trained LTA pilots, many in the Naval Reserve, on hand to pilot the new World War II blimps as they entered service and to train new personnel for combat duty (Figs. 16-1 and 16-2).

In the years between World Wars I and II, United States civil airship activity was largely limited to the operation of commercial and advertising blimps by Goodyear. Goodyear started off with their small "Pony" blimp and then began operating half a dozen helium inflated airships. These flights were a learning experience for their crews and designers in development of flight and ground-handling techniques.

Commercial Goodyear blimps ranged in size from 51,000 to 183,000 cubic feet. Most had a 123,000 cubic foot capacity and could carry approximately six passengers. From the beginnings of these commercial operations in 1925, until transfer of the Goodyear blimp fleet to the Navy in 1942, Goodyear airships made 152,441 flights and carried 407,171 passengers without a single passenger injury of fatality.

Fig. 16-1. The crew of the Goodyear blimp Pilgrim.

Crash of the Navy rigid airship *Macon* in 1935 ended the U.S. Navy's love affair with rigids and their LTA efforts switched back to nonrigids. At that time, the Navy was operating the 210,000 cubic-foot *J-4* (Fig. 16-3), the 320,000 cubic foot *K-1*, and the 202,000 cubic foot *ZMC-2* (Figs. 16-4 and 16-5). *J-4* was an open gondola airship built in 1924, while the *K-1*, built in 1931, used blau gas as well as gasoline for fuel. The *ZMC-2* was the first successful all-metal airship. It was built in 1929 by the Metalclad Airship Corp. of Detroit. Its hull consisted of 24 longitudinals and 12 circular bulkheads riveted to a .0095 inch thick outer skin of alclad sheeting. Though possessing some rigid construction characteristics, *ZMC-2* was in fact a pressure airship that depended on its internal gas pressure to maintain hull rigidity in flight.

The 183,000 cubic foot Goodyear *Defender*, named for an America's Cup racing yacht, was purchased by the Navy in 1935 and designated *G-1*. Two years later, on abandonment of the Army's airship program, the Navy received the former *TC-13* and *TC-14* nonrigids of 350,000 cubic foot capacity.

As American entry into World War II drew near, increased airship strength was authorized. When Japanese planes attacked Pearl Harbor, the Navy had operational four new K-type (Figs. 16-7 and 16-8) patrol airships, built from 1938-41, three small L-type (Fig. 16-9) trainers, the *G-1* Fig. 16-6, and the *TC-13* and *TC-13*.

More than a year earlier, on its own intitiative, Goodyear began a pilot training program at Wingfoot Lake with the Navy's future requirements in mind. Between September, 1941 and April, 1944, the firm

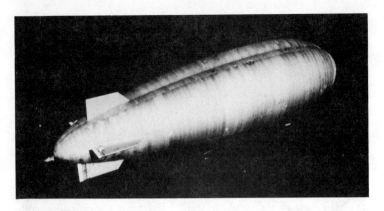

Fig. 16-2. The RS-1 was the only semi-rigid airship constructed for the U.S. Army by Goodyear.

delivered four modern airships (113-K, 10-L, 70-G, and 4-M) to the Navy. In addition, the Navy took over for war duty Goodyear's five commercial blimps and designated them *L-4* to *L-8*.

When the United States entered WW II there was only a single airship on the entire West Coast—Goodyear's Los Angeles based commercial blimp *Resolute*. At first, the *Resolute* operated on privateer status and it was the first such ship with the United States Navy to do so since the War of 1812. At the time, the *Resolute* was armed only with the pilot's hunting rifle. The ship and crew officially joined the service on March 10, 1942.

The last airship built for Goodyear's prewar fleet was the *Range R*, which first flew on August 13, 1940. It was deflated months later and sold to the Navy as the *L-2* on February 1, 1941.

THE MYSTERY BLIMP

Immediately following the sale of the *Ranger* to the Navy, Goodyear began building a replacement early in 1941 and it was still unfinished when war broke out. It was delivered directly to the Navy at Moffett Field in February, 1942 as the *L-8* (Fig. 16-10). In August that year, the *L-8* became the center of a mystery story so intriguing that the war was all but forgotten.

On the quiet Sunday morning of August 16, 1942 the sun was just beginning to warm the sky shortly before noon in Daly City, California. John Scotto had left home to stroll along the narrow suburban streets. Glancing upward, he suddenly stopped and stared. A partially deflated blimp was descending and drifting toward him (Fig. 16-11).

As he watched, the blimp scraped across some power lines (Fig. 16-12) and fell in a heap to the pavement (Fig. 16-13). A crowd quickly gathered and held the blimp down until police and firemen arrived. When the firemen got there, they were shocked to find no one aboard the blimp.

Fig. 16-3. J-4 and L-1 airships in Barnigate Bay, New Jersey.

Fig. 16-4. The U.S. Navy's ZMC-2 was an all-metal airship.

Anxiously, they slashed the gas bag open to see if anyone was inside. Nobody! The police called Moffett Field.

The Navy blimp *L-8*, the learned, had taken off at 6 a.m. on a routine patrol flight from the Treasure Island NAS, where the blimp was on detached duty. Aboard were two veteran LTA men, Lt. (j.g.) Ernest Dewitt Cody, 27, and Ensign Charles E. Adams, 38, both survivors of the crash of the *USS Macon* in 1935. After a routine radio contact with Moffet Tower, they began their routine ASW search procedure.

At 7:50 a.m., nearly two hours after takeoff, Cody reported to Moffett that he had sighted an oil slick, five miles east of the Farallon Islands, and was dropping lower to investigate. Fifteen minutes later, Moffett tried to make contact with the *L-8*, with no luck. After repeated effort to raise the blimp by radio, Moffett called NAS Alameda to report an emergency.

Two OS2U search planes scrambled from Alameda and headed west for the Farallons. Over the ocean, a thick overcast blanketed the Pacific with only a 500-foot ceiling beneath. The search planes radioed Moffett that they were pulling up and over the cloud deck.

The call from the Daly City Police Department came in at 11:15 a.m. The big blimp was lying on the street like a sick cow. Would they please do something about it?

Fig. 16-5. The ZMC-2.

Fig. 16-6. G-1 over the USS Falcon.

By now all hands were investigating the mystery. A Coast Guard cutter and a Navy ship were found to be conducting separate operations near the scene of the oil slick. Neither had taken much notice of the blimp.

However, a finishing boat skipper was located in the area who had taken a great deal of notice. He reported seeing *L-8* come down close to the surface of the ocean and drop two smoke flares. As the blimp turned toward the fishing boat, the fishing boat captain decided to stay clear of the area. He felt the blimp was on a bombing run. However, *L-8* just flew off into the overcast.

Nothing more was heard of the *L-8* for the next 2½ hours. During that time the two men aboard the *L-8* simply disappeared. At 10:20 a.m., a Panama Clipper pilot reported sighting the blimp flying aimlessly above the cloud deck at sea. Ten minutes later, a flight of Kingfisher search craft, which had departed Moffett Field earlier, reported seeing *L-8* break through the overcast at 2000 feet and then descend again into the mists.

At 10:45 a.m., the blimp was sighted from Fort Funston. It was flying low about a mile away and headed for shore. Fort Funston is located between the Pacific shoreline and Lake Merced and just north of Daly City.

The blimp drifted in on a strong wind and touched down on the beach near the Olympic Club golf course. Some swimmers in the area attempted to reach the blimp and hold it down, but the impact of landing dislodged one of two depth bombs carried aboard. Lightened, the *L-8* became airborne again and floated off into the clouds before anyone could reach it. Then John Scotto sighted her.

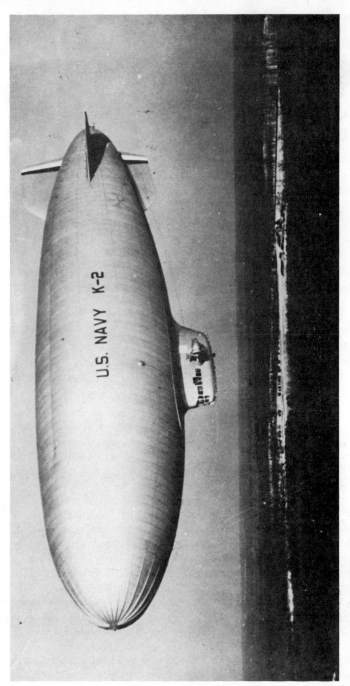

Fig. 16-7. A non-rigid K-2 airship.

Fig. 16-8. Vice Admiral Charles E. Rosendahl, USN, (Ret). gazes at the K-43.

Newspapers bannered the story: MYSTERY VEILS FATE OF WRECKED BLIMP CREW!

There was much hangar-flying over the incident. Some people felt that the *L-8* had struck the water and dumped the crew overboard. Others believed that they had simply fallen out or jumped overboard.

The Navy's investigation was interesting and puzzling. The *L-8* originally had been the Goodyear *Ranger III*. After delivery to Moffett Field, piloted by Cody, *L-8* rendezvoused with the aircraft carrier *Hornet* which was on its way to take part in the historic Jimmy Doolittle B-25 raid on Tokyo. The blimp dropped 300 pounds of navigation domes onto the deck of the *Hornet*.

As to the last flight of the *L-8*, much was left unlearned. It was obvious that at some time during the mysterious voyage the craft had reached its pressure height. This was indicated by its partially deflated condition. Automatically valving off some gas, the craft descended. This caused the strange buckling amidship.

The salvage party that picked the *L-8* up at Daly City found that the craft was in good condition. Windows of the car were all closed, but the cabin door was open. According to witnesses, it had been open when the craft landed. The engines were stopped when the craft hit. The two propellers were badly bent, but they had not been bent while turning. The radio was in good working order.

Parachutes and the rubber life raft were intact and the portfolio of classified documents were also intact. It was determined that the car had

Fig. 16-9. The U.S. Navy's L-1.

Fig. 16-10. The U.S. Navy's L-8.

Fig. 16-11. The L-8 breaking up before the crash.

Fig. 16-12. The L-8 drifting over Daly City, California.

not at any time been immersed in water. Plenty of fuel was left in the tanks. One throttle was wide open and the other was half open. This indicated that the craft had at some time been making a turn. Ignition switches were both on, but the engines simply were not running.

The only sign of the two crewmen was one officer's cap that was found on a window ledge. Finally, the Navy investigators gave up. On August 16, 1942, Lt. (jg) Cody and Ensign Adams were officially declared missing. They were never again heard from. On August 17, 1943, they were both presumed dead.

Hauled back to Moffett Field, *L-8*, the "Flying Dutchman" mystery blimp was repaired and returned to service as a training blimp. On May 15, 1946, Goodyear bought the craft back from the Navy and in 1947 it once more went into service with the Goodyear blimp fleet—a graceful lady with a secret that was never divulged.

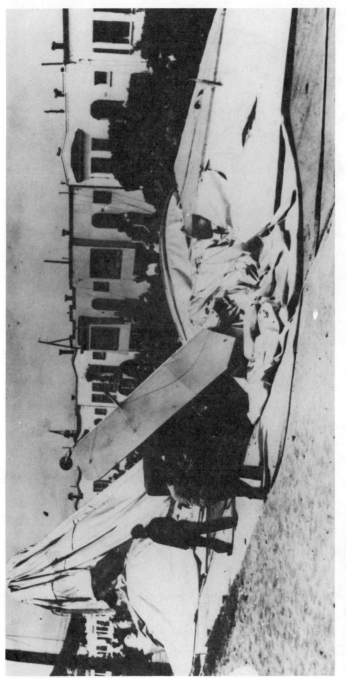

Fig. 16-13. The L-8 after the crash.

271

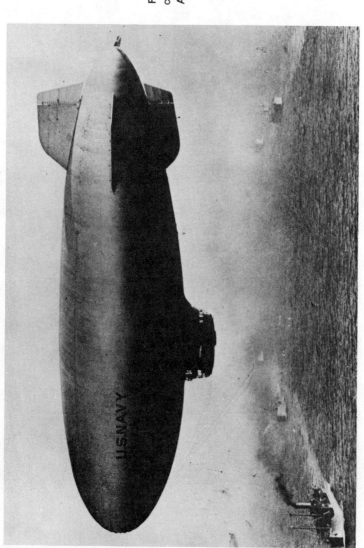

Fig. 16-14. An airship on convoy duty in the Western Atlantic.

ESCORT AND SURVEILANCE DUTY

It was during World War II that blimps enjoyed their finest hours in the sky (Figs. 16-14, through 16-24). Aside from those used primarily for training or experimental purposes, U.S. Navy airships of World War II were grouped into 14 fleet blimp squadrons. Operating from more than 50 bases, they performed antisubmarine patrol and escort operations over a 3,000,000 square mile area along the United States' Atlantic, Gulf and

Fig. 16-15. The surrender of the U-858 with a U.S. Navy blimp providing coverage.

Fig. 16-16. An airship lowers supplies to the crew of a life boat.

Fig. 16-17. The U.S. Navy blimp 2A-3W "Reliance."

Fig. 16-18. An attack on a submarine by K-58.

Pacific coastlines, in the Caribbean, along the South American coasts from Panama to Rio de Janeiro, and in the Mediterranean.

One United States fleet blimp utility squadron also operated from five different bases along the Atlantic seaboard. Together with the 14 other squadrons, they flew a total of 55,900 missions for 550,000 hours and escorted 89,000 merchant ships and troopships overseas, often through areas infested by wolf packs of Nazi U-boats, without the loss of a single surface ship. A total of 87 percent of the blimps assigned to fleet units remained in operational readiness at all times to establish a record of availability for military aircraft.

Despite their huge bulk, making them an obvious target for anti-aircraft fire, only one blimp was actually destroyed by enemy fire. In 1943, off the Florida coast, the Navy blimp *K-74* made a point-blank run over a surfaced German submarine. When the blimp's bomb release mechanism failed to function, the sub raised its guns and shot the blimp down.

The peak of World War II airship operations was 1944. In that year, naval lighter-than-air flight personnel numbered 1500 officer pilots and 3000 enlisted air crewmen. Ground and administrative personnel totaled 706 officers and 7200 enlisted men.

The first nonrigid airship transoceanic flight was made in 1944, 25 years after the aborted attempt of the C-5 to cross the North Atlantic. Blimp Squadron 14 was ordered based with six K-ships at Port Lyautey, French Morocco, for patrol of the Straits of Gibraltar. The blimps were ferried across the Atlantic in pairs from South Weymouth, Massachusetts, via Newfoundland and the Azores. The first flight, covering 3145 miles, was made on May 29-June 1, 1944 by *K-123* and *K-130* in a total flight time of 58 hours.

The following year, two additional K-ships were flown to Port Lyautey from Weeksville, North Carolina, via Bermuda and the Azores. The trip covered 3532 miles in 62 hours. Another transatlantic airship movement was planned in May 1945 when the Navy, recognizing the value of the blimps in visual and instrument detection of U-boats, ordered a blimp squadron based in southwest England. This move was cancelled, just prior to its execution, due to the capitulation of Nazi Germany.

While ASW operations were the main duties of the Navy blimps during World War II, it was found that their unique flight characteristics

Fig. 16-19. The first blimp landing aboard the USS Yorktown for passengers.

Fig. 16-20. The invasion of France. Balloon barrages float overhead to protect the ships from low-flying enemy strafers.

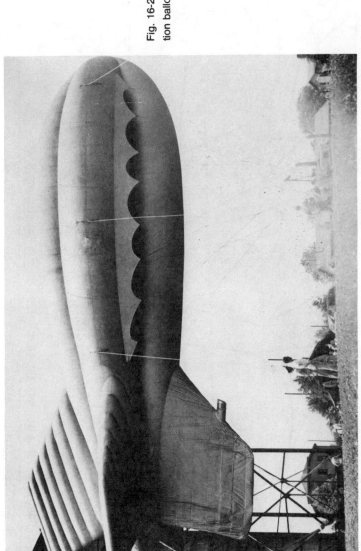

Fig. 16-21. A type R observation balloon.

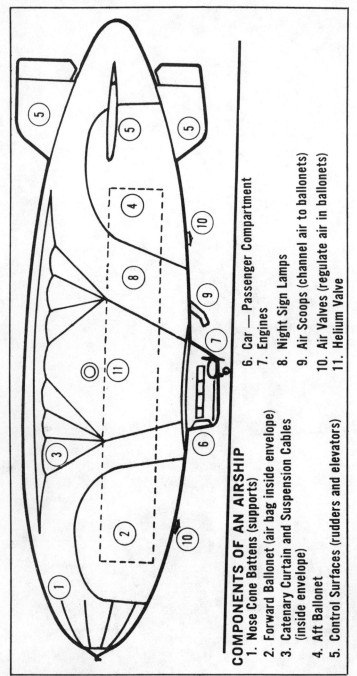

COMPONENTS OF AN AIRSHIP

1. Nose Cone Battens (supports)
2. Forward Ballonet (air bag inside envelope)
3. Catenary Curtain and Suspension Cables (inside envelope)
4. Aft Ballonet
5. Control Surfaces (rudders and elevators)
6. Car — Passenger Compartment
7. Engines
8. Night Sign Lamps
9. Air Scoops (channel air to ballonets)
10. Air Valves (regulate air in ballonets)
11. Helium Valve

Fig. 16-22. Airship components.

gave them value in the fullfillment of general utility missions as well. These included torpedo recovery, aerial photography, observation, special equipment calibration, search and rescue operations, and other missions that called for slow speed, low altitude flight over extended periods of time.

In the Mediterranean theater, blimps from Squadron 14 played a major role in minesweeping operations by spotting and marking otherwise undetected mine fields. A number of sweep vessels were saved by diverting them from collision courses with mines that could only be seen from above.

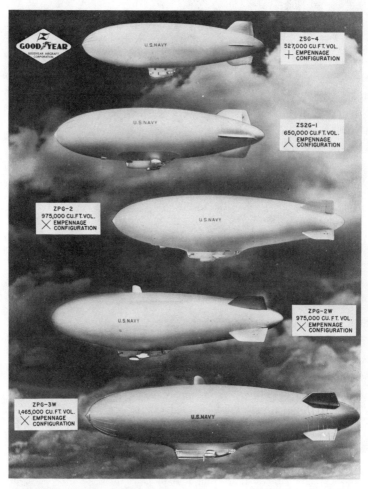

Fig. 16-23. U.S. Navy blimps.

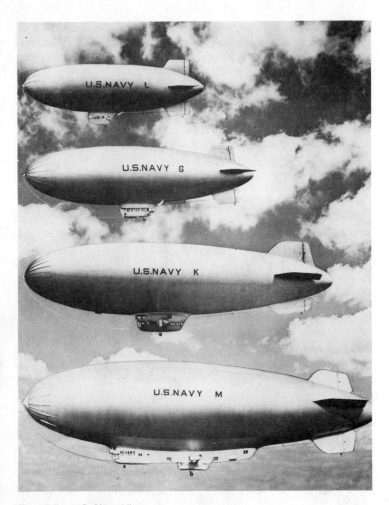

Fig. 16-24. U.S. Navy blimps.

In 1945, the end of hostilities caused reduction of the Navy's active airship organization. Two operational U.S. fleet blimp squadrons remained along with an extensive training and experimental airship program at Lakehurst NAS—the war and postwar headquarters for naval LTA activities. One such program to determine the sea-keeping and habitability features of airships resulted in the 725,000 cubic foot *XM-1* (formerly the 647,500 cubic foot *M-1*) establishing a 170 hour and 17 minute world's aircraft endurance flight record for continuous unrefuelled flight on November 2, 1946.

On July 22, 1954, the initial flight was made of the prototype Goodyear *ZS2G-1* blimp (Figs. 16-25, 16-26 and 16-27), successor to the wartime K-class naval airships, with an entirely new design of both the envelope and the car. This class was readily identifiable by the inverted-Y arrangement of its control surfaces that provided greater ground clearance for takeoff and landing maneuvers.

In 1955, the first of a newer, bigger class of Goodyear airships was commissioned—the 1,000,000 cubic foot *ZPG-2W* Fig. 16-28 and Fig. 16-29. One airship of this type set a new world record for continuous flight of more than 300 hours. The *ZPG-2W* measured 343 feet in length, was 108 feet high and weighed 48,000 pounds empty. It carried two 700-horsepower Wright R-1300 engines that were uprated to 800-horsepower at 2600 rpm takeoff power. Maximum speed was 70 knots and sea level rate of climb was 2200 fpm.

Fig. 16-25. The Goodyear ZS2G-1

Fig. 16-26. Note the inverted "Y" disposition of the control surfaces for the ZS2G-1.

The last of the giant nonrigids built for the United States government by Goodyear were the Navy's four *ZPG-3Ws* (Figs. 16-30 through 16-36). They were the largest nonrigids ever built and at 403 feet in length and 1,500,000 cubic feet volume they were designed for use in a new kind of defensive warfare—airborne early warning picketing. The first was commissioned in 1958.

On its first operational barrier flight with the Continental Air Defense Command, the huge *ZPG-3W* established a new world record for time spent on continuous patrol. Captain F. N. Klein, commander of Fleet Airship Wing One at Lakehurst NAS, reported that the blimp was on

Fig. 16-27. The ZS2G-1 airship.

285

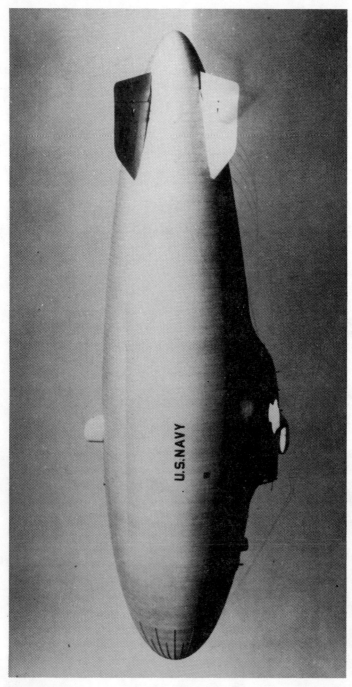

Fig. 16-28. The U.S. Navy's ZPG-2W airship.

Fig. 16-29. The U.S. Navy's ZPG-2 hovers over the USS Leyte.

Fig. 16-30. The ZPG-3W.

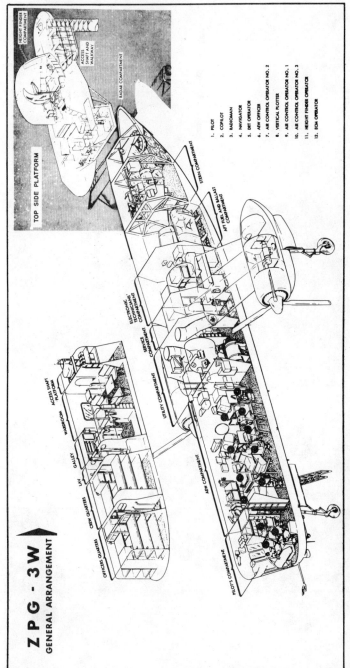

ZPG - 3W
GENERAL ARRANGEMENT

TOP SIDE PLATFORM

HEIGHT FINDER COMPARTMENT

ACCESS SHAFT AND WALKWAY

RADAR COMPARTMENT

STERN COMPARTMENT

AFT FUEL AND BALLAST COMPARTMENT

ELECTRONIC TECHNICIANS COMPARTMENT

SERVICE COMPARTMENT

UTILITY COMPARTMENT

ACCESS SHAFT PLATFORM

WARDROOM

GALLEY

LAV.

CREW QUARTERS

OFFICERS QUARTERS

AEW COMPARTMENT

PILOT'S COMPARTMENT

1. PILOT
2. COPILOT
3. RADIOMAN
4. NAVIGATOR
5. DRT OPERATOR
6. AEW OFFICER
7. AIR CONTROL OPERATOR NO. 2
8. VERTICAL PLOTTER
9. AIR CONTROL OPERATOR NO. 1
10. AIR CONTROL OPERATOR NO. 3
11. HEIGHT FINDER OPERATOR
12. ECM OPERATOR

Fig. 16-31. The general arrangement of the ZPG-3W.

289

Fig. 16-32. The gondola of the ZPG-3W.

Fig. 16-33. The ZPG-3W.

291

Fig. 16-34. The ZPG-3W made its maiden flight on July 21, 1958.

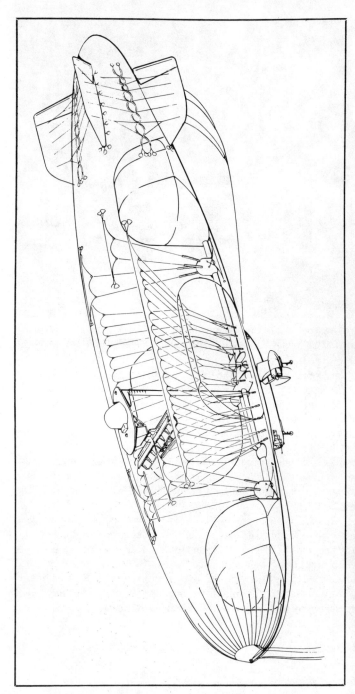

Fig. 16-35. A diagram of the ZPG-3W.

Fig. 16-36. Looking over the electronic technician's panel on the ZPG-3W airship are, left to right, AE/2 Woolfe, AE/2 Cook, AE/1 Bennett and ATC Frudenberg.

station continuously for 49.3 hours. That was more than double the amount of time logged by its smaller predecessor—the *ZPG-2W*.

Manned by personnel from Airborne Early Warning Squadron One, the *ZPG-3W* left its station on the evening of February 27, 1960, and remained on duty until March 1. It returned to Lakehurst 58 hours after takeoff.

The giant blimp was the first of four 3W models to join the smaller 2W airships in providing flying radar stations patrolling a 100-mile stretch of contiguous radar barrier for the Continental Air Defense Command. The New York and New Jersey coastlines were covered.

The 3W was equipped with the most advanced and largest flying electronic gear and could detect approaching jet aircraft at ranges previously unheard of. All aircraft inbound to New York and New Jersey coasts were picked up on the airship's radar, tracked for course and ground speed and reported to the Semi-Automatic Ground Environment System (SAGE) of the Continental Air Defense Command. Any targets not identified were intercepted by jet flights scrambled from coastal bases.

Chapter 17

U.S. Navy Rigids

The *ZRS-5*, better known as the *USS Macon*, resembled a giant silver cigar sliding along effortlessly through wisps of clouds. It carried men and airplanes in its belly and moved swiftly or hovered in one spot. Construction (See Figs. 17-1 through 17-14) was completed on March 11, 1933, and it was the last of a breed of strange American rigid airships that flew the United States Navy colors. When the craft went down off Point Sur on the California coast on February 12, 1935, it brought to an end the Navy's airship era.

The *USS Macon's* home was in California's lovely Santa Clara Valley, at a Navy base called Moffett Field, but its beginnings were far away. They were born of Navy interest in the World War I Zeppelins that had raided England and France with limited success. After all, a great future was predicted for rigids in naval reconnaissance work and they might even be used as flying aircraft carriers (Figs. 17-15 and 17-16).

THE USS SHENANDOAH

In 1919, the Navy was granted authority to acquire and utilize two airships. The first, *USS Shenandoah*, had yet to be designed and built. This would take considerable time since America was new at the airship game. But the second was already flying in England—*ZRS-2*, or simply *R-38* in British terminology. The craft never did receive a proper name.

R-38 had been built in the United Kingdom for the United States Navy and was a carbon copy of the German *L-33*—a high-altitude type featuring much lighter construction than standard Zepps. *R-38* had crashed and burned during a trial flight at low altitude. The Court of Inquiry learned that weather had nothing to do with the accident nor was there any problem with her structure. The Court found pilot error as the reason for the crash.

Fig. 17-1. The USS Macon under construction.

logged time, took the lives of 16 American Navy men and 28 others.

Efforts were now concentrated on the 2,115,174 cubic foot rigid airship *ZR-1*. Construction began in 1919 at the Naval Aircraft Factory in Philadelphia, Pennsylvania. Assembly following at the Lakehurst NAS in nearby New Jersey. Christened *USS Shenandoah*, the craft was largely a copy of the German Zeppelin *L-49*, but modified for mooring mast and helium operations.

The *L-49* has bravely set off on the last great airship "silent raid" of World War I on October 19, 1917, along with 10 other Zeppelins: the *L-41*, *L-44*, *L-45*, *L-46*, *L-47*, *L-50*, *L-52*, *L-53*, *L-54*, and *L-55*. They flew into the teeth of a low pressure system moving down from Iceland over England. The airships were headed for disaster. Four of them would never return to Germany.

At dawn the following day, three of them (the L-44, the L-49 and the L-50) were hopelessly lost in the storm over Lorraine, France—far behind enemy lines. Giant 75 mm. outaircraft guns of the French Army raised their muzzles skyward and opened fire. *L-44* was forced to climb hastily from 12,000 to 19,000 feet. Then at 7:45 a.m. an incendiary shell scored a direct hit. The craft burst into flames and went nose down.

L-49 and *L-50* were following close behind and witnessed the awful end. *L-49's* commander, Kapitanleutenant Hans-Karl Gayer, with only two engines working, believed this craft was over Holland when *L-44* was hit. Therefore, he turned back to the west. Dropping lower to get his bearings, Gayer was shocked to see a formation of five French Nieuports of Escadrille N-152 making intercept runs on his airship. Carrying only tracers and ball ammunition, according to historian Douglas Robinson, in his book *Zeppelins in Combat*, the fighters failed to set *L-49* on fire. But they did force the *L-49* to land on a wooded slope of the River Apance near Bourbonne-les-Bains (Fig. 17-17). The crew jumped to the ground and frantically attempted to set the airship on fire. While Gayer fumbled with a Very pistol that had malfunctioned, and elderly Frenchman carrying a squirrel rifle approached the German crew and heroically disarmed them.

Before the *L-49* was dismantled by its captors, detailed drawings were made of the design and distributed to all Allied powers. It was these

Fig. 17-2. The USS Macon under construction.

Fig. 17-3. The USS Macon under construction.

drawings that formed the basis for the design of *USS Shenandoah* (Figs. 17-18 through 17-22). As a result, the *Shenandoah* was slow in building. By the time it first flew on September 4, 1923, the design was already obsolete by more than five years. Nevertheless, it made a number of highly successful trips, included was a 9000-mile circumnavigation of the continental United States in 1924.

THE USS LOS ANGELES

With all the delay in completing the *Shenandoah*, the Navy found itself sorely in need of an operational airship. For this reason, the *USS Los Angeles* came into existence. It was built for the U.S. Navy at the Zeppelin Company works in Friedrichshafen under a contract signed on June 24, 1922 by Dr. Hugo Eckener, Commander Ralph Weyerbacher, USN and Captain Garland Fulton, USN. Fulton, the U.S. Navy's Inspector of Naval Aircraft, stayed with the airship during the two years it was built. Fulton became a close friend of Dr. Eckener and the designer, Dr. Karl Arnstein.

The German workers, believing the craft would be the last Zeppelin built outdid themselves in workmanship to make it the best dirigible ever. It had a 2,471,000 cubic foot capacity and was 658 feet long and weighed 77,836 pounds empty. It could carry a useful load of 101,430 pounds. Five engine gondolas each carried a V-12 Maybach engine of 400 horsepower at 1400 rpm. It was designed to carry 20 passengers and was the first dirigible equipped with sleeping accomodations for long cruises. The

Fig. 17-4. The USS Macon hangared at Moffett Field.

Fig. 17-5. The USS Macon at Moffett Field.

passenger quarters were combined with the control car in a single structure built onto the keel. A wind-driven generator provided electric power for the radios and for the ship's lighting.

LZ-126 was also the first Zeppelin to be painted with aluminum powder mixed with dope. This gave it the familiar silvery appearance of future airships. Primarily the paint was to reduce solar heating and thereby minimize the loss of helium gas. Prior Zeppelins had been clear-doped.

With Dr. Eckener in command, the maiden flight of *LZ-126* was made on August 24, 1924. He took the opportunity to show the craft off proudly by touring the *Reich* to the applause of crowds below her. Dr. Eckener was said to be apprehensive about the dangers of the delivery flight over the Atlantic. No Zeppelin had yet made such a trip. He decided to cruise on reduced power to extend the range of craft to 5350 miles in 96 hours.

Dr. Eckener was expert at pressure flying. When he encountered a low pressure area in midatlantic, he boldy turned north to pick up tailwinds that gave him a ground speed of 78 mph.

The *LZ-126* arrived at Lakehurst at 9:37 a.m. on the second day out. The crew was warmly greeted by U.S. Navy airmen. Hydrogen was valved off and the craft was immediately reinflated with helium. The craft's first flight from Lakehurst, on November 25, 1924, took it to Anacostia NAS. There, as the Navy's new *ZR-3* the craft was christened *USS Los Angeles* by Grace Anna Coolidge—the wife of President Calvin Coolidge. The *USS*

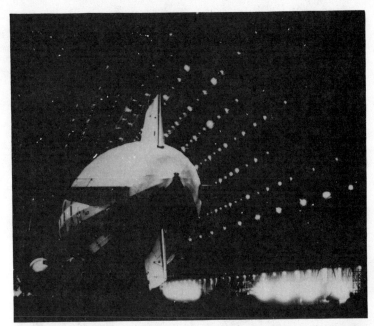

Fig. 17-6. The USS Macon hangared at the U.S. Naval Air Station at Sunnyvale, California.

Fig. 17-7. The USS Macon just prior to its first flight.

Fig. 17-8. The USS Macon approaching Moffett Field.

Los Angeles made 331 flights totaling 4320 hours without a fatality (see Figs. 17-23 through 17-28).

A disaster nearly occurred to the *USS Los Angeles* on August 25, 1927 while it was attached to the top of Lakehurst's controversial high mooring mast. A wing shear stood the craft up almost vertically on its nose (Fig. 17-29). The 25 crew members were visibly shaken, but no one was injured as the craft slowly settled back onto an even keel in the opposite direction.

It was the *USS Los Angeles* that pioneered the U.S. Navy's experimental use of dirigibles to pick up fighter planes on a hook and subsequently release them. This was a British idea that had been around for

Fig. 17-9. The USS Macon nears a mooring mast.

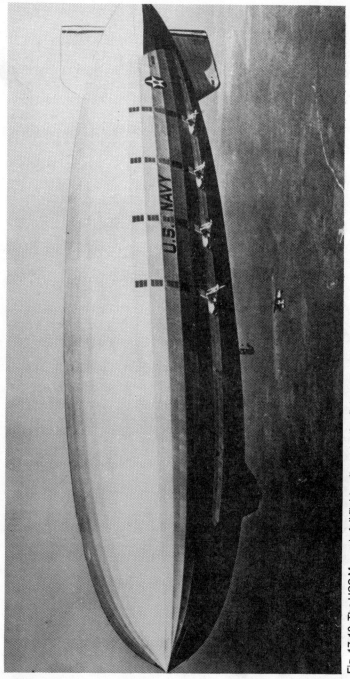

Fig. 17-10. The USS Macon in full flight as its protective fighters prepare to hook on.

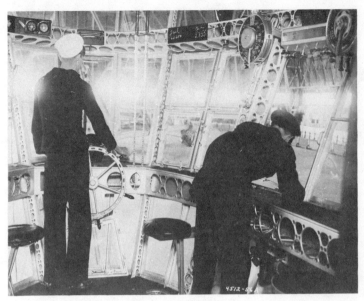

Fig. 17-11. The control car of the USS Macon.

some time and had been planned for use aboard giant scouting dirigibles of the future. The first hook-on was made by a Vought UO-1. Later, the Goodyear-Zeppelin Co. formed by acquisition in America of the German Zeppelin patents, designed a stout duralumin trapeze for this purpose. The device was installed in the *USS Los Angeles* in December, 1928.

Fig. 17-12. The control car of the USS Macon.

Fig. 17-13. The auxiliary control station in the lower vertical fin of the USS Macon.

First hook-ons with the smaller Curtiss XF9C-1 fighters planned for use aboard the *USS Akron* were made in October, 1931. When the *USS Akron* was commissioned on October 27, 1931, it was decided to decommission the *USS Los Angeles*. Decommissioning took place on June 30, 1932 at Lakehurst NAS.

Meanwhile, the *USS Shenandoah* was finally completed and made her maiden flight at Lakehurst on September 4, 1923. Being too small to be of real military value, it served basically as a laboratory ship, along with the *USS Los Angeles,* from which to work out more advanced airship designs.

HELIUM

The *U.S.S. Shenandoah* was the world's first rigid airship to fly with helium gas. While helium is nonflammable, it posed two major operational

Fig. 17-14. F9C-2 was carried by the USS Macon.

Fig. 17-15. A UO-1 Aztec light logistic support aircraft with a crane hookup.

problems. Its lifting power was less than that of hydrogen giving decreased performance, and it was very expensive. At that time, helium cost more than $120 per thousand cubic feet compared with $2 to $3 per thousand cubic feet for hydrogen.

Helium production at the government's Fort Worth plant in Texas could barely keep up with the demand. In 1924, it was impossible to keep more than a single airship filled at one time. The USS Shenandoah normally flew below 4500 feet with gas cells 85 percent filled in order to prevent the loss of gas through automatic valves. Also, it normally made landings in the cool of the evening instead of at midday. This way the helium would be supercooled and valving gas would be unnecessary.

On September 2, 1925, the USS Shenandoah departed Lakehurst NAS to undertake a series of public relations flights throughout the Midwest at a time when county fairs were being held all over. The skipper, Lieutenant Commander Zachary Lansdowne, USN, was apprehensive because of the normal summer thunderstorm activity in that part of the nation. Like a good officer, he followed orders and pushed on.

Early the following morning, near Ava, Ohio, the giant silver dirigible encountered severe weather. A huge flow of cold air from out of the northwest had formed an upper level front by overrunning warm air pushing up from the southwest. This created high atmospheric instability

Fig. 17-16. F9C-2 hooks onto the Macon's trapeze.

and turbulence. Ahead, the crew could see thunderstorms laced with lightning building across the horizon.

VIOLENT WEATHER

At 4:20 a.m., the *USS Shenandoah* was suddenly hurled upward at 1600 fpm despite efforts to keep the craft down with engines running wide

Fig. 17-17. The crash of the Zeppelin L-49 in France gave the Allies the latest information on German dirigible design.

Fig. 17-18. The USS Shenandoah in flight.

open and the nose down 18 degrees. Nearly a mile above the rolling hills of Ohio the craft encountered a blast of cold air and was sent hurtling downward—only to encounter another uprush of moist tropic air. The 682-foot hull, wrenched by these opposing currents, was spun around counterclockwise. The nose was canted up steeply and, with a thundering crash of torn metal, the hull broke in two.

The forward end, now lightened, was carried upward to roughly 10,000 feet with seven people aboard. The navigator, Lieutenant Commander Charles E. Rosendahl, kept his cool and valved off sufficient helium to free-balloon that part of the airship to a safe landing 12 miles distant.

In all, 14 members of the crew of 43 lost their lives in the tragedy. The crash was officially blamed on weather of rare violence. It was a tragedy

Fig. 17-19. The USS Shenandoah moored to the USS Patoka.

Fig. 17-20. A side view of the wreckage of the USS Shenandoah.

that would cause many people to wonder about the practicability of long, cigar-shaped dirigibles attempting to penetrate storm fronts and other weather anomoies where sharp vertical gust loads are frequently encountered. The "helium-heads," as the pro-dirigible people were called, countered that the answer was to fly like Dr. Eckener flew—around the storm systems, not through them, utilizing counterclockwise tailwinds of low-pressure areas to advantage and avoiding the hazards of frontal disturbances.

PATENTS AND PROCESSES

With the German Zeppelin patents and proccesses and key personnel acquired in 1924 by the Goodyear Tire & Rubber Company, a subsidiary firm, the Goodyear-Zeppelin Corporation, was formed in Akron, Ohio. Construction was undertaken in 1928 of two 6,500,000 cubic foot rigids for the U.S. Navy. Both measured 785 feet in length and 133 feet in diameter. They had a cruising range of 6500 miles and a maximum speed of 72 knots.

For power, both ships carried eight 560-horsepower German Maybach engines mounted in separate engine rooms within their hulls. Propellers were mounted on outriggers so that they could be swivelled to change from horizontal to vertical thrust. To compensate for weight lost by fuel burnoff, water recovery apparatus was installed with exhaust condensers mounted on the hull over the engine rooms. Each carried a trapeze for the landing and launch of airplanes. Internal hangar space was provided for five aircraft.

Fig. 17-21. Wreckage of the USS Shenandoah.

Fig. 17-22. The wreck of the USS Shenandoah near Sharon, Ohio showing the end view rear section.

Fig. 17-23. The USS Los Angeles.

Fig. 17-24. The USS Los Angeles over New York City.

316

Fig. 17-25. The USS Los Angeles moored to the USS Patoka.

Fig. 17-26. Landing of the USS Los Angeles aboard the USS Saratoga.

A GIANT RIGID

The *USS Akron* (*ZRS-4*) was completed in 1931 and on August 8 was christened by Mrs. Lou Henry Hoover, wife of President Herbert Hoover. These new airships were covered with sheets of 2.8-ounce cotton cloth, 74 by 24 feet in dimension and laced to the airship's framework. Half a dozen coats of clear and aluminum-pigmented dope were then applied to give a lovely, silvery appearance that would serve as a solar heat reflector.

As first of the Navy's really giant rigids, the *USS Akron* was built in a brand new giant shed at Sunnyvale, California—30 miles south of San Francisco (See Figs. 17-30 through 17-35) Sunnyvale came into the picture in 1929 when Congress ordered an investigation to select a new air station for LTA craft to serve the Pacific Fleet. The shed, with its orange-peel doors and steamlined design, measured more than 1,000 feet in length, 308 feet wide and 198 feet high. It was completed in March, 1933 and renamed Moffett Field after the three-time Chief of the Bureau of Aeronautics who was lost in the crash of the *USS Akron* that year.

The first flight of the *USS Akron* took place on September 23, 1931. Lieutenant Commander Rosendahl was in command. Among the 113 passengers were Navy Secretary Charles Francis Adams, Assistant Secretary for Air David S. Ingalls, Admiral Moffett (Fig. 17-36), 10 members of the Navy Board of Inspection, Goodyear President Paul Litchfield, Garland Fulton, Dr. Arnstein, airship designer Charles P. Burgess and Ralph Weyerbacher.

Trial Flights

Following nine additional trial flights, during which the craft's speed fell short of contract commitment by three knots, the *USS Akron* was placed in commission on October 27, 1931—not at Sunnyvale, but at Lakehurst NAS. The craft flew for two years with varying success. Early in 1933, it was taken over by Commander Frank C. McCord, a veteran LTA pilot who made a name for himself by saving the big airship during a severe East Coast storm that struck near Lakehurst at the end of a 43-hour flight. Rather than attempt a landing in the squall, McCord swung north up the Hudson River Valley, then swung west over Lake Ontario and Lake Erie to get behind the front. As the storm moved, out to sea, he followed behind it, and landed in clear weather at Lakehurst after a run of 72 hours.

Fig. 17-27. Vought UO-1 attached to the trapeze of the USS Los Angeles.

Fig. 17-28. Vought UO-1 equipped for "hook-on" experiments with the USS Los Angeles.

McCord was not so lucky on April 3, 1933 when he set off from Lakehurst to calibrate radio direction finder stations along the New England coast. Admiral Moffett was aboard. This time another cold front was rapidly approaching from the west and the sky soon was filled with black clouds laced with brilliant flashes of lightning. Again McCord tried to outrun the storm, then he finally headed out to sea to ride it out.

Shortly after midnight, the ship began losing altitude dramatically. Finally, the stern struck the water and soon water poured inside the control car. A lack of proper lifesaving equipment and the cold ocean water took the lives of 73 men—including Admiral Moffett and Commander McCord. Only three crewmen survived.

Fig. 17-29. The USS Los Angeles drifts toward a vertical position during an accidental "stand-up."

Fig. 17-30. The USS Akron's ring laying ceremony.

Fig. 17-31. The USS Akron over Union Station, the Post Office and the Government Printing Office, Washington D.C.

Fig. 17-32. The USS Akron.

Investigation

An investigation revealed that there was a possibility of "altimeter error" involved. McCord might not have realized he was as close to the ocean's surface as he was in the black night, due to the airship entering a region of very low pressure. The low pressure would have made his altimeter indicate that he was higher than he actually was—by several hundred of feet. Today, wise pilots are careful to set their altimeters to the nearest reporting station's pressure readings and follow the axiom: "Pressure low, look out below!"

THE USS MACON

The hard-luck sister-ship *USS Macon* was virtually identical to the *USS Akron*. It was lost due to structural failure—not weather. An incipient failure had been detected during a cross country flight, following its commissioning as *ZR-5* in the same month the *USS Akron* was lost. Temporary repairs had been made in flight. After the airship had participated in fleet maneuvers in the Carribean and returned to California, much time and study were devoted to determine the seriousness of this weakness and its implications.

It was finally decided that the weak point, a stern frame, should be reinforced with extra channels. Not enough time was available to ac-

Fig. 17-33. The USS Akron as mooring mast at Sunnyvale, California.

Fig. 17-34. The XF9C-1 Sparrowhawk has engaged the trapeze extended from the forward underside of the dirigible Akron and is about to be hoisted into the airship's five-plane hangar.

complish the job before the start of new fleet maneuvers in the Pacific, in which the *USS Macon* was scheduled to participate, and repairs were deferred until completion of the mission.

USS Macon (ZR-5), which has been christened by Mrs. William A. Moffett on March 11, 1933 at Akron, was the star of the new Moffett Field base at Sunnyvale. But the career of the *USS Macon* was spotty.

Fig. 17-35. A Curtiss F9C-2 "nests" inside the USS Akron.

Fig. 17-36. Rear Admiral W.A. Moffett.

On its first exercise, the craft came out from inside a cloud directly in the line of fire of a Navy cruiser and was "presumed destroyed" and ordered to continue the exercise as *"ZRS-6."* Another time, two "enemy" aircraft in the war games discovered the craft and a scout plane was launched from the dirigible to fight them off. The fighter did its job well and returned to hang up on the trapeze and be hauled inside the hull, but *USS Macon* again blundered out of the cloudland into the range of antiaircraft fire from a division of cruisers. Once more it was "destroyed" and finished the games in disgrace, as *"ZRS-7.'*

Later on the *USS Macon* became a naval showpiece. The crew learned how to better handle the craft in war games. But on February 12, 1935, just 22 months old, the *USS Macon* encountered a Pacific storm returning from fleet maneuvers without the stern post repair job completed. It crashed at sea, and of 81 men aboard, all but two survived.

This closed the era of rigid airships for the United States Navy and Moffett field was turned over to the Army. The Navy, at that time, had no further use for the giant hangar. However, as World War II approached, the Navy took Moffett Field back to serve as a hangar for blimps.

Chapter 18

Airships of the Future

Will the giant airship ever come back? This question has been asked many times and there have been many answers. The technology exists, space age materials are available and there appears to be a wide range of mission requirements for super-airships of breathtaking dimensions.

Yet there are those who cannot forget the frightful, front-page photographs of the *Hindenburg* that appeared in the morning editions of major newspapers on May 7, 1937. The fear of similar disasters has been given a name—the *Hindenburg Syndrome*.

THE ULTIMATE AIRSHIP

It was later that same year that one of the first proposals was made for a super-dirigible. It was called *The Ultimate Airship* by the designer, C. P. Burgess. He was a principal figure in drawing up the design of the Navy's first rigid airship, the *USS Shenandoah*, and in developing specifications for the *USS Akron* and *USS Macon*.

To Burgess' way of thinking, *The Ultimate Airship* would be a metalclad of 7,400,000 cubic feet displacement with a slenderness ratio of 4:1, 618 feet long with a 154.5-foot diameter and skinned with .0008-inch Alclad. This construction, he beleived, would offer the most efficient hull possible with no requirement for compartmentation or flight without pressure. He also envisioned using engines with liquid cooling. Helium would be used to cool the radiators, and the entire hull's surface would be used to, in turn, cool the helium.

METALCLADS

The Navy's interest in metalclads goes back to the 202,200 cubic foot *ZMC-2* laid down in 1928. By August of that year the thin-shelled duralumin skin was completed and two Wright Whirlwind aircraft engines were installed. On August 19, the 149-foot airship, on its maiden flight, covered 600 miles nonstop from the aircraft Development Corp. Factory to Lakehurst NAS. The craft flew well for more than a decade. But like the Slate all-metal *City of Glendale* dirigible (Fig. 18-1) and the Schwartz *"Tin Can"* airship of the 1890s, it was a one-and-only stepchild.

GIANT LTA'S

In 1972, The Navy took a new look at giant LTA's and a mission-oriented systems analysis of updated rigid airship design studies was recommended and reported on by the Naval Research Laboratory. For a starting point, NRL suggested considering a design authorized by Congress in 1938. That design was for the *ZRN* by Goodyear-Zeppelin, a 3,000,000 cubic footer, 650 feet long that was to have been used as a trainer for airplane crews and pilots flying scout planes from the *Akron* and *Macon*.

Next, said NRL, they should consider the existing design for a *ZRCV*, a 9,500,000 cubic footer able to transport nine dive bombers. If constructed, it would be the largest airship ever built.

Third in the study was *ZRCCN*, described as "a major step into completely new territory. It would be a vessel of 22,000,000 cubic feet capacity, more than twice that of ZRCV. No facilities capable of housing such a vessel exist," they warned.

Stepping bravely up the ladder another rung, NRL suggested consideration of a super-giant airship called *ZRCVN*. It was pointed out that "The ultimate development in the line of rigid airships might take the form

Fig. 18-1. The "City of Glendale."

of a large, nuclear-powered carrier of strategic bombers. The form would be that of a pair of *ZRCCNs* connected by a wing section, powered by large, helicopter-type rotors.

"Cargo space is available within the wing section," they pointed out,"in addition to that within the airship hulls, and dynamic lift is greatly enhanced. The two hulls would be spaced 800 feet apart (centerline separation) for an overall width of 1000 feet. The intermediate airfoil would have a span of 600 feet and a chord of 500 feet for an aspect ratio of 1.2, with a maximum thickness of 90 feet."

Such a behemoth carrier of strategic bombers, they reminded, "presents a glorious opportunity for nuclear propulsion, with flight power requirement of 85,000 horsepower translating to 63,000 kw, which would require a sizeable but not unreasonable reactor."

While the cargo capacity of the ZRCVN would be enormous, NRL pointed out, most of it would have to be flown on and off. Therefore, the obvious ideal cargo would consist of aircraft—"from 75 to 100 aircraft loaded with nuclear weapons and a stay in the air as long as desired. The *ZRCVN* would thus constitute a very fast aircraft carrier, immune to submarine attack, whose complement consists entirely of bombers deployed for response within seconds." In a masterpiece of understatement, NRL concluded that construction of such a huge craft would be "a formidable task."

FEASIBILITY STUDY

In 1977, the National Aeronautics and Space Administration completed a two-phase feasibility study of modern airships. NASA-Ames Research Center's 7 × 10-foot wind tunnel was used for exploratory evaluations. Participating industry firms supporting the study, made by Goodyear Aerospace Corp. included Neilsen Engineering & Research Inc., Battelle Columbus Laboratories, Piasecki Aircraft Corp., Sikorsky Aircraft Corp., General Electric Co., Radio Corporation of America, Summit Research Corp. and Northrop Research & Technology Center.

Three promising modern airship system concepts and their missions were studied:

—A heavy-lift airship, employing a nonrigid hull and a significant amount of rotor lift, used for short range transport and positioning of heavy military and civil payloads.

—A VTOL (vertical takeoff and landing) metalclad, partially bouyant airship used as a short haul commercial transport.

—A class of fully bouyant airships for long endurance Navy missions.

The heavy-lifter concept (Fig. 18-2) would be proven out, in NASA's thinking, with the development and construction of a research vehicle combining the lifting capabilities of four large helicopters and a large, helium-filled nonrigid airship for a total payload capacity of more than 75 tons. Gross weight would be 324,950 pounds, with 144,150 pounds of bouyant lift and 180,800 pounds of dynamic lift provided by the helicopter

Fig. 18-2. The Goodyear "heavy lifter" design.

rotors. These would consist of four Sikorsky *CH-54B* helicopters coupled, two on each side, to the bouyant envelope by means of a star frame. The resulting craft, half again as long as a Boeing 747, would fit snugly between the goal posts of a football field.

Prior to loading, the research airship would be slightly heavy in order to minimizing ballast requirements. The bouyancy would come from a 2,500,00 cubic foot nonrigid hull that would be 342 feet long and filled with helium. Its mission would be to short-haul very heavy, outsized cargo. A prime need, said NASA, is for off-loading of military surface ships in areas where deep water port facilities do not exist—as well as similar functions for removing civilian cargos in developing nations lacking deep water ports. Industries which could use such a monster craft include power-generation, petroleum, construction, logging and heavy equipment firms.

The VTOL, semi-bouyant concept would be used as an airport feeder vehicle for transporting passengers or cargo between major air terminals and suburban or downtown depots. An operational concept proposed by NASA would be 238-foot long pressurized metalclad envelope of 428,500 cubic feet, powered by four turboprop engines driving 30-foot prop-rotors, which could be gimballed to switch from VTOL lifting to forward thrust for cruise.

VTOL AIRSHIP

Had researchers at NASA gone to the trouble of checking U.S. Patent Office files (See Figs. 18-4A through 18-4E) they might have been amazed to find that the VTOL airship had been conceived and patented in 1908 by Simon Lake—inventor of the even-keel submarine. While researching the history of American aeronautics years ago, I received a warm letter from Lake, written from Washington, D.C. on September 15, 1940, in which he pleaded:

"Now please do not put me in the position of claiming to be an expert—I am simply one who believes, as I did 35 years ago, that it is possible to build flying machines that can rise vertically, hover in the air, and go anywhere above the earth or sea and land safely in restricted areas."

Backed by his experience in designing a successful submarine, Lake recalled that "my 1908 airship was a compromise between the gas-filled airship and the airplane, in which I incorporated direct lifting force by a large propeller which could be swung in gimbels so as to give an upward lift to augment the lift of the gas-filled hulls and could then be gradually changed so as to give a forward or backward thrust in horizontal flight.

"My next patent, Number 928,524, filed on December 10, 1908, operated in the same manner except that her I showed a single gas-filled hull and proposed to use a greater proportion of mechanical lift by using two or more side propellers. I have always felt this would provide a much safer flying machine than any yet produced if the gas used was helium. Such craft can be designed to rise or settle vertically, travel backwards or forward and travel on land or water, and with great static stability would always remain on an even keel.

"In case of failure of engines in the air, the planes could be manipulated to cause the flying craft to settle gradually to any selected spot where there was room to set it down. The heavy machinery would be carried in a combination boat and land vehicle which would contact land or water first and prevent shock to the passengers or upper light construction of the lifting elements of the craft; retractable wheels were also provided.

"I believe such type craft would be a far safer and superior type today for all commercial purposes, except, perhaps, that of my latest roto-plane, which operates on much the same principle as my early patent, but uses much greater horsepower and lifting plane area than that provided for in the early design."

The man who introduced the modern day submarine of even-keel design, looked far ahead and envisioned super-dirigibiles with hybrid VTOL capability that NASA got all excited about it in the mid-1970s. Perhaps the first actual VTOL hybrid airship should be named in honor of Simon Lake.

In its conclusion, the NASA study asserted that a "new class of fully-buoyant airships of approximately 11,000,000 cubic feet capacity could meet the Navy requirements for four missions studied, as a low-risk extension of previous LTA technology. These missions included: (1) submarine trail, (2) detection, classification, and surveillance of sub-

Fig. 18-3. The Goodyear hybrid heavy lifter design.

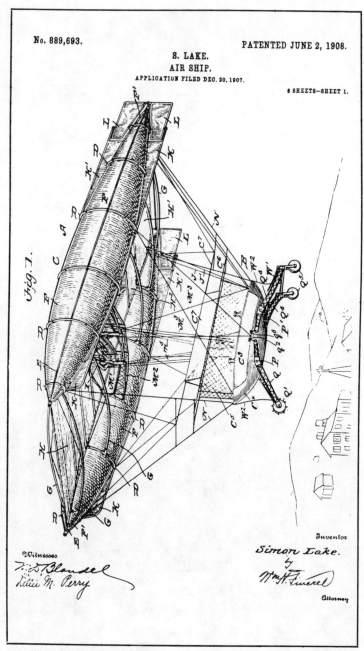

Fig. 18-4A. Simon Lake's dirigible patent (1908-1909) featured tilting propellers for VTOL or forward propulsion.

S. LAKE.
AIR SHIP.
APPLICATION FILED DEC. 20, 1907.

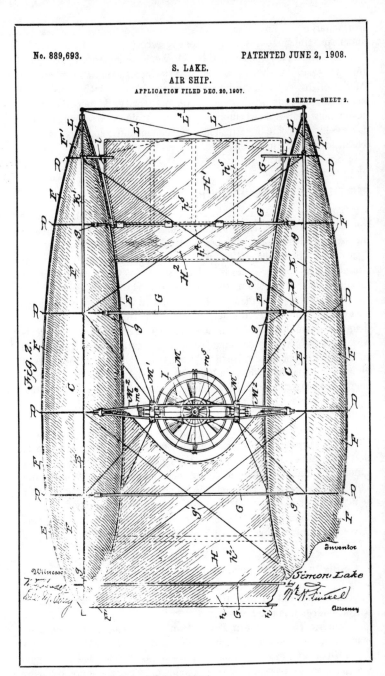

Fig. 18-4B. Simon Lake's dirigible patent.

marine targets, (3) maintenance of a counting or detection barrier across submarine transit routes, and (4) convoy escort.

Modern LTA vehicles, said NASA, would be superior to airships of the past—particularly with respect to dash speed and low speed control. Modern lightweight gas turbine engines would allow higher dash speed and cruise speeds with reduced weight penalty. Modern helicopter technology and advanced automatic flight control systems would make an LTA vehicle capable of vertical landings and takeoffs, and fully controllable at low speeds in hover mode.

Sound familiar?

PROPELLER LIGHTER-THAN-AIR VEHICLES

These theoretical studies by NRL and NASA were not all hot air. On February 27, 1979, a Congressional hearing was held on propeller lighter-than-air vehicles before the Subcommittee on Science, Technology, and Space of the Committee on Commerce, Science, and Transportation of the United States Senate. It began to look as if the government was finally turning an ear to the helium heads, who hoped to bring back the biggies.

In his opening statement, Chairman Howard W. Cannon reviewed the past studies and observed that "two areas for use of propelled lighter-than-air vehicles have emerged. An example from one of these areas deals with the transportation and emplacement of very heavy assemblies and subassemblies encountered in the construction industry. Such needs exist for items ranging in weight from 100 to 1000 tons. Another area of possible need is for long-endurance surveillance. An example would be patrolling the recent extension of the national fisheries rights to the 200-mile offshore zone."

Senator Barry Goldwater, a qualified jet pilot, pointed out that giant LTAs have attractive features: "They are fuel-efficient, they can remain aloft for extended periods of time, they are inherently safe, and they cause a minimum amount of annoyance. But these features alone do not justify building LTA vehicles. They must be able to do useful work that no other vehicle can, or be able to do the same work more efficiently."

Rear Admiral A. P. Manning, Jr., Chief, Office of Research and Development, U.S. Coast Guard, pointed to seven possible missions for LTAS:

Aids to Navigation. System surveillance, minor repair and small-bouy replacement.

Enforcement of Maritime Laws and Treaties. Surveillance, patrol, interdiction and boardings.

Marine Environment Protection. Surveillance, on-scene command, control, communications, equipment delivery and logistics.

Military Operations and Preparedness. Coastal and harbor surveillance, antisubmarine warfare protection of offshore assets and convoy escort.

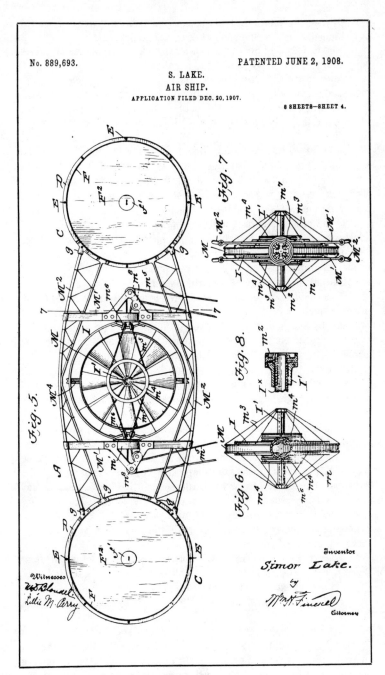

Fig. 18-4C. Simon Lake's dirigible patent.

Marine Science. International ice patrol, gathering of oceanographic data, service and support of oceanographic bouys.

Port Safety and Security. Harbor and port surveillance, hazardous cargo traffic control and escort, and logistics.

Search and Rescue. Search, recover, board, tow, deliver equipment and personnel, on-scene command, control and communications.

Manning admitted that they'd about reached the limit of paper studies and warned they'd have to "look to NASA to develop the technology for this concept."

Next, Frank N. Piasecki, president of Piasecki Aircraft Corp., made an estimate that a total of 14 heavy-lifters could be sold at contemplated prices. He warned that to become a primary transport system, a military craft must be able to carry the heaviest load required—specifically a battlefield tank weighing 60 tons.

"The United States has spent much of its wealth in the development of advanced aeronautical technology," Piasecki told the subcommittee. "What we need in order to capture this new and emerging potential market is the investment capital to build and demonstrate the flight and cost characteristics of heavy vertical airlift systems."

Piasecki went on to tout his company's heavy-lifter, the *Heli-Stat*, in which a single pilot can manage the large combination of thrust forces provided by four helicopters. Automatic flight control provides "synthetic" stability, in contrast to the older "pendulum" stability proposed by Simon Lake in placing the center of bouyancy well above the vehicle's center of gravity.

He further informed the congressmen that France was already well along with designs of heavy lifters in the 550-ton payload range. He recalled that a helicopter had been developed by the Piasecki firm for the Air Force in 1953 that was capable of lifting 7 tons. The craft was designed for possible rescue of B-36 bomber crews from the otherwise impenetrable terrain of Alaskan mountain ranges they might have to overfly on the way to Korea. This project, the Piasecki *H-16*, was taken over by the Army for air delivery of a 50-ton battle tank. In 1957, five design study contracts were issued and over 25 designs were actually developed for giant VTOLs before the Army forgot the idea and switched its budget for helicopters to support its bid for control of strategic missile operations— including the V-1 Redstone.

"Unless the entire Army transport requirements can be airlifted, there is no critical, primary role for HVAL (Heavy Vertical Air Lift)," Piasecki concluded. "Then the most economical solution is to make do with what is presently available—this was the reasoning behind the C5A sizing."

The Air Force, however, had a real "Achilles' heel" in airborne launch systems being considered for the MX missile. With an estimated weight of more than 50 tons, he warned that the Air Force's total dependence on long runways made it vulnerable to bomb crater damage that could take many days to repair. A heavy-lifter could do the job better and faster.

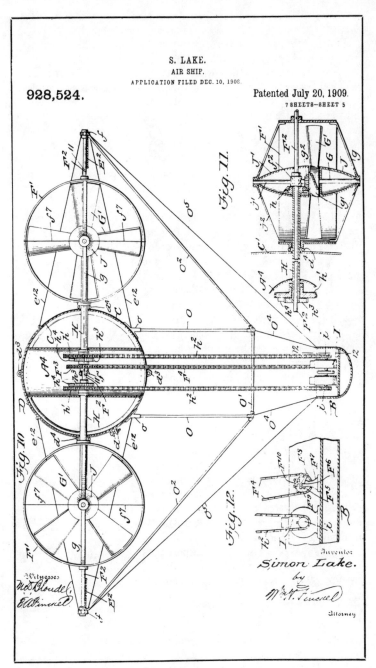

S. LAKE.
AIR SHIP.
APPLICATION FILED DEC. 10, 1908.

928,524.

Patented July 20, 1909.
7 SHEETS—SHEET 5

Fig. 11.

Fig. 10.

Fig. 12.

Witnesses

Inventor
Simon Lake.
by
Attorney

Fig. 18-4D. Simon Lake's dirigible patent.

339

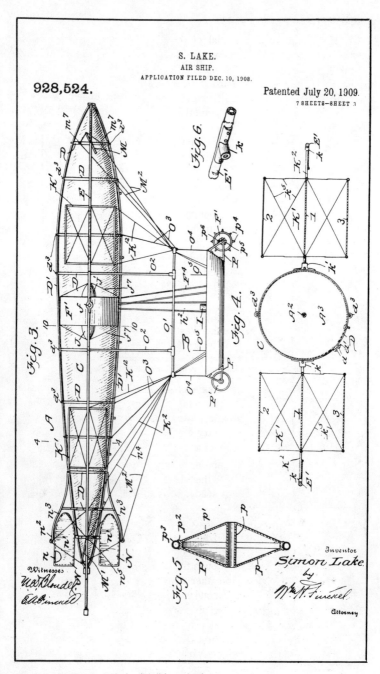

S. LAKE.
AIR SHIP.
APPLICATION FILED DEC. 10, 1908.

928,524.

Patented July 20, 1909.
7 SHEETS—SHEET 3

Fig. 18-4E. Simon Lake's dirigible patent.

COMMERCIAL HEAVY-LIFTERS

The commercial potential of the *Heli-Stat* are equally inviting, Piasecki pointed out. They included uses in forestry, the oil industry, mining, powerplant construction, maritime ship unloading, and for transportation where no roads exist.

To Senator Goldwater, the biggest market for heavy-lifters was the logging industry. He saw a potential for use of more than 1000 such aircraft.

Goldwater's views were seconded by another witness, George M. Leonard, assistant director of timber management for the U.S. Department of Agriculture. He told the subcommittee: "Throughout our mountainous forested areas of the national forest and on private lands as well, there are substantial tracts of timber where road construction is economically or environmentally unacceptable. Many of these tracts of timber are productive and can contribute to our Nation's wood product needs in an environmentally acceptable way."

Where conventional helicopters can economically increase the harvest area from the end of a surface road by some 3000 acres. Leonard pointed out, heavy-lift vehicles "could possibly increase this area to about 63,000 acres." A further consideration, said Leonard, was the heavy-lifter's potential for salvaging timber—"roughly 5,000,000,000 cubic feet of timber is lost annually in the West due to insects, disease, fire, and other natural causes," much in areas presently inaccessible to ground crews, but open to heavy-lifter salvage operations.

In addition to timber harvesting, said Leonard, "one of our major concerns is the protection of mountain country and the wilderness areas. Yet we know those areas do have mineral resources like oil that the nation needs. This does provide an opportunity for heavy-lifters to get heavy equipment back into the country for needed test drilling or whatever, without the permanent effect of a road into that area."

Leonard concluded by pointing out that the biggest helicopter in use in the logging industry today is the Sikorsky S64 *Skycrane*. It is capable of lifting 10 tons, while the legal load for a logging truck is approximately 35 tons.

When the question arose as to safety of heavy-filter flying in the face of sudden storms, William Koven, a technical expert with the Naval Air Systems Command, reminded that "operational utility and flexibility will be substantially enhanced through the use of advanced weather sensing and forecast techniques—weather satellites, for example—which will permit airships to operate near and around severe weather conditions with a confidence heretofore unavailable."

But much research and development still lay ahead to perfect the heavy lifter, Koven warned. First was the basic aerodynamics of ellipsoidal shapes equipped with a variety of low-aspect-ratio tail surfaces. This is particularly true in regard to scale effect. What works well in a model might not in a full-sized airship. Another problem was the proximity of

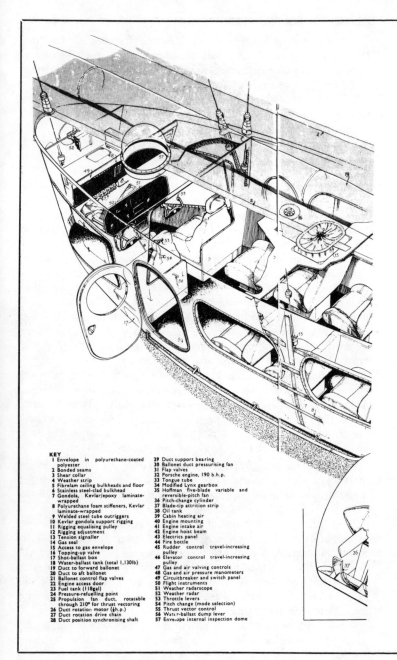

KEY
1 Envelope in polyurethane-coated polyester
2 Bonded seams
3 Shear collar
4 Weather strip
5 Fibrelam ceiling bulkheads and floor
6 Stainless steel-clad bulkhead
7 Gondola, Kevlar/epoxy laminate-wrapped
8 Polyurethane foam stiffeners, Kevlar laminate-wrapped
9 Welded steel tube outriggers
10 Kevlar gondola support rigging
11 Rigging equalising pulley
12 Rigging adjustment
13 Tension signaller
14 Gas seal
15 Access to gas envelope
16 Topping-up valve
17 Shot-ballast box
18 Water-ballast tank (total 1,130lb)
19 Duct to forward ballonet
20 Duct to aft ballonet
21 Ballonet control flap valves
22 Engine access door
23 Fuel tank (118gal)
24 Pressure-refuelling point
25 Propulsion fan duct, rotatable through 210° for thrust vectoring
26 Duct rotation motor (½h.p.)
27 Duct rotation drive chain
28 Duct position synchronising shaft

29 Duct support bearing
30 Ballonet duct pressurising fan
31 Flap valves
32 Porsche engine, 190 b.h.p.
33 Tongue tube
34 Modified Lynx gearbox
35 Hoffman five-blade variable and reversible-pitch fan
36 Pitch-change cylinder
37 Blade-tip attrition strip
38 Oil tank
39 Cabin heating air
40 Engine mounting
41 Engine intake air
42 Engine hoist beam
43 Electrics panel
44 Fire bottle
45 Rudder control travel-increasing pulley
46 Elevator control travel-increasing pulley
47 Gas and air valving controls
48 Gas and air pressure manometers
49 Circuitbreaker and switch panel
50 Flight instruments
51 Weather radarscope
52 Weather radar
53 Throttle levers
54 Pitch change (mode selection)
55 Thrust vector control
56 Water-ballast dump lever
57 Envelope internal inspection dome

Fig. 18-5. A cutaway of the AD-500 airship (courtesy of Airship Developments Ltd.).

342

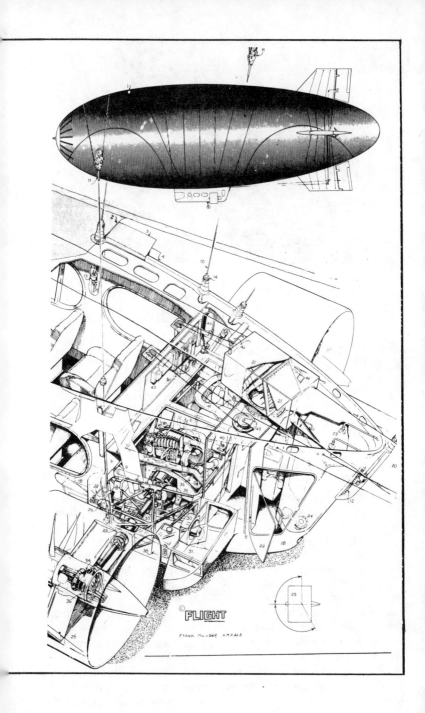

©FLIGHT
INTERNATIONAL

FRANK MUNGER AMRAES

Fig. 18-6. Heavy vertical air lift logging with Piasecki Heli-Stat aircraft.

propellers and large, slow-turning rotors to the very large airship hull—both in and out of ground effect. And then there was the matter of precision flying.

Senator Goldwater remarked caustically: "Listening to you fellows today, I get the hunch we have done just about all the paperwork we can. Somebody better get to work and figure out if the paper is right or wrong!"

Once built, where would you put a huge heavy-lifter airship? The answer was obvious. The proptotype heavy-lifter could be hangared at Lakehurst, Moffett Field or at the two airdocks of the Marine Air Facility at Santa Ana, in Southern California.

A picture was introduced in testimony about an unusual British dirigible. This craft was about the size of the Goodyear blimp and represented the latest state -of-the- art in airship construction. It was funded by Venezuelan interests and the craft was built of modern composite materials. The car molded in one piece from Kevlar. Supercharged

Porsche sportscar engines turned ducted fans able to tilt for VTOL operation. Located at Cardington, former home of the British *R-101*, the new ship was called the *AD-500* (Fig. 18-5). Its nonrigid envelope of Dacron was covered with a white urethane coating. The Maiden voyage of the *AD-500*, built by the small firm of Aerospace Developments Ltd., took place on February 3, 1979. Future missions contemplated for such craft, the senators learned, would be to transport natural gas from Third World countries across the Mediterranean to Europe and in Venezuela to operate 22 such craft as educational television broadcast platforms.

THE HELI-STAT

On January 24, 1980, Piasecki Aircraft Corp. announced that it had received a contract from the Naval Air Development Center to construct, test and demonstrate a heavy vertical airlift system—their *Heli-Stat*—funded by the Forest Service of the U.S. Department of Agriculture. The goal was to demonstrate the utility of timber harvesting with the VTOL craft (Figs. 18-6 and 18-7).

Initial funding of $680,000 would lead to a negotiated contract estimated to run to $10,000,000 over the next two years. The first phase of construction would be at Piasecki's Philadelphia facility and at Lakehurst NAS. The 240-foot long *Heli-Stat* would have a bouyant lift of 25 tons, coming from an envelope of 1,000,000 cubic feet filled with helium to offset the weight of four H-34 helicopters of 1525 horsepower each.

By bringing the *Heli-Stat's* weight to near zero, total thrust of the helicopter rotors would be applied to lifting the useful load—with precision hovering possible. A single pilot will operate the vehicle from the left rear helicopter cockpit. A flight engineer would be in each of the other three cockpits.

Measuring 111 feet in height and 149 feet wide, the *Heli-Stat* would easily fit into standard blimp hangars at Lakehurst, NJ, Elizabeth City, NC, Santa Ana, CA, Moffett Field, CA, and Tillamook, OR.

Fig. 18-7. Piasecki Heli-Stat hybrid ship of the future.

345

Fig. 18-8. The Aereon Aerobody hybrid heavy lifter concept (courtesy of NASA).

THE DYNAIRSHIP

One other novel heavy-lifter concept (Fig. 18-8) was developed by Aereon Corp. of Princeton, New Jersey. In 1973, they submitted to NASA a joint proposal with Aeronautical Research Associates of Princeton for a delta-shaped, semi-bouyant aircraft called *Dynairship*. It was to be some 600 feet long, able to operate up to 40,000 feet for several days without refueling and travel at speeds from 30 to 200 knots. The design called for diesel-powered turboprop propulsion. However, the very size and shape of the *DYNAIRSHIP* design lends itself to requirements for nuclear power.

Aereon's name was borrowed from Dr. Solomon Andrews' Civil War period dirigible. While a triple-hulled version was developed, the new Aereon Company soon abandoned it in favor of the deltoid "aerobody" airship. A small test version flew successfully. This was a 1140-pound lifting body of welded aluminum tubing fitted with a plastic canopy salvaged from a glider and powered with a McCulloch engine uprated from 70 to 93 horsepower. On March 6, 1971, this craft, *Aereon 26* (Fig. 18-9) was flown by test pilot John Alcott to an altitude of 500 feet for several orbits at the FAA's NAFEC research center in New Jersey.

Named *Project Tiger*, the mission climaxed a four-year research and development cycle by establishing aerodynamic proof of the concept prior to proceeding with a large, semi-bouyant type. The subsequent Aereon *Dynairship* design was later evaluated by Boeing Vertol Co., under contract to NASA, as being representative of lifting-body concepts because of the background of information developed by Aereon on the delta planfrom lifting-body shape.

William McE. Miller Jr., Aereon's president, submitted the Project Tiger Evaluation Report on *Aereon 26 (Aerobody 001)* to professor D. C. Hazen of Princeton University's School of Engineering and Applied Sciences. Hazen found that it contained "impressive" results. He reported: "Given the limited range of lift coefficient that it was possible to achieve with the configuration flown (.23 to .41) and the relative simplicity of the test instrumentation employed, the tests were obviously skillfully designed and flown.

"As far as the results themselves are concerned, there seem to be no great surprises. The handling qualities seemed adequate and should certainly provide assurance that a full scale machine should not experience undue problems. Except for severely Reynolds number-dependent quantities, such as aileron effectiveness, the flight tests confirmed the predictions made on the basis of relatively small-scale tunnel tests."

Miller had other theoretical inputs from government research sources that gave him confidence. For example, the *DYNAIRSHIP* was rated higher than several alternative hybrid concepts in the Boeing Vertol modern airship feasibility study, published in May 1975, for NASA.

"The Aereon *DYNAIRSHIP*" the study concluded, "appears to be a most representative concept in this category. Characteristics of the other body shapes would probably vary little from this baseline. While of some

Fig. 18-9. Aereon's Aerobody-26.

Fig. 18-10. The Raven thermal dirigible.

technical interest, the more complex concepts appear to suffer many technical uncertainties . . ."

BACKYARD INVENTORS

Meanwhile, America's backyard inventors today are pushing ahead on their own and are designing and building homemade "thermal airships" for pure sport flying (Fig. 18-10).

Typical of this new breed of LTA enthusiasts is Brian J. Boland, an art and photography teacher at Farmington High School in Connecticut, who with his wife, Kathy, designed and built hot-air balloons and then produced a hot-air airship, the *Albatross* (Fig. 18-11). It was first flown on October

Fig. 18-11. The Albatross is a homebuilt thermal dirigible.

Fig. 18-12. The Yellowstone thermal dirigible flies at 15 mph.

11, 1975. By January 1978 they had accumulated 24 grand hours of fun flying, low and slow, over the lovely New England countryside.

Boland's *A-1 Albatross* has an envelope made from 32 separate strips of polyurethane-coated ripstop Nylon. The gondola, which holds four persons, is built of light alloy around which wicker walls are woven. Underneath are oaken landing skids. The gondola is suspended by 28 flexible steel cables attached to two catenary suspension curtains. The gondola's tubular framework serves as mounting for three 8,000,000 BTU propane burners—with 60 gallons of liquid propane fuel contained in half a dozen low-pressure cylinders. Another 6-gallon tank holds a fuel-oil mixture for the propulsion engine. The engine is a 40-horsepower Rockwell JLO 2-stroke powerplant that drives a Banks Maxwell 2-blade ducted pusher propeller.

Raven Industries Inc., of Sioux Falls, South Dakota, are veteran balloon makers. In June, 1977, they launched a thermo-blimp, the *Enterprise*, to share the sky with another factory-built hot-airship, the *Yellowstone* (Fig. 18-12), built by Cameron Balloon Works of Bristol, England, for James "Buddy" Thompson. Thompson is a sports balloonist and Chairman of Glenmore Distilleries Co. of Louisville, Kentucky. His children—Lisa, Emery, Jim Jr., and Sam—not only serve as part of the flight crew, but they also designed a startling paint scheme showing a bunch of LGM's (Little Green Men) grinning down on mere earthlings. Again, propane burners provide hot air for lift, while a 40-horsepower engine, also propane powered, propels the craft along at an exhilerating 15 mph—the only way to fly! Says Thompson: "The *Yellowstone* is the only airship in the world which has both a National Park and a superb Kentucky Bourbon named after it!"

I'll drink to that!

Index